ENTER, CONVERSING

By Clifton Fadiman

Essays and Criticism

PARTY OF ONE (1955)

ANY NUMBER CAN PLAY (1957)

THE LIFETIME READING PLAN (1960)

Anthologies, Collections, and Symposia

THE VOICE OF THE CITY AND OTHER STORIES BY O. HENRY (1935)

I BELIEVE (1939)

READING I'VE LIKED (1941)

THE THREE READERS (WITH SINCLAIR LEWIS AND
CARL VAN DOREN) (1943)

THE SHORT STORIES OF HENRY JAMES (1945)

THE AMERICAN TREASURY (ASSISTED BY CHARLES
VAN DOREN) (1955)

FANTASIA MATHEMATICA (1958)

CLIFTON FADIMAN'S FIRESIDE READER (1961)

Inner Sanctum Editions

LEO TOLSTOY'S WAR AND PEACE (1942)

CHARLES DICKENS' PICKWICK PAPERS (1949)

Translations

FRIEDRICH NIETZSCHE'S THE BIRTH OF TRAGEDY (1926)

FRIEDRICH NIETZSCHE'S ECCE HOMO (1926)

DESIDER KOSTOLANYI'S THE BLOODY POET (1927)

FRANZ WERFEL'S THE MAN WHO CONQUERED DEATH
(WITH WILLIAM A. DRAKE) (1927)

Enter, Conversing

CLIFTON FADIMAN

Cleveland   *New York*

The World Publishing Company

Published by The World Publishing Company
2231 West 110th Street, Cleveland 2, Ohio

Published simultaneously in Canada by
Nelson, Foster & Scott Ltd.

Library of Congress Catalog Card Number: 62-9053

FIRST EDITION

Grateful acknowledgment is made to the following publishers for their kind permission to reprint from the works indicated: Bantam Books, Inc.: introductions to *The Red and the Black* and *Typee*, copyright © 1958 by Clifton Fadiman. George Braziller: "On Limited Warfare" from *Subverse: Rhymes for Our Time*, copyright © 1959 by Marya Mannes and Robert Osborn. City Lights Books: "Loud Prayer" by Lawrence Ferlinghetti from *Beatitude Anthology.* Curtis Brown, Ltd.: "Oafishness Sells Good, Like an Advertisement Should," copyright © 1956 by Ogden Nash; first published in *The New Yorker.* The Curtis Publishing Company: copyright © 1957, 1958, 1959, 1960, 1961. Harcourt, Brace & World, Inc.: "The Hollow Men" in *Collected Poems 1909-1935* by T. S. Eliot, copyright, 1936, by Harcourt, Brace & World, Inc. Harper & Brothers: "The Newlyweds" from *The Carpentered Hen* by John Updike, copyright © 1955 by John Updike, which originally appeared in *The New Yorker.* Holt, Rinehart and Winston, Inc.: "Fire and Ice" from *Complete Poems of Robert Frost*, copyright 1923 by Holt, Rinehart and Winston, Inc., copyright renewed 1951 by Robert Frost. Indiana University Press: "David" from *The Reckless Spenders*, copyright 1954 by Walker Gibson. Little, Brown & Company: "The Private Dining Room" from *Verses From 1929 On* by Ogden Nash. Little, Brown—Atlantic Monthly Press: "The Case for Basic Education" from *The Case for Basic Education*, edited by James D. Koerner. Mills Music, Inc.: "Huckleberry Finn," copyright 1917 by Mills Music, Inc., United States copyright renewed 1945. The Viking Press, Inc.: "The Day After Sunday" and "Girl's-Eye View of Relatives" from *Times Three* by Phyllis McGinley, copyright © 1952, 1959 by Phyllis McGinley. These poems originally appeared in *The New Yorker. The Wall Street Journal* and Georgie Starbuck Galbraith: "The Product" by Georgie Starbuck Galbraith.

WP362

814
F

FOR

Ed and Bill

Contents

Contents

Men, Books, and a Pianist

Journeys in Time and Space

Contents

To Teach the Young Idea How To Shoot

Prefatory:

An Essay on an Essayist

A SMALLISH BOOK lies before me, containing a selection from the essays of Leigh Hunt. The title page is undated, the flyleaf inscribed "C. M. Baker, Dec. 25, 1892." This edition was probably published sometime in the eighties, which would make my volume at least a septuagenarian. It has weathered well, the sturdy blue cloth binding and brownish label are unimpaired, the heavyish paper with its uneven fore edge is hardly discolored. Yet any bookman would at once recognize this shilling reprint (Camelot Series) as surviving from another age. To it there clings the odd pathos attaching to objects that are period pieces but not yet quite museum pieces, objects whose connection with us lies just this side of evanescence. They touch us as a dying odor in a room we vaguely remember faintly challenges the nostrils of memory.

We all prefer to believe we are intended for some purpose. Leigh Hunt (1784-1859) might have been born to illustrate the word "minor." A pretty-pretty romantic poet and an essayist of just barely the second order, he was associated with the circle of Byron, Shelley, and Keats. If remembered at all, beyond the Eng. Lit. class, it is because he wrote "Abou Ben Adhem," which I trust children are no longer forced to memorize, and "Jenny Kissed Me," the near-triolet that confers upon him a feeble anthological life. He also enjoys a dim fame as the original of Harold Skimpole in *Bleak House.*

As an essayist he is, though charming enough, of such low voltage that probably only another essayist could take much interest in him. And even that interest is apt to be largely archaeological.

I list a few of the titles of Leigh Hunt's sketches: "Pocket-books and Keepsakes," "Deaths of Little Children," "On the Graces and Anxieties of Pig-Driving," "Spring and Daisies," "Windows," "Shaking Hands," "Coaches," "Tea Drinking," "Of Sticks," "Getting Up on Cold Mornings," "A Chapter on Hats," "A 'Now'" (Descriptive of a Hot Day), "A 'Now'" (Descriptive of a Cold Day), "Of the Sight of Shops." . . .

The kindly reader may smile at these titles, the tough-minded scorn them. Perhaps they are useful only as evidence of the vast gap that separates us from Leigh Hunt's readers of, say, 135 years ago, willing to sentimentalize with him over the Deaths of Little Children, to listen to him gossip about My Books, to consider gravely his opinion of Anacreon. They must have been members of the comfortable, fairly cultivated middle class, with considerable leisure time on their hands, able to appreciate Hunt's copious flow of poetical and classical references, and bearing a relationship to the author quite different from that felt by us toward our own essayists. They appear to have been content merely to take pleasure in the mild play of Leigh Hunt's graceful, second-rate mind as it composed variations on nonweighty matters. They asked for nothing more than to be charmed. They did not demand that the essay *do* something, change the angle of mass opinion, or contribute to public debate. They did not require the challenge of controversy, the pressure of the topical, the stimulus of instruction. Or I should say that they did ask for these things from their political journalists (Leigh Hunt also wrote a good deal of political journalism, enough to land him in jail) but not from their informal essayists.

Something in the atmosphere of the time permitted small men like Hunt and larger ones like Lamb and Hazlitt to flourish. Something in the atmosphere of our time, it is often noted, works counter to the familiar essayist, so much so that during the next quarter of a century we may witness his liquidation. (A few years ago I myself wrote for him a premature exit march.) Yet even if he should vanish from the scene it is consoling to realize that he has had a long and happy run. It was almost four centuries ago that Montaigne in his "tower raised above but not removed from men's follies" first laid down the indulgent laws of the essayist's art. Four centuries are a long time.

Nor can we be positive that the line Montaigne fathered is coming to a dead end. Among the living there are at least two masters, E. B. White and Aldous Huxley. Among the recently departed are Thurber, Morley, DeVoto. In England there are many sons of Chesterton and Beerbohm. (Whatever cartel it is that writes the fourth leader of the London *Times* is of the true breed.) And it would be easy enough to name several dozen talented current native practitioners of this admittedly non-crowd-pleasing art, who somehow manage to get published and to search out amid our immense population the few thousand readers still by nature responsive to the essay's uninsistent charms.

The "essayist" in the heading of this preface refers to the present writer. If, during these comments, the perpendicular pronoun seems to erect itself unduly, that is because it is the stock in trade of my guild. "It is myself I portray," said our man Montaigne, without apology. For the rest, just as a plumber is one who plumbs well enough to get paid for it, so an essayist is simply one who writes essays that are good enough to achieve respectable publication. Beyond this I make no claim.

The present volume is the third such collection. The total number of essays in the three volumes works out to a little over a hundred. It sounds like too many (Lamb wrote only seventy-four). One recalls what the self-doubting Dvořák once said to Sibelius: "*Ich habe zuviel komponiert.*" Still, to have passed, if only by dint of application, the century mark is perhaps enough to warrant a little retrospection, as we might grant the Oldest Living Inhabitant the right to maunder through his repertory of anecdotes.

I should begin by saying that I was not a self-starting essayist, as many of the real masters were and are. Some men actually do appear to be what most men like to imagine themselves—architects of their own destinies. But not me. Again and again, when I wasn't watching, someone has slipped into my back pocket a blueprint of part of my future. Thus about a decade ago Ted Patrick, editor in chief of *Holiday* magazine, suggested that I try to work up a new monthly department. Being an unusual editor, he laid down no conditions except that I write acceptably about what interested me. He was, in other words, requesting me to turn myself into a familiar essayist, a request sufficient to freeze the marrow of one who knew and loved Hazlitt and Santayana and Virginia Woolf and Belloc and the rest of that fair company.

For some years I had been a journalist and sedulous writer of introductions. I had managed a number of more or less formal literary essays, some of which have reappeared in these collections. But the familiar essay, written without the aid of the crutch of another man's words—this I had not attempted.

Basically the problem of the essayist is one of self-assessment. He must establish a measure of the scope, the dimensions, and the intensity of his interests. That is what Montaigne worked at all his writing life. Had it not been for Mr. Patrick's casual invitation I might never have discovered that I could put together intelligible paragraphs on such diverse matters as privacy, conversation, house-hunting, cheese, mathematics, eccentrics, children, wine, puns, letter-writing, television comics, education, Mother Goose, fireworks, and Judy Garland. I do not claim that I wrote well on these heads; merely that I derived great pleasure from discovering that I could write on them at all.

One of the most attractive and prolific essayists of our time (he is also a distinguished scholar) once remarked to me, rather ruefully, that he was now so well trained that he thought he could, if challenged, write 2,000 publishable words on almost any topic. An exaggeration, of course; yet in a way such versatility marks the natural essayist, though he may be of the second or third rank. Choose a few subjects at random: the color blue (Melville wrote, in *Moby Dick*, what amounts to an essay on the color white); a revolving door; insomnia; one's first childhood friend. The natural essayist, a Chesterton, a Christopher Morley, a Robert Lynd, confronted by these four themes plus a deadline would probably do pretty well with any of them.

There are people who have inborn mechanical skill. They know at once how to fix the toaster or drive a strange car. There are men similarly skilled in the field of nonobjects: ideas, words, fancies, opinions. Their minds are so well stocked (and, more important, they are so intimate with those minds) that they can, almost at will, turn on the spigot of entertaining commentary. Not opinionated, they are rich in opinions.

These are the virtuosi of the art, and it goes without saying that I am not one of them. I have never finished an essay without surprise that I had done so, or without an inner conviction that it was my last one. Hazlitt's mind was a well; mine, like most men's, is more like a storeroom containing a finite number of objects. So far I have been able to ticket and describe over a hundred of these objects. I am not sure that there are another hundred lying about on the shelves.

This collection displays thirty-two items from the storeroom.

First, as to the title: I make no secret of the fact that I have consciously tried, where it was appropriate, to convey a sense of actual talk. This, as I have painfully discovered, is more complicated than it sounds. One must somehow merge three elements: one's own style, the basic but indefinable speech patterns of one's countrymen, and a cunning set of departures from and variations on these patterns. In poetry Robert Frost has done this supremely, perhaps uniquely, well. I have tried to transpose something of his method to the lower plane of my own prose; and every once in a while I fashion a sentence or two that seems to do the job.

Creating the illusion of a man talking does not necessarily involve the use of the vernacular or an incessant bowing to the loosely informal. Lamb's "Dream Children" is a highly wrought piece of prose, full of calculated literary tricks. Yet somehow Lamb's voice pervades the whole glittering performance; and if "Dream Children" moves you at all (it leaves many cold) it is the very pitch and tonality of that living voice which is affecting you, even more than what the voice is saying.

An essayist can be great, like Francis Bacon, and still we may not be able to hear his voice. Or he can be great, like Montaigne, and give the effect of being overheard rather than read. The whole matter has something to do with the dramatist's art: the essayist whose voice is audible is projecting himself as a character more than as a mind. Aldous Huxley is a marvelous essayist; but it is the movement of his intellect rather than the rise and fall of a personal voice that arouses our admiration.

I have tried, in many of these essays, to give the illusion of talk not only because the technical problem involved is interesting to a writer, but for reasons of a more general nature—I should perhaps say of a sociopolitical nature. Our democracy rests on a variety of supports, and one of them is communication. I do not mean the communication provided by our highly efficient public-address systems, though that too is essential. I mean the communication that comes of people quietly talking with each other, perhaps of matters of no great moment, pleasures, opinions, whims, memories. Most of us agree that in this area something in the nature of a breakdown is occurring. We live in an era of efficiency; and conversation is not efficient, performs no work.

And yet we know that our political and social system, based on the idea of freedom, links with the free flow of private as well as public statement. Sometimes an informal essayist, though he supplies only one end of the dialogue, can make a tiny contribution toward starting that free flow. The more formal thinkers say more important things and can move men's minds in matters of great pith and moment. But the Montaignes help to keep those minds sweet, well aired, and merely human. Such minds belong to free men. And so an essayist who introduces conversation by the backstairs of his own writing may be performing a small act of good citizenship. I should like to think so.

Tocqueville, looking us over in 1832, perceived and valued our activism and foresaw the impressive future it would help to create. But he also remarked, "No men are less addicted to reverie than the citizens of a democracy"; and the judgment contains its minim of acid. For reverie, and its brother, the free play of the mind divorced from practical goals, are elements of civic health. A life, like furniture, can be too functional, as we of the technical age are already discovering. Some room must be left—it need not be much—for reverie, speculation, floating free in mental space.

The informal essayist is one of those representing this world of casual speculation. His business is to make trial after trial of his mind, not to arrive at final truths, but, more simply, to discover what is there so that he may hold it up for the observation of any whom it may concern. He is concerned of course to present his notions in the best possible light and, if he advances any arguments, hopes that the reader will find them persuasive. But he is less interested in changing the reader's mind than in stimulating it to movement. I suppose most informal essayists are content to be Non-Influentials.

The present collection, accordingly, is not electric with the charged air of controversy. Only one essay, "The Case for Basic Education," takes what is called a stand on an issue of overwhelming importance. I hope it will persuade some readers that the case is a good one. But I did not write it with that idea in mind. I wrote it for the simplest of reasons: I was full of the subject and was relieved to get it off my chest.

Certain fairly apparent prepossessions lie back of most of these pieces. They are the prepossessions of one who greatly admires the scientific culture so eloquently defended by C. P. Snow, but who feels uneasy at the turn it has taken during our lifetime toward what might be called totalitarian technology. Only sentimentalists hanker after a return to the past; but there is a large body of Americans, vocal or nonvocal, who believe, or at times only hope, that some of its values may still be incorporated in our future, assuming that we have one. The reader may interpret these essays as minor commentaries on those values.

It may be, as some say, that we are moving toward a world imperium headed not by a man or a class but by the machine itself. Perhaps we are all scheduled to become part of a stupendous filing system. But even if this should turn out to be the case, the writer by his very nature cannot acquiesce. He cannot tolerate anonymity for himself. Still less can he tolerate it for others, partly for the professional reason that universal anonymity would destroy his very reason for existence, which is to dramatize people and ideas in continuous and exciting process.

All our writers, except a few who find an odd salvation in the exploitation of despair, are nonacquiescers. Among them is a minor group of informal essayists. They may be on the way out, but meanwhile they are able to suggest that, while there is much facelessness, there are also many odd faces; that the mind is still free to play; that one can recover the literature of the past without making the gesture of retreat; that men like Artur Rubinstein not only exist but are generally admired, and for the right reasons; and that the new leisure, though it will open to some the gates of boredom, may stimulate many others to an increased and happier cultivation of their own minds.

In most societies the writer is a sniper, not a cheer leader. In our time, agreed, there is plenty for him to snipe at. But this challenge brings with it a certain exhilaration, and if he is lucky and skillful enough some of this exhilaration will communicate itself to the reader.

Most of these essays have appeared during the last few years in *Holiday* magazine. I have made a few changes, deletions, and additions, none of a consequential character. Some of the references may seem a trifle dated, but it seemed better to leave them that way, in their original state of nature.

'Tis of Thee

American Humor in the Jet Age

I HAVE JUST FINISHED reading my forty-seventh book of recent American humor and am about ready to let normal cheerlessness break in. I have been so be-slapsticked with the laughableness of psychiatrists, beatniks, children, commuters, second lieutenants, and organization men that I can't tell my brain from my *os humerus*. Still sunk in the torpor produced by massive doses of hilarity, I set down these notes. Probably the reader need not be warned against taking them too seriously—assuming that he is willing to take them at all, for most of us are wise enough to flee like startled deer at the first symptom of an essay on humor.

Furthermore, I have the uneasy feeling that a mere literary critic has no right to discuss the subject. It should be handled by a *Fortune* expert. For humor is now rationalized, organized, packaged, distributed, reprocessed, and redistributed on the awesome scale of Big Business. It is almost a part of technology.

American humor seems to have passed through several stages, somewhat like industrialism itself. Its premachine or cottage-manufacture phase, folk-rooted, lasted well into the nineteenth century, culminating in Mark Twain at his best. It is marked by a handmade quality. Most attempts to revive it today distill a factitious, Grandma Moses aroma.

Country humor in the IBM era is illustrated by Mr. Cliff Arquette, television comic of the moment. He portrays what the jacket of *Charley Weaver's Letters From Mamma* calls "a likable old codger who reads sidesplitting letters from his 'Mamma!'" Mr. Arquette's old country-store crackerbox is filled with side-splitting plastic pretzels: "As I said before, last night Grandma threw a big party. They say he may live."

On the other hand, the genuine Mark Twain tradition survives in a man like William Faulkner, who draws his nourishment from roots sunk in a soil far removed from Hollywood or Radio City. Faulkner's *The Hamlet,* though its villainous Flem Snopes is hardly a laughable character, is none the less a work of high comic art in the frontier tradition. Its wonderful grotesque tale, *Spotted Horses,* is the simon-pure article. There's no canned laughter in it.

Free-swinging, private-entrepreneur capitalism finds a certain reflection in the individualistic, taboos-be-damned school of satirists, of whom Finley Peter Dunne remains a fine example of the early, and Ring Lardner of the later, phase. (The first Marx Brothers films belong to this period too.) The period of luxury-product manufacture coincides with the emergence of the glittering *Académie Comique* of *The New Yorker,* which has done so much to civilize, and also to standardize, our national sense of humor.

The early phase of true mass production corresponds to the peak of the radio era—the assembly-line gags and "situations" of Bob Hope, Eddie Cantor, Jack Benny. We are now swinging into the electronic age. In tempo with the shift, American humor begins to superorganize, or, as we shall see, to react in ways of its own against the smooth constrictions of the System.

Numerous are the signs of humor in high-speed orbit. An infallible fun machine, untouched by human hands, ejects, like missiles, an endless stream of best-selling joke books and anthologies. Humor, carefully graded and varied, is applied like Duco to dozens of normally neutral products such as ash trays, table napkins, earrings (one marked IN, the other OUT), toilet paper (Rib-tickling Toilet Rolls Spin Out Riotous Sayings). Funny books are produced with reflex immediacy to exploit in business-like fashion any current subject of serious thought—so that the Organization Man, for example, has now been so efficiently kidded that, in our neatly induced state of amused superiority, we have forgotten that he persists, multiplies, and keeps right on having social consequences. Humor is gimmicked and pack-aged so as to suggest a "product" rather than an immortal spirit: a confection called *Ad-Liberties* mismatches slogans to repro-ductions of art masterpieces; *Captions Courageous* does some-what ditto; *Did Anyone Bring an Opener?* offers stills from old movies, bound up with interchangeable "Choose-Your-Own" captions; in *These Are My People* Mr. Arquette, who pervades the air and the bookshops like a gas, supplies his avid audience with photos of himself impersonating, with the help of funny costumes and what children call "funny faces," various imaginary relatives. (Uncle Percy "used to do imitations of birds. He could do a sea gull so real you'd be afraid to look up.")

Our emergent ideal of a frictionless technological culture hangs the Do Not Touch signs on a whole herd of sacred cows: Negroes, Jews, Irishmen, Senators are no longer permitted to seem funny. (Though there is always Mr. Hyman Kaplan.)

The same high ideal accounts for the decay of the irreverent political cartoon, except for Herblock and a few others who cock snooks in the class magazines. The statesman who permits him-self humor cannot, and quite properly should not, be permitted to become President, for he might cast a mocking shadow on the Jet Age Big Brudder image. Finally, that political-scientific gift to our time, the venerated Team, now supplies humor with its underpinning: according to the credits on the last Oscar show, it took eight strong men to provide Mr. Hope with a score or two of gags—gags whose tired look was perhaps the natural result of overhandling by eight masseurs.

I am not being snooty about Organized or Commodity humor. Some of it is very funny indeed. Some not. I do not know, any more than the next man, what humor is, and am quite content to settle for the proposition that humor is what makes people laugh or smile, inside or outside. Naturally what makes *me* laugh or smile seems to me to be nearer to humor, whatever humor happens to be, than what makes the other fellow laugh or smile. I am concerned only with some rough litmus test that may distinguish current Organized humor from the more traditional Unorganized humor, a kind which, despite handicaps, still flourishes among us.

There should be a word other than "humorist" to denote the purveyor of Commodity or Applied humor, as opposed to the creator of Pure humor. The pure humorist is a rare bird, and not always, in the simple sense of the word, a funny bird. He is a man with a special fix on life. That fix is skewed, seemingly oddly, yet it rarely fails to reveal truth. The oddness of the skew does not preclude the utmost seriousness. It seems built in, largely beyond the writer's control. It often produces laughter, but rather as a by-product, not a deliberate objective.

Humorists of this order, though of varying merit, are Aristophanes, Rabelais, Montaigne, Cervantes, Shakespeare (sometimes), Lamb, Dickens, Beerbohm, even (if read properly) Henry James. In our time we have the late James Thurber, E. B. White, Ogden Nash, Frank Sullivan, S. J. Perelman, and a few others who, though they produce humor for the commodity market, are nevertheless not commodity humorists, but pure humorists. The others, often writers of talent and charm, are not so much humorists as humor-writers. That is not an adequate word either, but let's use it for short.

The fact that we have so few pure humorists is no reflection on our times, for there never have been many in any period. But the fact that we have so many applied-humor-writers, as against their relative scarcity in previous eras, may have some meaning. I would suggest that the meaning is linked with our commodity-civilization, which sooner or later finds a way to turn even the secretions of the imagination into neatly packaged, shrewdly graded, properly priced products.

The humor-writer is a craftsman who selects a small segment of experience and then hooks a pair of spectacles over his ears and nose through which to look at it. But in the case of the humorist the spectacles and the eyes are one and the same.

His kind of imagination has something to do with the poetic gift. It is a special vision. It is found only in men of notable depth of temperament, often of temperament precariously balanced: think of Dickens, Lamb, Mark Twain, all "abnormal." Such men breathe humor; it is the atmosphere in which they live. They do not, except in their less inspired moments, "produce" it.

The humor-writer knows just what he is doing. He is out to make you laugh. Hence he is apt to come up with discrete, intentionally funny lines, passages, situations.

The humorist, though like the poet a highly conscious artist, has a rich, loamy unconscious for his consciousness to work with. He is not out primarily to make you laugh but to express a personal comic vision. Hence it is hard to find in an E. B. White essay many designed funny sentences. Yet the effect of the whole is to produce in the reader that sudden delighted irradiation of the mind that we call humorous awareness.

Jean Kerr and Jack Douglas, for example, both seem to me to be good, though quite different, humor-writers. I enjoy them greatly. But that enjoyment is limited by my sense that they are working hard at the business, whereas Montaigne seems to be playing an uncalculated game. The humor-writer is a marksman, the humorist a dancer. One works with separate fragments, mirroring the fractionation of our culture; the other works with wholes, complete visions, mirroring his own mind. Because fragments decay, TV funnymen cannot afford to repeat themselves. Because visions, seemingly evanescent fragrances, nevertheless subtly resist dispersal, *Pickwick* remains a masterpiece.

As poets and novelists deal in visions, we sometimes find more pure unorganized humor in them than we do in the professional humorists. I have often thought that Robert Frost, in certain of his moods, is a truly great humorist; in a few lines he can set the world aslant. Let me take a couple of examples of a lower order of genius. Edwin O'Connor's *The Last Hurrah* is full of pure humor; so is Jessamyn West's tender study of adolescence, *Cress Delahanty,* with its unforgettable scene of the hat that fell into the fishbowl. Yet these writers probably do not think of themselves as humorists, in the sense that the diverting Max Shulman or the equally diverting H. Allen Smith so think of themselves. Among the newer novelists I think Peter DeVries has the root of the matter in him, particularly when he forgets to hone, burnish, and style his wit and gives free relaxed play to his odd genius for fantastication.

The American humorist or humor-writer has to create nowadays under a peculiar set of pressures. The nature of these pressures accounts in part for the nature of our humor.

The first pressure I have already touched on. It is that of a society blindly driving toward an advanced state of technology and universal-jointed communication. This is the pressure of a machine. Therefore it produces mechanical humor—that of the air waves (with some wonderful exceptions—but I don't see Mr. Caesar around much these days), the jokebook, the gimmick book, the celebrities' wisecracks cranked out by publicity robots and transmitted by the endless belts of the gossip columns. This is our equivalent of the classic Roman circus. Like those vacation resort apartments so aptly called Efficiency Units, this is Efficiency Humor.

Its purpose, not necessarily known to its makers, is to neutralize the enormous boredom bound to ensue, as Aldous Huxley has pointed out, should we persist in bringing the Brave New World to birth. It is for all of us. But it is not folk humor. It is mass humor. About it clings the stink of something worse than death, the stink of dehumanization.

The second pressure is unique to our time. It is that of the imminence of planetary disaster. The humorist can work joyfully with a world in a jam. He always has, because the world has always been in a jam. In fact the jam is his bread and butter. But he has never before been asked to work with a world that may be shot out from under him. He can handle trouble well enough; Don Quixote is a man of troubles. But now he is required to handle, not the rich tragicomedy of trouble, but the ungraspable specter of annihilation.

What does he do? Well, sometimes he does what many of

us would do in such impossible circumstances. He goes a little wild. We get the humor of *Angst*, beat humor, nihilist humor. The *Mad* books, for instance, have sold over a million and a quarter copies. What they are selling is complete rejection. Nothing is sacred. Enjoy a good howl before atomizing. The young are particularly fond of *Mad* humor, perhaps because it is the young who sense annihilation more keenly than the rest of us. They haven't had a chance to live; we at least have had a few years.

Consider also the Greenwich Village humor of the pitilessly witty Jules Feiffer. He calls one collection of his destructive cartoons *Sick, Sick, Sick: A Guide to Non-Confident Living*. Non-confident is the operative word. Another, *The Explainers*, tears the hide off every fat cliché that hopes to disguise the possibility that we are going to hell in a uranium handbasket. The very lines of Mr. Feiffer's drawings are nervous. His people are demons; his humor is not that of the grin, but of the rictus. He is the poor bohemian's Breughel.

And here comes the talented Roger Price with a satire: *J.G.— The Upright Ape*, a *Candide* gone semidemented. And here is the brilliant cartoonist Alan Dunn, with *Is There Intelligent Life on Earth?*, in which some Martian visitors look us over in utter amazement. Even Charles Addams, who has been ladling out grue for some years, seems, as a master of the comedy of morbidity, more in tune with the time than ever. And the wild *non-sequitur* humor of Jack Douglas' *Never Trust a Naked Bus Driver* or his *My Brother Was an Only Child* holds a note of frenzy not to be found in its immediate ancestor, the "nut" humor of the Donald Ogden Stewart school of more than a generation ago.

Finally we can see how far out we've gone by comparing the often brilliant nihilist social and political commentary of a Mort Sahl with the relatively good-natured topical satire of the peaceful, hopeful era of a Will Rogers.

To the pressures of the Brave New World and of possible annihilation we may add a third, already alluded to: the pressure of the New Respectability.

Corey Ford, who has himself written first-rate applied humor, complained in a magazine article a couple of years ago that American humor is in a bad way, that we hadn't produced a genuine new humorist in ten years. Mr. Ford thinks the trouble is that we're afraid to laugh. The New Respectability, with its taboos and its One-Happy-Family sloganeering, is pressing too hard on the jocular vein. He figures you can't milk laughs out of sacred cows.

There's something in this. But not everything. The reason the explanation is only partial is that humorists are by nature artists of evasion, Houdinis trained to escape from the locked trunks of conformity. There's a lot of escaping going on at the moment.

It's true that, except in the better country clubs, we've stopped telling jokes about Pat and Ikey; and the blackface comedian is a thing of the past. It's true also that Mr. Hagerty's hackles rose when Art Buchwald (who turns out commodity humor often touched with genius) dared to write a spoof of a Washington press briefing. Naturally Mr. Hagerty didn't know that Mr. Buchwald was kidding—you don't laugh in church, especially when the church is on Pennsylvania Avenue.

But take another sacred cow—Big Business. Mr. Caskie Stinnett, no mean funnyman himself, recently charged that "business will permit itself to be discussed only in the noblest terms." I can quite understand this, for profit-making on a decisive scale involves a kind of fanaticism incompatible with humor.

Yet my desk is awash with books deriding, sometimes effectively, sometimes with that edginess that comes of improperly controlled indignation, the absurdities of superorganization, the tribal fetishes of production, all the hollow solemnities of sell. The existence of this school of humor evidences a deep split in the business psyche itself, for most of the writers are Madison Avenue types, and know what they're talking about.

The disease of the New Respectability stimulates other antibodies. The quasi-religion of Togetherness produces writers like Jean Kerr and Shirley Jackson, whose stock in trade is the Little Monsters, and whose pictures of American family life should drive any reflective young man to sterilization. Similarly the New Respectability is challenged by the New Bawdiness, illustrated by any number of explicit books of cartoons and by openly Rabelaisian funny novels. A good example of the latter is George Albee's *By the Sea, By the Sea*, a riot of libidinous hilarity for two-thirds of the way, at which point it turns into straight commodity humor with an eye on Hollywood.

Mr. Albee's extravaganza is about some crazy people (or sensible, depending on where you sit) who have withdrawn completely from competitive society, like Mr. Steinbeck's Tortilla Flat amiable bums. This withdrawal gambit (it started with Huck Finn, of course) is the main feature of dozens of books of contemporary humor. It illustrates vividly one evasion technique of the humorist. Not allowed to laugh straight into the face of his society, he does the next best thing—he portrays a society which does his laughing for him indirectly.

And so we have George Price's priceless lunatics. We have Richard Powell (*Pioneer, Go Home!*) and Mac Hyman (*No Time for Sergeants*), whose heroes lick the system by simplemindedly staying out of it. We have Pogo and Peanuts and other symbols of unconventionality. We have Edmund Love's *Subways Are for Sleeping*, presenting in the most sympathetic light assorted members of the outgroup, the nonjoiners.

Finally, we have parody. It is my conviction that a score of years that can produce a Thurber, a White, a Perelman, a DeVries, a Wolcott Gibbs (and there are many others) can justly be called an age of great parody. Parody is partly a literary exercise, one of the most difficult forms of literary criticism. But it can also be a subtle mode of evading the constrictions of convention. There is a certain kind of writer who, forbidden to kid the President, will take out his humor on his own colleagues and the art forms of his time. By so doing he establishes himself, in the most indirect way, as a critic of society. Under the kinds of pressures now operating, parody flourishes. It is the literary man's impudent gesture par excellence.

As is clear from the foregoing, the future of American humor, like the future of anything else, is linked to our physical survival.

Assuming that we do survive, it is linked to the tempo of mechanization. At present we produce large quantities of machine humor; smaller quantities of humor satirizing the machine and machine living; and still smaller quantities stemming from an older, relatively timeless, philosophical view of experience. The humor that continues to delight, to console, and indeed to survive is hearted with wisdom. Of this kind of humor we are not without magnificent examples. But its future is hardly what you would call assured.

What Is a Great Man?

A Conversation

SCENE—*Lounge bar of the United Nations Headquarters, New York City.*

TIME—*The present.*

CHARACTERS—*Tascheraud, Campbell, and Thompson, minor UN officials from France, Great Britain, and the United States respectively.*

TASCHERAUD: While our hardier colleagues within are undergoing the eloquence of the Soviet delegate, I propose we enjoy the most universally welcomed product of our friend Campbell's native heath.

CAMPBELL: Tascheraud, you have the prose style of an ambassador.

THOMPSON: Make it three. Speaking of your native heath, Campbell, I recently came across an interesting remark about Scotsmen in Churchill's *History of the English-Speaking Peoples—*

CAMPBELL: Thompson, you've been *reading* again?

THOMPSON: Wasn't caught at it, though. Actually it's winked at among us backstairs functionaries. Among the real brass, of course, the habit's not encouraged.

35

TASCHERAUD: Of course. And so you get things done more quickly. I shudder to think of how much we French have failed to accomplish, solely because of our national weakness for reflection.

CAMPBELL: Buck up, Tascheraud. Communication will soon be so instantaneous no interval will remain for reflection. Thompson, you were talking about the Old Man.

THOMPSON: Yes. Well, in this passage Churchill's discussing art and letters in eighteenth-century Scotland. He mentions the philosopher David Hume, the economist Adam Smith, the historian William Robertson, the poet Burns—and winds up with "the great Walter Scott." Now why did he reserve "great" only for Scott?

TASCHERAUD: Interesting. One would have thought it more appropriate to the so vastly influential Hume and Smith.

CAMPBELL: Not at all. Churchill's quite right. Of the five Scott *is* the great man. For us Britishers, I mean. Churchill knows perfectly that as a *mind* Scott—how do you chaps put it, Thompson?—Scott isn't in the same league with Hume or Smith. But he was the one with *character*. Read his life. Stood up to things, you know—rather like the Old Man himself.

THOMPSON: You would make courage the test of greatness?

CAMPBELL: I said character. Much bigger thing. Includes courage, naturally, but also self-discipline, patience, the capacity to command events, the ability to endow your inferiors with your own qualities and—this is crucial—to act grandly with no touch of grand opera. That's why Hitler and Mussolini can never seem truly great to us—they're grandiose, not grand.

TASCHERAUD: But do you not admire Churchill's intellect?

CAMPBELL: Despite what our critics say, we do not object to intellect. But it must keep its proper place. Churchill's intellect was as notable at fifty as at seventy. But he wasn't great at fifty. He was great in the Blitz. Put it this way—do you chaps think much of Churchill as a writer?

TASCHERAUD: Formidable!

THOMPSON: Terrific!

CAMPBELL: Agreed. We were pleased as Punch when he wangled the Nobel prize. Still for us it was only a side show, a bit like winning the ribbon at the fair for the largest mangel-wurzel. His intellect doesn't make him great. What makes him great (I mean of course supremely great) is that when everything looked a shaky do, he knew almost without reflecting (sorry, Tascheraud, old boy) how to talk and *act* for the country. In a way—don't let this go any further—Churchill is not a man of ideas. But he is something better—he *is* an idea: Britain. Rather the British *character*. Let me make it even clearer. Who is the greatest Englishman that ever lived?

THOMPSON: Shakespeare.

TASCHERAUD: Newton.

CAMPBELL: I suspected you'd name them. That's what history and the books say. But we don't worry about history—we've made so much of it, it doesn't overawe us. Of course we *know* they're great. But they're in the *public* pantheon. The private pantheon—that of the people as a whole—shows a different set of busts: Churchill's ancestor Marlborough. The elder Pitt. Wellington. Nelson. Queen Elizabeth. Even Cromwell, though he speaks for only part of us. We can't *feel* Newton's greatness—overpowering intellect makes us ordinary folk a bit uneasy. Isn't that true of your people too, Thompson?

THOMPSON: Not precisely. It has less effect on us because we don't generally know it's around. Take the physicist Willard Gibbs—I have a journalist friend who thinks he's the greatest intellect ever produced in this country. But we haven't heard of him yet, though he died over fifty years ago. Poor Gibbs—he had no apple to make him famous. Or take our Presidents—the finest *mind* among them was probably John Quincy Adams. But he means little, except to historians and other Adamses.

TASCHERAUD: But surely, Campbell, your Shakespeare——

CAMPBELL: We know nothing of his character. He's great, but not what you might call *alive great*. In a way Shakespeare isn't a man at all. He's a national resource, rather like your Grand Canyon, Thompson——

THOMPSON: Or Kleenex.

CAMPBELL: He's part of the Empire—pardon, the Commonwealth. He's a public utility, laid on, like hot water——

TASCHERAUD (*softly*): Or the Pierian spring.

CAMPBELL: Pardon?

TASCHERAUD: No matter. Pray continue.

CAMPBELL: No, I've had my innings. You're up, Tascheraud. Who are your greatest men?

TASCHERAUD: All our pantheons are public; it is the French way. We are never quite certain of anyone's rank until it has been made official, just as we are never quite certain of the morality and good reputation of a word until the Academy has passed on it. Our national passion for order——

CAMPBELL: Vastly overrated thing, order. Should be reserved for the military, where it belongs. Englishmen are law-abiding largely because we've rarely had order preached at us. Sorry, Tascheraud.

TASCHERAUD: As I say, we have only one pantheon. But it has two divisions and most Frenchmen are never quite certain which of them merits the purer devotion. As you know, we pay great attention to words—indeed, we are so inept at politics that we often prefer to be ruled by words rather than by parties. Two of these words are *l'esprit* and *la gloire*. They exude an almost religious aura—as at the moment, Thompson, the words "team spirit" and "adjustment" do for your fellow citizens.

THOMPSON: You've been listening to our sociologists and magazine thinkers, Tascheraud. In general we not only do not reverence words, we suspect them. We even vote down men who use them clearly.

TASCHERAUD: For a Frenchman it is not the same. Perhaps it is a fault in us. We do not mind deceiving ourselves with a word as long as that word can enlarge our imagination. For example, *la gloire. Le jour de gloire,* you recollect, *est arrivé.* I suppose the two Frenchmen who incorporate the word for us are Louis XIV and Napoleon. They are among the supreme greats in the French pantheon. Every schoolboy knows them by heart. Yet in our soberer moments we know also that, along with the magnificence of Louis' court and the magnetism of his mistresses—

for with us such mistresses are bound up with *la gloire*—went a series of blunders that impoverished the country and in truth made our revolution inevitable. As for Napoleon, we are still recovering from him.

THOMPSON: Then why are Napoleon and the Sun King great?

TASCHERAUD: One must think not in terms of the facts, as you Americans say, but in terms of art. Louis and Napoleon were dramatic successes—in their careers, their magnificence, the magnitude of their arrogance, the intensity of the spotlight with which each in his time bathed France. Campbell's great men— Pitt, Elizabeth, Marlborough—actually achieved substantial results for England. A businessman would say that they brought in a profit; and, my dear Campbell, though you omitted this crass detail, I suggest it is a factor in their national greatness. But Napoleon and Louis are for us not men of strong character who advanced our country's fortunes. They are rather heroes of Glory, actors in a grand pageant. We are very fond of the theater, we Frenchmen.

THOMPSON: But how about the other part of your pantheon, the *esprit* part?

TASCHERAUD: Ah, there you touch the division in our souls. For though we adore Glory, which we know to be unreasonable, we also adore Reason as if it were glorious. Indeed, if the Russians, who invented everything, have not already staked out a claim, some of us would list France as the birthplace of Reason.

CAMPBELL: The devil of it is it's true. That's what makes it hard occasionally for Englishmen and Frenchmen to communicate. You are rational, we are sensible—how is one to bridge so vast a gap?

TASCHERAUD: Alas, there is no other way but this. We must continue talking with each other, for centuries and centuries——

THOMPSON: But get back to your great men of reason——

TASCHERAUD: There it is: we revere Napoleon and Descartes at the same time and with equal fervor: a humiliating illogicality. We are as much moved by a display of intellect as you English are by a display (properly underplayed, of course) of character. When we are so moved we say our greatest man is Voltaire or

Descartes. We have a natural reverence for writers, even for bad writers, precisely because, my dear Thompson, they deal intimately with those very words your countrymen so shrewdly distrust. Even those who disagree with De Gaulle have a certain admiration for him, because he still stands for the tradition of *la gloire;* and they admire him the more because he has shown himself to be a writer. The point is even clearer in the case of Malraux—not only a great writer but a man of heroic action. But remember, we are quite capable of making a hero out of a poet no less than out of a conqueror. We are prouder of Racine and Baudelaire than of Turenne. French boys still dream of becoming poets as American boys dream of becoming—what, Thompson?

THOMPSON: Account executives.

TASCHERAUD: You speak too ironically of your great country, Thompson.

THOMPSON: That is our habit when we love it most dearly. Never having had a Racine to study, we do not so easily come by the language of passion.

TASCHERAUD: You are overmodest. A country that has produced a Melville, a Poe, a Whitman need not envy us a Racine.

THOMPSON: All the same they're not our great men, not our greatest.

CAMPBELL: Who are?

THOMPSON: The funny thing is, we're not sure. Englishmen know who theirs are; Frenchmen are even more certain about theirs. We're still searching for the right gods. It used to be the Founding Fathers, but they've now become the property of the historians—they're hardly even quoted on the Fourth of July any more. Then it was the great industrial barons of the nineteenth century, but they, too, are old hat. And, as I said, the intellect itself does not command our immediate reverence. It would surprise most of us to be told that among our very greatest men are Willard Gibbs, William James, John Dewey, though it would not surprise any Frenchman to be told that Laplace, Pasteur, Carnot are among *his* country's greats.

CAMPBELL: Then who *is* your greatest American?

THOMPSON: Most of us would say Lincoln. It is difficult for me to say why this is so without seeming fatuous. You see, just as there are two strains in the French soul, Tascheraud, one stressing Glory, the other Intellect, so there are two in the American soul. They have often been pointed out: the idealistic and the practical. Our great men are usually one or the other. In Lincoln's case, the two merge—for Lincoln was probably the most practical, even the most ruthless, politician in our history up to the time of the second Roosevelt.

First of all, our heroes must be truly of the people. I don't mean a *representative* of the people, as you say Churchill is. You English seem to *like* your heroes to come of superior stock —even Cromwell was petty gentry, wasn't he? We don't. We want a certain homeyness, a certain commonness of touch. That's why Washington and even Jefferson are what Campbell calls public pantheon figures to us. But Lincoln's different. And so— I imagine this name will surprise you—so's Henry Ford.

Lincoln and Ford. How to make sense out of such a combination? Well, we seem to make heroes out of men with a sense of the American mission. Does that seem vague? It is. But it has meaning for us. You see, all Americans live in a strange state of excitement. We know that Destiny has pitchforked us into a position—which we don't understand very well and exploit very badly—in which we can actually be of help to the whole world. I don't mean by "leading" it—that never works, as the Russians are finding out and—here I beg your pardon, Tascheraud—as Napoleon found out. I mean by *giving* it something. The thing we think we have to give has a dozen handles. One big handle is called freedom; another big handle is called machinery. One kind of American great man—Lincoln pre-eminently—knew how to work the first handle. Another kind of great man—Ford, perhaps—knew how to work the second one. But both Ford and Lincoln are popular heroes not because of their *achievements*— saving the Union, making good cheap cars—but because each had a sense that he was doing what he did so that the world might as a result be joggled just the least bit in the direction of greater decency and comfort and happiness. It's the sense of American *mission* that the American feels in his greatest heroes. Not character. Not glory. Not intellect. Rather hard to talk about. Shall we finish these and order another?

Who'll Take the Hi-Road?

In his book *Good Behaviour* the English critic and former diplomat Harold Nicolson examines twelve patterns of civility, from classical Chinese ceremonialism to the code of the British public school product. His discourse is delightful—delightful even in its insularity, for at his most urbane Mr. Nicolson is tempted to judge other types of courtesy by his own admirable one.

American manners, however, floor him completely. "Americans appear to belong," he writes, "not to a different race merely, but to a different planet." The judgment is not one of disapproval: indeed, he admits, with slightly nervous cheerfulness, that our manners may soon supply the model for the rest of the world. Furthermore, he admires, with as little reserve as his training permits, our helpfulness, our hospitality, and our "sweet equality." Yet on the whole we baffle him. He is, for example, astonished by three American traits that other visitors have also noted: the license accorded youth, the position of power we grant to our women, and our general disregard of personal privacy.

I could no more explain to Mr. Nicolson why we behave like Americans than he could explain to me his affection for "the excellent institution of fagging." But, if I cannot enlighten him, perhaps I can offer him the trivial consolation that comes of knowing that others share his bewilderment. For there are a few phenomena of the Casual Era that buffalo me as much, I am sure, as they would buffalo Mr. Nicolson.

Take the simple matter of salutation. Now, I know the correct form as well as any man. I know I should jettison all that phraseological lumber of a bygone epoch when, according to circumstances, one said "Good morning," "Good afternoon," "Good evening," or even (it *does* sound quaint) "How do you do?" How corny, how square, to preserve from my youth the tendency to use the fossil word "sir" when addressing an older person, or one whom we used to call a superior. I shall try again. Dear reader, I do not know you, you do not know me, let us swear eternal friendship. Hi.

Or take the matter of introductions. In certain alert-eyed, locker-room circles this formula rules: "Meet Bill Haskins, Union Carbide." I may like Bill Haskins, I may admire Union Carbide, but my fuzzy brain is unable to relate the two sentiments. Plain Bill Haskins is a fellow man. Bill-Haskins-Union-Carbide awes me into a social stupor. What is worse, being myself almost unintroducible, I am a burden to others. All I own is two names, the first rather resistant to brisk curtailment, the second not notably attractive. My Union Carbide is Me—a small firm, raggedly managed, quite unlikely to expand. I feel keenly my lack of Company manners.

Of the diverse elements that go to make up the New Behavior, I list three that most unman me.

1. FEEDING CAN BE FUN

Shall we start with garlic bread? As Fluellen was recognizable by his leek, so today the smart, the traveled hostess is known by her affection for its powerful relative. Any timorous guest who, though he may like the staff of life well enough, prefers not to be felled by it, is viewed as a spoilsport. He is not Gay. I—I am not Gay.

I draw an even chillier glance when unmasked as Anti-Dip. With a certain distaste we read of the courtiers of Louis XIV who used to plunge their bread into the sauceboat. We rate our manners superior to those of the Noble Arabs (they are turning up with monotonous regularity these days in every Near East travel book) who thrust their hands into the common platter of torn-up mutton in the hope of emerging with the sheep's eyeball. The Dip, of course, is different. Out of the primitive solitary ceremony of the mere Dunk our higher religion of Togetherness has evolved this cocktail hour Agape. The Dip is not only a conversation starter but a kind of ritual Urn of Fun. I wish I were more adept at the rite, but, alas, I dip poorly. I must leave to others the rapt pleasure of inserting an oil-exudant potato chip into an unidentifiable viscous mass, enriched by detached pieces of other guests' oil-exudant potato chips, and then extracting and devouring the now highly socialized tidbit.

The Dip must be part of that new community sense dictating so many of the shifts in our behavior. So is Food-sharing. Any observer of manners in our public eating places must have noted the growing tendency to offer some of the contents of one's plate to one's fellow diner. Occasionally the transfer is forced, with much hilarity. One's plate of food used to be a private possession, like an Englishman's home. It is now becoming a gastronomic extension of the Community Fund on the one hand, and game equipment on the other. To illustrate the progress we have made I quote from della Casa's *Galateo,* an absurd manual of etiquette as practiced four hundred years ago: "I do not think it right to offer food from one's plate to anyone else."

2. THE CULT OF INFORMALITY

Each society creates its own image of bad, as well as of good, manners. The reverse of Castiglione's Courtier is the Boor. Indeed, since the chivalric era rudeness, shifting meaning with each age, has usually been considered basic to bad behavior. Among us today, however, it is not so considered, except in certain antiquated milieux.

Our pet abomination is less the Churl than the Stuffed Shirt. We tolerate offhandedness sooner than pomposity. The great sin is not vulgarity but affectation. The Gentleman fades; the Nice

Guy takes over; and everybody works twenty-four hours a day at being Sincere.

Sincerity may manifest itself in various ways, one of them being reserve, even taciturnity. But for us the signal mark of sincerity is friendliness.

And so, with our characteristic efficiency, we are beginning to work up a wholly new system of approach-behavior, a 360-degree, universal-jointed amiability that seduces some foreign visitors and stuns others. (Mr. Nicolson, for example, rather likes it.) As the spontaneous overflow of powerful feelings, such friendliness can be heart-warming. When the pistol of cordiality is held to the other fellow's head, it can be less so.

Ceremonious manners need not, any more than a business contract, imply falseness. A contract acknowledges and tries to minimize the essential unknowability and unreliability of human beings. It is not based on an elevated view of human nature. Neither is it based on a distorted one. The same is true of formal courtesy. Such courtesy merely codifies and systematizes a chilly but sound insight: that people though held together basically by communication, occasionally get along better by keeping their distance, at least for a time. There are occasions when Donne's statement will not stand up, when we *are* islands to ourselves. Traditional good manners are in part an agreed-upon system of signals flashed from one island to another. They do not necessarily issue from kindness of heart (though often their effect is to make everyone feel happier than he would be without them) but rather from a fear that the human race, were it to abolish all bars, gulfs, and reserves, would become less human, and might indeed fall apart. It is this same fear that leads us to prefer any government, however unjust, to none at all.

The Nice Guy, carefully cultivating his sincerity, is not happy with this rather un-Fun view of the race. Believing in bridges, not gulfs, he is an expert at constructing them forthwith out of chance materials. Unless he does so, he feels, he might run the risk of indictment as a Stuffed Shirt, than which and so forth.

And so, instead of greeting, we hail each other as if we were taxicabs.

And so too we have the present torrential upsurge of First-naming.

The James-Lange theory of the emotions tells us that we do not clench our fists because we are angry but that we are angry because we clench our fists. In the same way perhaps Mr. Jones and Mr. Smith, shortly after their first meetings, call each other Tom and Joe not because they like each other but because they believe that they *will* like each other as a consequence of saying Tom and Joe.

Sometimes this works. But not always. A couple new to the town may within a few weeks find themselves on a first-name basis with five hundred presumed friends. In a few years they are still on the same basis, but now they may have discovered that they don't care much for four hundred of the first-name friends, or perhaps themselves aren't much liked by them. It makes for difficulties.

The virtue of First-naming lies in the saving of the time and energy of a busy, mobile people. Its danger lies in the premature fixing of relationships that perhaps should remain for a while in a fluid state.

Traditionally the English have been most conscious of this danger. Their reserve has nothing to do with whether they are cold, hot, or lukewarm. It is simply a form of social accident insurance worked out over the course of centuries by a realistic race. We, on the other hand, are an optimistic race, willing to take the risk involved in a sudden oversupply of intimacy.

The increasing use in the business world of first names, regardless of age, rank, salary, ability, or length of service, entails certain perils. On the surface it produces an atmosphere of happy familyhood. Underneath, it often generates unconscious tensions arising from uncertainty as to one's actual status in the happy family. To those innocent victims of cordiality, the employees, who may have been under the impression that they held four aces, it may come as a surprise, once the chips are down, to discover that the boss really has the cards.

However we look at it, we are a long way from Jane Austen's world in which, as Mr. Nicolson recalls for us, Emma was filled with ire at the thought that Mrs. Elton might be so unrefined as to dare to "go about Emma Woodhousing me."

3. TEENOLATRY

The essayist Frederic Morton recently contributed to one of our magazines what the editors billed as a "shamelessly opinionated view of the teener."

Mr. Morton pictured the teen-ager as in effect dominating the entire country. This domination is exercised over a vast variety of fields, from TV programs to the educational system. As for politics, when the eighteen-year-old gets the vote, as of course he will, we Americans will boast the first hot-rod President in our history.

For the moment, however, let us limit ourselves to his effect on our manners.

When, at a recent convention, the American Legion, instead of acting like teen-agers, comported itself as grown men normally do, the fact was thought worthy of front-page notice, as if somehow the Legion had reverted to an extinct form of behavior.

It has often been noted, and most of all by ourselves, that we, a magnificently gifted people, do not count among our outstanding talents a talent for aging. Deep down we have never cared much for that dull law of Nature decreeing that embryos shall become men, and not vice versa. The only character in our fiction who has grown into a true culture hero (our Aeneas, our Siegfried) is Huckleberry Finn—and not because of his genius for expression, but because of his genius for irresponsibility.

The teen-ager (Huck Finn remodeled by Charles Addams) has enormous energy, great ability to command publicity, and the Hitlerian capacity to dominate through incessant demands. He is, in a word, a *success*. His success confirms and encourages our disinclination to accept the fact that the only essential reason for being young is to outgrow it.

In the domain of manners the results are evident, and to me (I have no teen-age children) startling. Our table manners are influenced by those of a dominant group whose etiquette derives from the manipulation of the pop bottle, the ketchup-smeared hamburger, and the omnipresent cigarette. Our oft-noted aversion to privacy has as one of its roots the breezy code of the teen-ager for whom the double concept of private property and the private person is as unimaginable as walking; for whom noise and sound are identical; for whom a house is an adjunct to a garage; for whom the telephone is a way of life. Twenty-five years ago our highways were not littered with debris. If they are so today it is because our youthful mentors have taught us that it is more dashing to chuck away than to dispose of. From whom have our mature female citizens, parading a thousand Main Streets, borrowed their short shorts, their halters, their blue jeans? From whom have our mature male citizens borrowed their tielessness, their coatlessness, their open Hollywood shirts, as they dine, sweat glands in magnificent working order, in public restaurants? And if grown men no longer offer subway seats to women they may well be influenced by their masters, the teen-ager, to whom such a gesture would seem corny.

Having at last found the Fountain of Youth, we are delighted to discover that it spouts Coca-Cola.

Of course, I am not talking of the millions of decent-mannered teen-agers to be found throughout the land. It's only that it's the others who are noticeable, the others who seem to be managing the show.

To sum up, these days I seem to be encountering, simply bred as I am, a few of the same difficulties that baffle Sir Harold Nicolson, whose nurture is quite different from mine.

Move over, Hal.

Tinker's Itch

THOUGH SOME THINK the wheel mankind's greatest invention, I prefer Kleenex. I use the wheel once as against a dozen employments of this indispensable tissue. What is Modern Man? He is a Wiping Animal.

No, like Mrs. Micawber, I never will desert Kleenex. But of late my devotion has been tested. How? Not long ago the withdrawal of the first piece of Kleenex from a new box was a fairly simple operation. Tearing off a perforated strip, you removed the tissue from a wide slot in the box top. But time and designers march on. The fact that Kleenex itself is perfect throws the designer into a frenzy of frustration. Maddened, he descends on the container. Now the first piece must be elicited through a small oval opening. As the shape of a piece of Kleenex is not by nature oval, you cannot effect an exit without pulling along with piece number one at least five more tattered and torn Kleenices—I assume *Kleenex*, like *Index*, comes from the Latin. (Note of apology: the manufacturers have, since these indignant words, kindly improved their container.)

This improvement mania, known medically as Tinker's Itch, is part of the progress of modern design. Our gullible great-grandfathers believed in the Perfectibility of Man. Faced with considerable contrary evidence we have replaced this doctrine with a belief in the Perfectibility of Things. If we cannot make a better man, let us make a better mousetrap. But, just as the delusion of the Perfectibility of Man got us into certain jams, so that of the Perfectibility of Things entails its own dangers.

The Condorcets* and Lenins of the drawing board and testing lab are guided by one or more sacred dogmas. I list a few.

1. NEVER LET WELL ENOUGH ALONE

This is the basic commandment. We have already noted its application to the Kleenex container. I offer another example. Before me lie two nutcrackers. One is a stone-age implement that will do nothing but crack nuts. It consists of two homely movable straight legs, connected at one end. The inner surfaces are evenly corrugated so as to hold firmly any conceivable nut. The other is a chrome beauty, streamlined so as to offer no resistance to the air, a property of untold value should you desire to propel a nutcracker beyond the earth's gravitational field. It also offers little resistance to the nut. Its Dietrichian legs boast three beautifully scalloped internal curves, for large, medium, and small nuts. It is designed so that only a very few fortunate nuts of exactly the right size can be gripped at all, much less actually cracked.

2. MAKE IT INACCESSIBLE

Kleenex is again a case in point. But a finer example is the Jiffy Bag, used for enclosing books. The Jiffy Bag boasts two main features: (1) staples that yield only to the fingers of Hercules; (2) soft sides stuffed with dirty shredded paper. As book covers have sharp corners they usually penetrate the shredded paper. Should they fail to do this, the struggle to dislodge the staples will accomplish a similar result: even, universal shred distribution. I hold in my hand, ladies and gentlemen, another book container, designed entirely without ingenuity, for it is a simple cardboard box,

---

* Marquis de Condorcet (1743–1794), philosopher and mathematician, author of an essay on the progress of the human mind, foretelling the ultimate perfection of mankind. His death in prison was due to the energetic efforts of the Jacobins, who also believed in perfectibility.

openable at once by the pulling out of a small tab. But this one merely permits you to get at the book. It is devoid of the advantages of the Jiffy Bag which guarantees "protection under the most hazardous conditions. Picture a mail car on fire—extinguished by cascades of water. Picture a book in a Jiffy Bag inside that car."

(Parenthetically we may note that, like the Jiffy Bag people, many modern designers belong to the Disaster or Ultimate Hazard or End-of-the-World School. This school attaches little importance to ordinary utility. The essential thing is to build in powers of survival proper to Mount Everest or the giant sequoia. A radio is recommended because it can be dropped harmlessly from a helicopter. A woolen scarf is tested by passing it through fire. A watch taped to Mickey Mantle's bat is still running after Mickey has lined out fifty drives.)

The Law of Inaccessibility operates with machine-turned precision in the case of many common objects: sardine cans, flip-top cigarette boxes, any number of things mummied in cellophane so as to pose interesting problems in topology.

We possess a graceful brass-and-copper grated-cheese shaker. Obeying the Law of Inaccessibility, its holes are too small to allow the cheese to come through. I should qualify: they *will* allow ready-prepared, packaged grated cheese to come through.

But as my household finds this inedible, the result is the same: we have the shaker and the shaker has the cheese. This leads directly to the next Law:

3. THE RIGHT SIZE IS THE SIZE TOO SMALL

I pass over such obvious illustrations as the exits of our railroad cars, so designed as to divide a trip from Blankville to New York into two equal time intervals: about forty-five minutes from Blankville to New York and about forty-five minutes from interior of car to platform of station; or taxicabs (except Checker) that involve a struggle for emergence that has developed into my sole remaining form of violent exercise; or standard beds, still constructed in bland disregard of the fact that the average American male is three inches taller than his grandfather, and growing all the time; or step-on weighing scales in which the pressure-sensitive portion of the platform is just large enough for the feet of a midget.

Allow me to dwell on commoner, less complex objects. Nothing could be commoner or less complex, for instance, than a pair of pants (male). Now I, like many other men, like to keep my wallet in my left rear pocket. This is usually provided with a button or buttonable flap to reduce the security risk. About three out of four pairs of pants provide pockets big enough so that you can, with a fairly full wallet, take advantage of the button. The fourth will hold an *empty* wallet, just barely. But not a full one.

Pass to the wallet itself. Most wallets are devised on the assumption that modern man never carries about in his billfold anything more than a single bill or perhaps, in flush times, two bills. But what is the truth?

The truth is that modern man, uncertain of his own identity anyway, is compelled to bear with him whatever scraps of evidence he can rake up to convince himself and others that he is someone. I, for example, currently have in my wallet: two thick commutation-ticket books; social-security card; two hospitalization identification cards; two small checks I have been meaning to cash for eight months; terse instructions as to the immediate disposal of my sudden corpse; two railroad schedules; twenty-three bills; an assortment of business cards bearing the names of various acquaintances now quite unrecallable; and a moderate quantity of fuzz. The wallet does its best to abide by the doctrine of containment. But if the bills are crisp and new and the wallet is removed briskly, the bills will fall out. And as stated, the wallet itself stands in constant peril of depocketization.

My wife, an uncaptious lady who makes modest demands of life (she married me), states that ladies' evening bags are constructed on the same principle of spatial economy. It is taken for granted therefore that during a festive evening the male escort must carry any amount of feminine gear—matches, cigarettes, keys, change, and so on—in addition to his own personal load of five martinis.

Why are return envelopes from our most efficient institutions, such as banks and department stores, *just* large enough for a single enclosure, but not sealable if you wish to add another? Why are men's wooden pants hangers (the kind built roughly like a triangle) neatly devised so that the pants at the fold are always too wide to be draped over the horizontal bar? It is in obedience to Commandment Number 3, already cited: *The Right Size Is the Size Too Small.* Which leads us to a related law involving an interesting postulate in the theory of numbers.

4. IF IT WORKS IN NINE POSITIONS OUT OF TEN, THEN 9=10

I have a floor lamp operating on the elbow principle, so that the upper illuminating section can be swiveled out and around. That is, it can be swung out and around up to an angle of 135 degrees. Dare to pass beyond this point, that is from 135 degrees to the maximum of 180 degrees, and the lamp can be relied upon to topple over. I shall not labor the point, noted by millions, that as a general thing no floor lamp exists at once efficient and pleasing to the eye. But it does not matter much; the floor lamp is doomed in favor of the civilized lighting to come. Even industrial designers have at last taken note of the fact that if God had wished to place the sun on a stilt, He would have done so.

5. THE COMPLEX IS ALWAYS PREFERABLE TO THE SIMPLE

Perhaps this is a corollary of (1).

Convinced as I am that the decay of common English prose is partly due to the invention of the typewriter, I have always tried to protect my style by using a fountain pen. The one I am now writing with is thirteen years old. I bought it from a man in Tuxedo Park who does not advertise, but instead makes fountain pens, which he sells for about two and a half dollars. They are terribly old-fashioned. You unscrew the top half and then pump in the ink by alternately squeezing and releasing a rubber sac that must cost about one-tenth of a cent. It has no springs, levers, hydraulic motors, streamlining, irium, barium, thorium; it cannot be dropped from a plane without breakage;

it comes unjeweled and only in black. All it does is write. This is more than can be said for some of its complex competitors.

6. FORM IS THE ENEMY OF FUNCTION

I adduce the example of the soup spoon. The bowl of the soup spoon is either round or oval. In neither case is soup, whose character is wayward at best, conveyed neatly from disinterested spoon to expectant mouth. Inasmuch as the mouth tends to assume the shape of a smallish hole rather than a wide horizontal mailbox slot, the soup *should* be tipped out of the spoon in a thin stream rather than a broad waterfall. It follows, therefore, that the proper shape for a spoon is that of a miniature ladle, narrower at one side (the mouth side) than at the other. In a longish lifetime of soup ingestion I have only once encountered a spoon suitable to the human oral orifice. This was at the home of the brilliant actress Adrianne Allen. It was a pleasure to eat her soup. Upon inquiry my hostess explained that these spoons were a family heirloom, having been invented, but never patented, by her grandfather, a noble spirit whose genius commands my admiration as much as his lack of business enterprise inspires my regret.

The whole doctrine of the Perfectibility of Things stems from a delusion suggesting infantile behavior. The infant moves his hands and arms, not on purpose, but simply because to his delight he finds he can move them. Similarly when we ingenious "grownups" discover that our marvelous new power tools *can* change almost any object, we conclude that therefore we should change it. I believe the economic motive is secondary, or even a mere rationalization. I believe that at least some of the more baffling experiments in modern design are the result of an infantile desire to apply power just because power is available.

Some years ago, to pass from one part of New York's Pennsylvania Station to another, the traveler had to open and go through a door. Then the doors were equipped with a magic toy, the Photoelectric Eye. Now, the Eye opened the door. But in order for the Eye-opener to work, the traveler had to approach the door, not at his own pace, but at one pleasing to the

Eye. This caused trouble. Today they have not only removed the Eye, but the door too, which nobody needed in the first place.

My garage doors are electrically operated. A miracle. But when power fails (as it does in the country) I'm stuck.

If my car is *in* the garage, I can't get it *out*. If *outside*, I can't get it *in*. Of course, if one dismantles the mechanism (which I do not understand), manual operation is possible. But this takes a strong man (not available in my household) and in the meantime I miss the 8:10, unless it is late, which it generally is, on account of technical difficulties.

Another thing: we have two small children. But our ownership of them is rather a precarious thing. If Child Number 1 happens to be under the open door and Child Number 2 presses the button, Child Number 1 is changed into jam. Hence they are forbidden to play near the garage. Hence again, they play near the garage.

Of course I can relapse to ordinary doors, but this costs three hundred dollars. More important, my neighbors would not like it. It would be a subversive gesture, for modern technology has already attained religious status, and I wish to profane no man's altar.

Are power-worked car windows or electronically worked refrigerator doors *true* improvements? Or are they the consequences of the free operation of the play instinct, about on a level with thumb sucking? Do tail fins really make for a better car? Or are they the consequences of gleefully fooling around with a billion-dollar Meccano set?

And—to bring us up to date—are satellites the issue of a basic scientific curiosity? Or is this attempt to communicate with the nonhumanity of outer space merely a confession of our failure to communicate with each other, a cry of despair that we pretend is a shout of triumph?

I Know What You Mean

DR. ELLSWORTH BARNARD of Bowdoin College recently proposed that high schools throughout the country revamp their English courses to teach rules "that conform to actual usage." Doctor Barnard went on to say, "Anything is all right if it fits the occasion and expresses the intended thought." The *New York Times*, reporting this pronouncement from the college once attended by Hawthorne and Longfellow, headed the dispatch: PROF. SAYS BUM ENGLISH AIN'T SO BAD AFTER ALL. The professor himself, by the way, teaches English, presumably Bum or Fancy, following the actual usage of the moment.

There seems little doubt that the Levelers, increasingly backed by the authority of the Learned, have won their war. Our language has been made safe for democracy. What would, let us say in Mr. Hoover's time, have been thought of as illiteracy, has been promoted to the rank of homespun American. The Levelers' thesis is now generally accepted: as our tongue is at any point merely the product of an infinity of small folk-initiated changes, the nasty notion of "correctness" falls to the ground, and there, we may well say, it lays. The king's English is dead; long live King Usage.

The victory of the Levelers and the Learned (always an irresistible political combination—see contemporary Russia) would appear to relieve me, and I presume other writers, of an oppressive responsibility. I must conclude that I spend too much time anxiously pruning these essays of what I had always considered personal faults of style: for example, a tendency to periphrasis, overuse of adverbs, reluctance to employ short sentences. It is a consoling idea that anything is all right if it fits the occasion and expresses the intended thought, for this would seem to make no great call on whatever writing ability I may possess.

Unfortunately, this consolation is academic. My editors are still mired in the pre-Leveling era. Thorough reactionaries, they insist that their writers have an obligation to their readers to write as forcefully, as elegantly, as amusingly, and (I blush for the word) as correctly as possible.

The Usage-Is-All school may, however, make my life as a broadcaster somewhat easier, for radio and television, being truly democratic arts, dispense with editors of speech. I have never, for example, been corrected for what I had these many years thought of as flaws in my diction and delivery: the belaboring of "very" and "well," the use of "ahm" for "I'm" and "ahr" for "our," needless complication of sentence structure, and other small sins of which I am now happily absolved. The Levelers are replacing an obligation to the language of Shakespeare and Lincoln with an obligation to the language of the juke-box gentry; just as the theologians of Cheerfulness are replacing our obligation to God with an obligation to Community Effort. Things get easier every day; we've never had it so good.

In one of my articles I once discussed the influence of the leaders of the Levelers, i.e., the mass communicators, particularly in radio and television. The response (or, as these fuglemen *preferably put it, the reaction) was surprising in its volume and intensity. Not all of it by any means was fan mail. Many of my readers accused me of that blackest of present-day sins, "a superior attitude." I had always thought that a thin but precise line could be drawn between feeling superior and feel-

* First Commandment of the Levelese Decalogue: Never use a word any one of your audience might have to look up in the dictionary.

ing distaste. The first involves the exercise of the ego, the second that of the judgment. I would have pleaded not guilty on the first count, guilty on the second; but it appears I have been deluding myself.

Other correspondents, bowing to the inevitable, suggest that it is time to make Televenglish retroactive, that is, to revise the English of the past much as the Stalinists revised the history of the Russian Revolution. Just as the latter substituted Stalin for Trotsky, so ought we to substitute the Winstonian "like" for the fascist-reactionary-imperialist "as." Examples:

> 1. Like the hart panteth after the water brooks, so panteth my soul after thee. King David
> 2. General: I received your letter of this date containing the terms of the Army of Northern Virginia like proposed by you. As they are substantially the same like those expressed in your letter of the 8th instant, they are accepted. R. E. Lee, General

One of my readers, under the delusion that the battle is still being waged, suggests that we do something about the doomed adverb. A billboard bearing three giant words: GULF STARTS WONDERFUL has given him a shock * for the consequences of which, I fear, there is no known cure.

Nor have I any consolation to offer other valued but unfortunately thin-skinned readers. It is best to bow, not rear the head (in fact, it is best not to use the head at all) when you hear Billy (I'm-just-plain-folks) Graham's benediction: "And may the Lord bless you *real good*." The Lord Himself, reputed by many to be guilty of that unhappy example of pre-Levelese, the Holy Bible, would do well to attend to Billy Graham.

Do not feel bad when you hear the broadcaster say he feels badly. Just remember that all men are created equally. When the friendly M.C. shyly confides to his millions of listeners that he feels nauseous, do not misinterpret this as self-criticism. As the United Nations slowly transform themselves into the YOO-nited Nations (often belittled as a lug-zury) give, as the broadcasters put it, a listen, and roll with the punch. Applaud the

---

* Learned Levelese: trauma

Televenglish teacher who reiterates that Ford Is America's Win-
ningest Car; who describes gorilla warfare, and mentions that
it occurred quite a ways back; who brings into your livin' room
with his *Waaarsh daay bluues?* the fine gamy accent of the picturesque street crier; who reports that so-and-so flew *into* Chi-
cago today.

From here on in we should accept with equanimity the Levelese law by which the originally jocular becomes the universally
mandatory. Thus always say *Longtime no see, How's about a
drink?, He's scared but good* (at Gimbels, Mr. Sigmund Roths-
child, A.S.A., "appraises everything but everything"). Those kind
of people are high-type fellas, just like you and I, and you can
say that again.

Some time ago, on a TV show dealing with words, I was properly taken to task by a distinguished professor of English because
I objected to the rate at which sounds were being dropped from
the language. He informed me that such snobbish purism had no
basis in logic. To be consistent, for instance, I should pronounce
gossamer as *goose summer*, of which the word is a contraction.
I accepted the rebuke, both to my scholarship and my character.
Hereafter I shall speak Televenglish. If I wish to be helpful I
shall be kwopertive. Traveling by air will become fling; speaking will become sāng; the state of being safe will become scurty
(ū as in cure); I shall soon be goeen to Washeenton to attend a
weddeen, unless I have a temperatoor, or perhaps a tempchur.
And, as more and more New Yorkers exchange the distasteful
you will in favor of the elegant *yizzle* (yizzle have to see Radio
City) I shall follow their lead. After all, I don't pronounce all
the letters in Cholmondeley, do I?

One of my correspondents, Miss Esther L. Johnson, sends me
a paragraph lifted from an editorial comment in an old *Youth's
Companion*, dated March 1, 1923. It reads:

> There are several engaging thoughts as to what the outcome
> of the widespread use of radio will be. Not the least pleasing of
> them is the idea that thousands of boys and girls will listen
> for an hour or more a day to a fair sort of spoken English, clearly
> enunciated. Youth is quick and imitative. Let us hope that on

the waves of the ether may come lessons that will enlarge our vocabulary and improve our pronunciation.

How pleasant for Miss Johnson and for us all that it has taken only thirty-nine years for this pious hope to become a shining reality.

Huck Finn and

the All-American Boy-Man

ONE AUGUST DAY I asked my son, aged eight, whether he was looking forward to school. "No, I wish I didn't have to go," he replied, looking me straight in the eye. Experience teaches us that the man who looks you straight in the eye, particularly if he adds a firm handshake, is hiding something. Aware that my son really likes the fine school he attends, I asked, "Where did you get that idea?" Holding out his little hatchet my young Washington replied bravely, "From television."

He was of course merely demonstrating the power of a minor myth familiar to us all. This myth, courtesy of television, had suggested to him that it was square to like school. That it was better to be an All-American Boy than to be himself.

In a way it all began with Huckleberry Finn.

Linguistic scholars note, among certain classes of words, a minor but steady drift toward degradation of meaning. Thus "silly" comes from the Old English *saelig*, or "blessed." An "innocent" is now a fool. "Lewd" once meant ignorant, and before that merely lay, or unclerical. This semantic Gresham's law, by which bad meanings drive out good, also at times governs imaginary characters. We can call a man quixotic only by blotting out the whole, complex Don Quixote and isolating one not overcreditable trait.

We did this with Huck Finn too. We took the one native fictional character who is part of the blood stream of the national imagination, and turned him into the All-American Boy. This Boy we then set in our folk pantheon. There he helped mold our actions, along with dozens of other popular heroes and heroines, including the Rugged Individualist (also the Team Player, for mythology makes strange bedfellows), the Mousetrap Maker, the Broad-Gauge Businessman, the Clean-Cut Young Fellow, the Good Egg, and Miss America. Finally, when we may have been just about ready to topple the idol from his pedestal, the Persuaders decided there was life in the young Boy yet. It looks (if I may drop into All-American) like they were right.

The original Huck Finn, Mark Twain's Huck Finn, was a genius. A genius of language—of language never "correct," always clear, poetic, powerful, and fitted to anything he wanted to say. A genius in his feeling for his country—the Mississippi flows north to south by way of Huck's heart. A genius, finally, of virtue achieved through struggle. His resolve not to inform on the escaped slave Jim (although his "conscience" tells him he should) marked a decisive moment in our history, a Gettysburg of the mind.

But it was easy to forget that this boy was a great man. It was easier to remember only that he disliked "sivilization." Gradually a popular Huck Finn image emerged, akin to the real Huck Finn only as "quixotic" is akin to the real Don Quixote. Cutting out Huck's brain and heart, we left the freckles and the fishing pole. Result: the All-American Boy, the Henry Aldrich of the old radio days.

To find out what had happened to Huck I visited Tin Pan Alley. ASCAP informed me that over a *dozen* Huck Finn songs were still in copyright. (They could unearth none about Captain Ahab, Hester Prynne, Roderick Usher, or Daisy Miller.) The best of these songs, by Cliff Hess, Sam M. Lewis, and Joe Young, was a hit in 1917. The date may point to the high-water mark of our uncoerced worship of the All-American Boy, just as our own time encloses the high-water mark of worship by persuasion. Cliff, Sam, and Joe's song is still in print and it's still a good one:

> There was a rascal in the town where I came from;
> The people thought that he was dumb,
> Because he couldn't do a sum.
> That's why they nicknamed him,
>   "Huckleberry Finn";
> But he believed in fun,
>   Laughed at everyone;
> How I wish I were him.

Chorus:

> Huckleberry Finn,
> If I were Huckleberry Finn;
> I'd do the things he did, I'd be a kid again.
> You'd always find me out fishin' beside a shady pool;
> Wishin' there never was a school;
> If I were only Huckleberry Finn,
> In ev'ry mischief I'd be in;
> And on my freckled face you'd always find a grin.
> I wouldn't put my shoes and stockings on for any man;
> And all I'd ever wear would be a coat of tan;
> If I were Huckleberry Finn.

Let me head you off. We need not wax too solemn over this ditty. I realize it voices a mood all of us, not merely we Americans, at times naturally fall into. Yet I think it does a bit more.

It illustrates, with touching unconsciousness, the downgrading I mentioned. In its guileless lines the real Huck has evaporated.

Furthermore it contains a number of familiar elements composing our present powerful All-American Boy-Man image. Thus:

1. *Youth worship.* The song is not about a boy called Huckleberry Finn. It's about a man wishing he *were* that boy.

2. *School phobia.* Lines 2 and 3 of the quoted verse imply a link between inability to learn and "real" smartness. Some lines in the second verse suggest this even more forcibly: "When I

begin to earn, Then I'll start to learn, How to count it." The general attitude is summed up nicely in "Wishin' there never was a school." Now I am not saying we Americans are antischool. I am saying that one of our treasured images is an antischool image.

3. *Fun morality.* That's the latest sociological slang for the song's "he believed in fun." They shall beat their school desks into sports cars and their altars into barbecue pits.

4. *Amiability,* or the idolatry of the grin.

5. *The religion of sport.* For the sake of our argument we'll call fishing—sorry, fishin'—a sport.

We've seen the image operating on my young son. Now, without trying to make any systematic application of the five elements above noted (for they combine and merge inseparably), let's see how the image works in rather more important areas.

Some years ago Mr. Nixon appeared on television to answer certain charges. I'm not concerned with his defense. The fact remains that most of us thought he did well; otherwise we wouldn't have elected him. I'm concerned with that dog, about which Mr. Nixon spoke with such charm. The Persuader inside Mr. Nixon (or more probably the Persuaders outside Mr. Nixon) suggested that a dog and integrity are indissolubly connected. The dog calls to mind a Boy, the kind of Boy who would make a good Vice-President. And—let's not kid ourselves—we loved it. That little ole Huck Finn image was right in there doing its bit. Mr. Eisenhower paid it homage when he responded in kind: "Dick, you're my boy."

Let me square myself with the Republicans. I wish I didn't have to lug in a dead one, for this is not a party-line essay. Reading Margaret Leech's distinguished biography, *In the Days of McKinley,* I was struck with how few sports-filled vacations McKinley took. During his infrequent recuperative periods he seems to have spent most of his time on a rocking chair on a hotel porch. Incidentally this is a form of exercise remarkably conducive to solid reflection, which is of course what we most want in a President.

Though McKinley actually was the kind of small-town boy who's part of the Huck Finn image, he refused to act like one.

But maybe McKinley shouldn't be given too much credit. He politicked before the religion of sport had made it necessary for him to show that he was All-American. Being American was enough.

Nor could I discover, from Miss Leech's book, that McKinley ever made a public, three-act, Good-Guy production out of eating the 1896 equivalent of pizza. Nor that he ever spent two and a half hours of executive time greeting Boy Scouts. The *New York Times* reported that during a Scout tour the Governor of the Empire State "never lost his smile." No one objects to good humor. (Also I happen to admire Mr. Rockefeller.) It's only when good humor is institutionalized, when it petrifies into the dogma of Goodscoutism, when the Huck Finn grin is made statutory, that I am made uneasy. The brute fact is that you and I grin only a few minutes of each day. When our great political leaders are never shown except grinning, the unworthy but natural suspicion arises that they are unaware that it is largely up to them to see that the earth is not blown up.

I am not convinced that the common run of us really prefer geniality to genius. A book by Dr. George H. Waltz, Jr., called *What Makes a Scientist?*, contains biographies of outstanding Americans in the field. Doctor Waltz trips over himself in his eagerness to assure us that his subjects are "very approachable human beings as well as trained and often highly creative people." But do we want our scientists to waste their time in approachability? Do we really care that they have wholesome hobbies and the mandatory five healthy children? Are they not worth more to us if they're as crusty as Newton, as odd as Pascal, as remote as Willard Gibbs? Shouldn't they be let alone so that they can do their work instead of being compelled to placate us with that ole fishin' pole?

We might call the following story *The Scientist and the All-American Boy.* For the authenticity of the facts I rely upon *Men and Atoms,* by the science writer William L. Laurence.

Once there was an All-European Boy named Enrico Fermi. On March 17, 1939 (yes, that early), Fermi tried to see Admiral Hooper in the office of the Chief of Naval Operations. All Fermi had in mind was to save civilization by explaining to the proper authorities the military importance of uranium fission.

He got as far as two young lieutenant commanders. They listened politely. According to legend, after Fermi had left, one turned to the other and said, "That wop is crazy!" There things rested for quite a while.

The story, if true, is interesting because it illustrates the intrusion of the All-American Boy mentality into a situation calling for its opposite. I am thinking of those young lieutenant commanders. Admitted, Fermi's English was poor, as contrasted with the elegance of their All-American "That wop is crazy!" Still, they might have been taught that not everyone speaks English. (The authors of *The Ugy American,* a book about the Huck Finn image in our diplomacy, recently pointed out the dangers of the monolingual complex.) More important, they might have been taught that there is in the world such a thing as high-order intellect. Had anything in their wholesome, fun-filled universe taught them that another universe existed, they might at least have made a five-cent local call to the Library of Congress or the Smithsonian Institution and established Fermi's world-famous position in five minutes.

Happily, once an abstract idea has slowly forced its way past our defenses, we become the highly intelligent people we basically are. It is improbable that the Fermi episode will be duplicated twenty-five years from now, because both West Point and Annapolis have announced plans to broaden the study of the sciences and the humanities.

I am not arguing for a nation of intellectuals. Nothing could be duller. I am arguing for a change of hero. The day of the All-American Man-Boy is over. We can't afford him, charming though he is. We can't afford to spend valuable time listening to influential grown-up Hucks who believe you can cure juvenile delinquency by inducing all the delinquents to spend their time throwing large balls into a rope-lined hoop. Nor can we any longer call "wholesome" and "healthy" the fact that a recent national survey of 5,000 teen-agers showed three times as many

objected to being called "egghead" as objected to the next most
disliked word.

When an otherwise excellent sports magazine tells us that
"every move in sports brings new thrills, new challenges, new
unknowns," the statement may have some justification. But when
it goes on to tell us that every such move gives "always the same
sense of living fully and successfully," we ought to be sufficiently
free of the Huck Finn image to recognize that this is nonsense
dangerous to the Republic, because it equates the whole man
and the good citizen with someone who can handle a noisy
powerboat, or who can kill, with the help of an expensive lethal
weapon, such powerful, savage, and inimical creatures as quail.

Civilizations are measured in many ways. One is by the height
of their heroes. We might keep that in mind whenever we find
ourselves falling for the grin, the studied bad grammar, the
Good Guy approach, the fishin' pole, and the freckles.

Private Thoughts on Public Faces

You may recall Private Mulvaney from Kipling's *Soldiers Three:* "I was a corp'ril wanst—rejuced aftherwards, but a corp'ril wanst." I was a celebrity once—reduced afterward, but a celebrity once. This match flare of fame sprang from my employment on a radio quiz show called *Information Please.* For a time I became a minor and expendable cog, but still a cog, in that glittering celebrity machine which is one of the many technological triumphs of our epoch and which compelled a few *maîtres d'hôtel* to half-recognize me on second sight. Even today elderly ladies and gentlemen will glance uncertainly at my face, then start as if at a ghost. Though now a mere fossil embedded in the Pleistocene stratum of the Celebrity Era, I was a corp'ril wanst, and speak of the celebrity system out of a mild familiarity with the way it works. So much for credentials.

I have been reading two books, one little, one big, about celebrities. The little one, *Operation Elvis,* a diverting, appalling treatise by Alan Levy, describes the graceful deference of the United States Army to the requirements of the celebrity system, as represented by then Pvt. Elvis Presley. This process was partly financed by our tax dollar, just as Mr. Presley's civilian career was and will be financed by the allowances we give our teen-age sons and daughters.

Any bookstore will sell you Mr. Levy's little book on the celebrity system, Yahoo division, for $2.95. But the big book may be bought only by those who have $26.00, which would seem to restrict the circulation of the *International Celebrity Register* largely to celebrities themselves. However, they are a numerous crowd. Far from being snobbish, the *Register* is as matey as a Presidential candidate. Everybody's in it, from Bertrand Russell all the way down, down to King Farouk. Even me. Me and Clara Bow.

Operation Elvis informally, the *Register* formally testify to the celebrity's growing power. The *Register* in particular dims with its authority all other more traditional lights, all Who's Whos, Blue Books, Social Registers, Halls of Fame. Its 864 pages of thumbnail biographies, as insidiously readable as Macadamia nuts are nibblable, comprise our Burke's Peerage, and steerage too. Albert Schweitzer cheek by jowl with Herb Score, here are the idols of a quantified society, each in his neon-lit niche not because of what he has done but because we have heard about him. Like those fabled city walls that rose to the sound of music, this new pantheon was called into being by adapting to various gadgets the invisible waves and pulsations of light, sound, and electricity.

The statement, of course, is unfair to you and me. The machines make, but we take. Did we not need celebrities, they would wither on the Hollywood-and-Vine. Like motorcars, however, they are called for on two fronts: the spiritual and the economic. The motorcar ministers to our spiritual comfort: if we cannot lift ourselves by our bootstraps, we can at least extend ourselves by our tailfins. But the motorcar, geared to a dozen major industries, also keeps men and dollars at work. So with celebrities. On the one hand, they satisfy a quasi-religious need: as the Olympians were to the Greeks, they are ourselves writ large and haloed in Technicolor. On the other hand, they are the neatly packaged and efficiently merchandised products of a vast industry, tying in all the instruments of mass communication and entertainment. Celebrity-making, celebrity-selling, and —when it becomes either needful or profitable—celebrity-assassinating: all are vital to the economic system. If the 2,000 celebrities listed in the *Register* were to vanish overnight and the publicity mills be enjoined by law against grinding out replacements, our country would suffer a considerable business dislocation.

I am speaking here of 2,000 *celebrities*, not 2,000 *persons*. As persons, perhaps over a third do work of great value to the world. Thus the late Nobel prize-winning physicist P. W. Bridgman had high human-being value—but only modest celebrity value. As for hundreds of others—vice versa. But all, whether a Bridgman or a Liberace, have, *purely as celebrities,* a special economic, as well as a quasi-religious, function, only vaguely related to the worth of their achievements.

To anyone who has ever even touched the coasts of communication, entertainment, philanthropy, and especially politics, the point is obvious. But I offer a minor illustration. In 1952 our State Department refused biochemist Linus Pauling a passport because it disapproved of his political associations. This may well have been a proper decision—I am incompetent to judge. In 1954 Doctor Pauling won the Nobel prize for chemistry. The State Department issued him an unlimited passport. This policy shift cannot be related to Doctor Pauling's worth as a scientist, which the State Department lacks the scholarship to estimate. Nor can it be related to any change in his associations, which would remain unaffected by receipt of the prize. It must have been related to his sudden jump in celebrity value, an increase to which the State Department is as sensitive as the Army was sensitive to Mr. Presley's semisacred status.

Celebrities therefore have a certain economic worth in that they save the *time* of the authorities. They short-cut the necessity for time-consuming reflection. They make decisions easier. Thus Hollywood can relieve itself of the painful need to determine whether or not an actor can act (which would involve expert judgment by trained and therefore expensive minds) by using instead the simpler yardstick of box-office or celebrity value.

As an interesting footnote to the Pauling case I might add that recently his celebrity value was enhanced when he was rescued from a rocky ledge on which he had contrived to get himself stuck. The rescue was chronicled on the front page of the *New York Times*. From the viewpoint of the anatomist of celebrity two consequences flow from this publicity. First, as a celebrity, Doctor Pauling now becomes a little more useful than he was before. Almost anything he henceforth does, especially if it is unconnected with the proper use of his brain, may be worth a stick of type, an air wave mention, a smallish photo in a picture magazine. Second, the law on quantification begins to work on us: as we hear and see Doctor Pauling's name more and more often, we unconsciously begin to confuse his value as a scientist with his value as a celebrity. Once we found out that Einstein played the violin, sailed a boat, and boycotted barbers, his scientific reputation among us nonscientists rose several points.

What is a celebrity?

Cleveland Amory, the editor in chief and Ward McAllister of the *Register*, offers as his rule of thumb for election to the pantheon "celebrity recognized outside of one's field," which seems fair enough. He is debonairly illusionless: ". . . it often means simply accomplishment in the sense of popular, or highly publicized temporary success." He further particularizes: "Names which, once made by news, now make news by themselves."

These are reasonable definitions provided you make two assumptions. The first is that "accomplishment" and "success" can always be equated. Often they can be, but it might prove a slippery task to pin down the precise accomplishment of an Elsa Maxwell or of any of the celebrated caterwaulers whose records are bought (always with your money) by teen-agers. Second, you must assume that names really *do* "make news by themselves" instead of merely making the air waves or the news columns, which is not quite the same thing. Are they "news"— or are we just trained to accept them as news?

I should like to qualify Mr. Amory's businesslike description of a celebrity with a less professional one. The celebrity (as distinct from merely a famous or distinguished human being) is a person who all by himself, or more usually aided by the system technicians, creates and maintains a public image. The public image may be a complete fake. Or it may be fairly close to the real person. Or it may alternate with the real person— Mr. Murrow used a public image on *Person to Person*, cast it aside on his less trivial programs. Or it may be a set of tricks deliberately and occasionally manipulated for some good end— F.D.R. might be an example here. But *some* distinction between the public image and the private person there must be to permit the manufacture of the true, the unblushful celebrity.

The *Register* includes a number of men of high achievement whose acquaintance I chance to possess. Two that occur to me are the novelist John Hersey and the historian Allan Nevins. By my lights they are not simon-pure celebrities because they have never been able, nor have they ever wished, to impose a public image on us. They are no more virtuous, I judge, than many others in the *Register*, but they are men of integrity in the literal sense—that is, integers, wholes, powerless to divvy up their personalities between themselves and us.

Mr. Hersey and Mr. Nevins are intellectuals. As a general thing intellectuals make poorish celebrities—they don't seem to have the brains for it. Also, they're inadequately motivated. That is, their business—which is to mold important matters into artistic forms, or to reflect upon and reach valid conclusions about them —is usually not helped much by owning and operating a public image. (There are exceptions: Bernard Shaw concocted a public image—The Paradoxical Showman—as a device for persuading us to accept the products of his intellect. Salvador Dali, an absolutely first-class celebrity, is an intellectual who can maintain a successful public image because he is also by nature an actor and a brilliant salesman.)

The most proficient celebrities tend to be idlers, entertainers, or politicians. Idlers often become A-1 celebrities, because the manufacture of an "interesting" public image is essential to disguise their vacuity. Entertainers must contrive a public image (the best one is an image of wholesome sincerity, like Mr. Godfrey's) because their living depends on being liked or "followed" by large groups of people, and most of them, like the rest of us, are by nature no more than normally likable or magnetic.

To achieve success in our time the politician must, or should, become a celebrity. This is less true in other countries. Though one of the most celebrated of men, Churchill is not a 100 per cent celebrity in the sense that, say, Barbara Hutton is one. That is because, from all reports, his public image and his private person coincide. Perhaps only an aristocrat, to whom it would never occur to demonstrate his superiority by rearranging himself for public consumption, can afford the luxury of such political stubbornness.

Finally, who makes celebrities?

Considered as a business, the celebrity network, on the glamour level, is created and run by able, mature professionals. Considered as part of our culture, however, I would guess, as have many others, that it is largely a response to the needs of teenagers.

The rate of current celebrity production seems to be inversely related to the intensity and maturity of the potential consumer's mental life: that Albert Schweitzer reads gossip columns is improbable. Of the many powerful blocs now operating in our country one of the most powerful is the teen-age bloc, or rather that dominant part of it which has adopted fun-morality as a religion. This group, plus the many grownups who find the teen-age outlook congenial, represent mental life at its phase of minimal intensity, short of feeble-mindedness. It is they who probably call into being the hard core of the celebrity system.

This hard core does not consist of the many distinguished businessmen, public servants, scientists, artists, educators, publicists, and so forth who actually do the vital work of the world. They are in the *Register*, of course. But the hard core, at once dynamo and show window of the celebrity system, is drawn mainly from the fields of entertainment, mass communication, fashion, sport, and Society, whether high, café, or occasionally para-criminal. Were this core to disappear, the system as a going concern would disappear with it. We might then revert to the barbarism of fifty years ago, when a man was judged by the genuineness either of his achievements or his family tree, or, more crassly, by the bulge of his bank account.

The teen-agers and their adult allies cannot afford to let this happen. For them the Sinatras and the Presleys, the basketball heroes and the film favorites are exactly what the solemn psychiatrists say they are—psychic necessities. Such celebrities perform the rituals which the teen-ager cannot perform for himself.

It works somewhat like this. The teen-ager chooses a celebrity to deify, or is ably maneuvered into doing so. But the celebrity god is not a jealous god, nor a wrathful one, nor even a watchful one. He is an approving, a jovial god. The god tells the teen-ager that teen-age standards are good, that fun-morality is moral, that rapid movement is progress, that play is virtue, that disk-jockey noises are music, that the world is not a time bomb but just one big neon-lit juke box.

Furthermore, he demonstrates, by his own financial success, that these standards pay off. Thus, at relatively little and always exclusively parental expense, the teen-ager gets a celebrity-god who at once entertains him, approves him, and allows him to experience a vicarious triumph. This seems to me an arrangement both theologically attractive and, from the celebrity system's viewpoint, commercially sound.

At the Sign of the Fork
in the Road

How are we eating these days?

Any discussion of our gastronomic condition must try to compose dozens of disparate facts, trends, tendencies. I submit a handful:

Never have we had so many restaurants that are first-class, good second-class, or working hard to become first- or second-class. One can flush them out not only in our plushier cities and exurbs but in less likely places. For example, Dallas—which I name as less likely because vituperative letters from Texas are so much more interesting than those from the more restrained states of the Union. And Skaneateles, New York; and Dania, Florida; and Manchester, Vermont; and Meridian, Mississippi, a region where the problem has usually been to find not edible, but simply nonregurgitant, food. All this information I glean from a sumptuous new restaurant guide, *Great Restaurants of America: A Personal Selection,* by Ted Patrick and his colleague, the New World Curnonsky, well-girthed Silas Spitzer. In it you will find loving yet candid descriptions of 103 restaurants, together with a treasury of whatever favorite recipes the proprietors could be teased into surrendering, plus delightful talk about wine, waiters, cookbooks, and kindred belly matters. In sum, a fanfare of gastronomic triumph. On the other hand:

Not long ago I quick-lunched on a stool at a "superior" New York hamburger emporium. (Nightmare vision: at this moment millions of proud Americans, born with the right to pursue happiness, are ranged on small tiddly stools, their heads hunched forward, feeding like pigs or horses at long troughs, their chompings punctuated by the swish and slap of the bar rag.) My nude hamburger—the roll is for connoisseurs of those etchings made by the thumbs of countermen—was almost inedible and, as the old joke has it, such small portions! The iced coffee consisted of a great deal of tired ice, some quite palatable water, and another ingredient of which one can say only that it was neither ice nor water. The bill totaled ninety-five cents plus tip. Some of this, however, may have gone for background: I consumed my ounce or so of corpse de hamburger in the heart of Madison Avenue, atmosphere supplied by the roar and stink of New York's toniest motorcars.

Only a few days before, my wife and I had had a late-afternoon snack on the Eiffel Tower's second *étage*. You can hardly call this a modish restaurant address. Still, we were given gratis a clean table to ourselves, overlooking the most beautiful city in the world. At 4 P.M. the Eiffel Tower menu could offer only cheese or ham sandwiches. That sufficed. My ham was fatless, generously portioned, embedded in a gigantic crusty French roll spread with fresh sweet butter. It was exactly what it has by tradition been for hundreds of years: delicious. As for my wife's Gruyère sandwich, its size and nutty richness astonished her. My glass of table wine was pleasant, which is all one could ask. My wife's coffee was French coffee, that is, characterful. Our bill amounted to less than four new francs, including tip, or about eighty cents.

In sum: the Eiffel Tower restaurant, operating on a humble gastronomic level, none the less as if by reflex followed a simple tradition of honest food, decently served, at a fair price; the Madison Avenue restaurant, operating on no clearly defined level, following no tradition whatsoever, served poor food badly at an absurd price. However:

Take a look at a magnificent new volume, *The Holiday Magazine Book of the World's Fine Foods,* by various authors, containing those articles on food, drink, and restaurants, both home-grown and European, that *Holiday* over the years is proudest to have published. In this Pavillon of food books the American palate, to toss a salad of metaphors, puts its best foot foremost. A sentence by Mr. Patrick, who wrote the introduction, sounds the keynote: "Enlightenment and sophistication have finally brought their benevolent influence to American eating habits."

If this book, along with *Great Restaurants,* be admitted as evidence, we must set down Mr. Patrick's judgment as accurate. And other confirmations of its truth are not lacking: the marked multiplication and apparently successful sale of cookbooks of all kinds; the development of a widespread market in what has come to be known, rather hideously, as gourmet foods, which include such snobbish nonsense as stuffed larks, grasshoppers in honey, and jet-planed *fraises des bois;* the popularity of cooking schools; the entrance into the restaurant business of young Americans who are serious about food; the activity of wining and dining clubs; the (very slow) growth of an appreciation of wine, without which no first-class gastronomy can exist, unless you want to plump for China, which I do not; the refining effect of travel on the tastes of some—as well as its tendency to confirm the barbarism of others, for we have all known patriots who, after sampling Paris' best, returned home even more devoted to their steak, potatoes, apple pie, and Scotch; the faint pink dawn of an acceptable motel cuisine—the restaurant attached to the lovely Motel-on-the-Mountain at Suffern, New York, for example, offers imaginative, well-cooked food at suitable prices. I could run on for several paragraphs, reciting happy experiences in support of Mr. Patrick's thesis. But I find myself suddenly derailed by the sound of a train whistle down in the hollow, triggering less happy memories, in this case memories of railway gastronomy. Question:

Why is the dining car on virtually any Eastern train rapidly turning into a chamber of horrors? As it confirms my relation to my proper habitat, the earth, I happen to love railway travel; and, to keep my love warm, I have resolved henceforth to make no journey of any distance without carrying a packet of sandwiches.

What does the Eastern dining car offer these days? A tableful of clattering, needless silverware. A slew of unrequested appetizers, crackers, potato chips, oozy salads, all usurping badly needed space on the crowded table. Waiters who seem to have embraced indifference as a way of life. Finally, a menu offering a wide choice of badly prepared and occasionally repulsive foods.

Whatever may be placed on a dirty, limp lettuce leaf is so placed, though what relation there can possibly be between a cold, drippy piece of lettuce and a hot veal cutlet is difficult to understand. The moment cheese is brought, your dinner roll —which might conceivably make the cheese palatable—is whisked away from you. On my last trip I encountered a Liederkranz that was blackish-brown mold virtually all the way through. When I remarked mildly to the steward that it would almost surely poison any rash guest, he accepted the statement as unsurprising and replaced the Liederkranz with some "Camembert" so chalky you could hear it squeaking against a blackboard. If you order a domestic wine, why must you be served one of the worst domestic brands instead of one of the many honest native wines that are readily obtainable? To the railroads (at least those in the East) I say: take back your damnable mints in their untearable nasty little bags and give us something we can eat!

As for the prices—it is truly painful to watch a decent middle-class citizen, perhaps traveling with his wife and one or two children, studying the menu's right-hand column in utter disbelief and sometimes in real panic. There is simply no longer any relation between what you get and what you pay. The diner has become a traveler's trap. The Donner Party ate better.

On some trains the disagreeable food may be part of a set policy of discouraging nonprofitable passenger travel. Also we must remember that many railroad executives, by nature and custom twenty-five years behind the times, may not yet have heard even a rumor of the "enlightenment and sophistication" Mr. Patrick so properly hails as obtainable in other areas. But at least part of the trouble is, as usual, our own fault. So long as we prefer spurious opulence and profusion to a few dishes honestly cooked and served, we will get what we want. If we insisted on a virtually choiceless *prix fixe* based on what a diner's narrow galley can feasibly produce in the way of food fit for human beings, we would get that. The French want it and the French get it.

Let us contemplate still another aspect of our split-level gastronomy. Nowadays the big-city businessman can command a complex restaurant lunch ranging from the interesting to the superb, with the expense-account system encouraging him to order any elegant kickshaws he fancies. After the excellent Commodore bar Martini at 5 P.M., he returns to a harassed wife who would like nothing better than to match at home the fare her beloved provider is used to at lunch. But can she keep him in the style to which he is accustomed? The litany is familiar enough: the devices supposed to save labor require the attention of the full-time engineer into which the wife is being rapidly transformed; the children, formerly useful domestic assistants, are now by common consent the masters of her time; cooks and kitchen help do not exist, or are unteachable, or represent an infinite series of problems in psychiatry. Result: the can, the tasteless efficiencies of the freezer, the commercial loaf, the packaged TV meal, the short-order hamburger dinner. In brief, an unavoidable relapse to mere basic nutrition, varied by sporadic, desperate forays into expensive "gourmet" foods, or on mild-weather weekends by the barbecue cuisine which is step by step leading us back to the open-fire gastronomy of our Stone Age ancestors.

The contrast between the increasing excellence of (male) public eating and the increasing dismalness of family private eating shows up as an outstanding feature of our gastronomic chaos. Eventually the middle-class city worker may evolve two completely separate alimentary tracts, one adapted to lunch, the other specialized for home use.

Our little gastronomic chaos is of course but a minute part of a larger one. As everyone is busy pointing out, we are not quite sure whether to revert to traditional civilized values—or to advance toward a new set of values proper to military-technical-industrial Man. The baffling thing is that the individual can't go whole hog for one or the other: a part of me seems to opt for the first, another part for the second.

The dispute over education, for example, is a large matter. The dispute over what and how we should eat is, I suppose, a small one. But they show similar faces. Should an American child be educated so that he may become a liberated human being, it being understood that there is then a danger of his throwing a monkey wrench into the social machinery? Or should he be educated to become a self-adjusting part of that social machinery? Similarly, should bread, the cornerstone of food, be baked in the French manner—that is should traditional, civilized virtues be baked into it? Or should flour be transformed, as it is with us in general, into a machine product, easy to produce, handle, sell, and insert into the alimentary canal, an object quite fit (I do not deny it) for military-technical-industrial Man, but quite unfit for that old-fashioned entity, the human being? We are torn both ways: we can, if we look for it, get finer bread than was available twenty years ago; we can also, without looking for it, get worse.

Our psyches have split palates. On the one hand, our puritan heritage frowns on "fancy" foods as somehow immoral, and we embrace the banality of steak as if it were a guarantor of virtue. On the other hand, the ladies' magazines swarm with fantastic recipes related less to gastronomy than to interior decoration; and we further compensate for our culinary repressions by a voluptuous gorging on an unbelievably varied mass of swill in the form of commercial candy and doctored pop. You can buy a hundred kinds of exotic canned soup—but not many of them taste good, and most of them taste the same. We have the best oysters in the world, and we accompany them with that concentrated dust which is the average American cracker, when it would be easy enough to provide what the English restaurant automatically gives you: a few thinly buttered thin slices of delicious brown bread.

Perhaps part of the trouble is that we have no gastronomic models. Having said farewell to isolationism, we now agree that our political leaders should be able to meet other world leaders on terms of equal sophistication. Yet possibly the only moment in which F.D.R. was beloved by virtually the entire population, Democratic and Republican, was when he served hot dogs to royalty. We insist that our Presidential candidates prove their ability to save us from destruction by devouring the crudest of popular foods in public, a kind of ritual eating of the wafer of democracy. Suppose Mr. Kennedy (whose favorite dish, it has been reported, is baked beans) or Mr. Nixon (whose favorite dish, it has been reported, is meat loaf) had said loudly: "I am not, I have never been, I never will be anti-Semitic or anti-Italian—but these knishes, this pizza you hold to my lips are garbage, and I refuse to win a vote by submitting my stomach to them." A reign of terror would have ensued and the political managers, emitting a cry of despair, would have fled to the hills.

Somewhere in Nietzsche, I think, there is a sentence to the effect that it takes chaos to give birth to a dancing star. We have the chaos. But it is a question whether you and I will live to see that star dance, at least in the cosmos of gastronomy.

Buyways of Cataloguia

I AM AN ADDICT, or victim, of mail-order catalogues. I don't mean those vast and wonderful department-stores-in-print put out by the big outfits, such as Sears, Roebuck and Montgomery Ward. I allude to the catalogues issued by hundreds of less famous but no less ingenious smaller houses, the bush leagues of the business.

Was it about eight years ago that I received my first infection by mail-order catalogues? It must have been, for it was just about then that they seemed to offer a pair of bewildered new parents a solution to the heart-freezing problem of what to get the children for Christmas. From their pages, it developed, one could conveniently order a whole floorful of the gaudy junk that today passes for toys and is part of the excreta of our age of plastics.

Starting on a shoestring of three or four catalogues, we have now run our annual intake up to about 150. The additional ones were, of course, not requested. Apparently all these firms, in a frenzy of noncompetition, take in each other's sucker lists: our original catalogues were so many Typhoid Marys. Moreover, once one's name is embedded in the files there is no known method of extricating it. A request to be dropped is invariably interpreted as a new inquiry from a potential customer. Hence our 150-odd include many duplicates, triplicates, and even quadruplicates. The first rule in running a mail-order house is: use every effort to increase the outlay for postage.

However, I have long since stopped playing King Canute to the flood. The fact is that, were this incessant spate of news from the weird country of Cataloguia to dry up, I should miss it. As another nibbles candy or explores a hollow tooth, I pore over my catalogues. Transported to Cataloguia I feel like a primitive suddenly set down in Radio City. Indeed I am a kind of primitive in time, for my rude and simple tastes were formed in the pregadget era. Hence the tens of thousands of objects proffered by the catalogues have for me the same fascination pocket mirrors and colored beads were once supposed to exert on savages. Far more than poetry does, or artificial satellites, they help to keep alive in me the faculty of wonder, or at least amazement. To my laggard mind, quite powerless to keep pace with its century, they are a kind of science fiction of the in-animate.

(Connoisseurs of explosions are aware that the proliferation of objects is just as staggering to contemplate as is the prolif-eration of people. Doubtless some profound meaning lies hid in the circumstance that three explosions should have occurred simultaneously: the people explosion, the thing explosion, and the Big Bang uniquely designed to annul both the people and the things.)

Cataloguia's export trade, though it derives from the old-fashioned novelty business, is of a different order entirely. Its scale, scope, and power of appeal are incomparably greater. Far more than a commercial side line, it is a vast social institution, with its own folkways and even what we writer chaps call a *mystique*. Insofar as we are developing a religion of things, the mail-order catalogue is its Word.

Shall we wander down a few of Cataloguia's buyways?

Let us start—as, come to think of it, we all do—with Sex.

The principle ruling Cataloguian sex is that machine produc-tion can aid, or even replace, the old-fashioned imagination our grandparents relied on. The world of the gadget, the household appliance, and the toy invade the world of the libido. You may, for example, buy an ice-cube tray emitting four cubes designed as exuberant female torsos. A hot-water bottle, made of durable blushing-pink vinyl plastic, duplicates Jayne Mansfield in miniature. It is guaranteed, says the Word, to please the old man, the grouchy boss, the office bachelor, and the convalescent male. For anglers there is Miss Bobbie, a float that is mainly mammary glands. The handyman will go for Able Mable the Workbench Wench, a similarly designed screwdriver. One of the best sellers last year—it must have been, for it appeared in innumerable catalogues—was the World's Shortest Nightgown, only ten inches long. Another was a timesaving device, quite in the spirit of our efficient age, a pillowcase with YES on one side, NO on the other, both sides embellished with pictures of small rabbits in appropriate situations. In tolerant Cataloguia even the deviate's needs are cared for—the smoker-sadist may drop his hot ashes into a tray concealing a small female nude plastic masochist.

Sex has always had, quite properly, its diverting aspect. But only in our time, I should think, has it been so systematically introduced into the field of mechanized "fun."

In Cataloguia, however, sex-gadget fun runs a poor second to bathroom-gadget fun. The industry has taken over the humor of the privy, just as it has with sex. It has organized scatology into an endless array of concrete objects. We may now buy our snickers and guffaws in gadget form: Brussels' Manneken Pis statue redesigned as a bottle dispenser-stopper—Little Squirt is his name; a mug or an ash tray shaped like a toilet bowl; a wall trivet patterned like a familiar seat cover bearing the legend: The Next Time You Have To Go Mention My Name—You'll Get a Better Seat; "Gotta-Go" bathroom gongs hung outside to speed up traffic ("Hilarious little skunk cartoon illustrates the point"); toilet tissue printed with suitable funny sayings; and hundreds of other asembly-line ribaldries. The elimination obsession touches all possible body areas—you can buy a belly-button brush, too, not to mention an ornate ear cleaner.

At one time the humor of Eugene Field and even of the later Chic Sale had a certain naturalness. It was rooted in the

rural fact that the outdoor privy was a dominant institution.
The New Scatology is interesting because it is contemporaneous
with an era in which the bathroom has become so efficient that
its function hardly any longer intrudes on our daily lives. The
recrudescence of water-closet humor is puzzling. I merely cite
Cataloguia as its current seminary.

As one might expect, Cataloguia is also headquarters for
practical jokes. It is hard to believe that these Laff gadgets
actually exist. Yet they do, and in staggering variety and mul-
tiplicity. Candy dishes in the shape of a hollow tooth; transparent
vests for watching's one's waistline; combs for bald-headed men;
forty-two-inch ties, "printed with screechingly funny mottoes";
sweat shirts stenciled "U.S.A. Drinking Team"; bathing caps
with grotesque faces appliquéd in felt on the back; highball
glasses whose base reveals a movable, lifelike eye—as Mr.
Durante puts it, I gotta million of 'em.

These surrealist fantasies would appear to reflect our national
sense of humor at its most basic level. It is clear that they
are eagerly bought by millions of us, the same millions who,
according to the sociological dopesters, should long ago have
been raised above the Yahoo level by the sophisticated pressures
of Hollywood, television, national magazines, and other expres-
sions of the glossy way of life. I should add that the Laff
gadgets are aimed not at youngsters (as they were in my childhood) but at the mature—and at the fairly well-heeled mature
at that.

Many of them cater to the morbidity marking any culture
that, like ours, feels itself in dire peril. On a serious plane the
shadow of this morbidity falls over a large part of our art and
literature. On the plane of farce it may be detected in a hundred
unsettling objects, designed, as one of my gift guides puts it,
"for every taste (some are weird)." There is apparently a heart-
felt need for plastic ears, toes, and fingers, sealed in apothecary
jars; for Black Boxes from which a ghostly hand arises, turns
off a switch, disappears (you can get this for only $4.98); for
grisly arrow earrings that seem to pierce a large portion of the
ear; for "happy jars" labeled "Opium" and "Marijuana." The

slope of the catalogues' gag merchandise is toward the bizarre, the macabre, even the sadistic. This was also true in simpler eras —the novelty shops still sell stink bombs and sneezing powder— but Cataloguia has raised Sick gadgetry to a high power of complication and intensity. It has fewer affinities with the innocent world of Peck's Bad Boy and many more with the less innocent world of Dali, Norman Mailer, and Tennessee Williams.

Many of Cataloguia's offerings, however, do seem aimed at the child who lingers happily inside so many of us grownups. What youngster has not obeyed the urge to stamp or write his name on all available clean surfaces? Understandably—for, in a world run by the large and powerful, his identity is constantly threatened. He scribbles his name to reassure himself. Many mail-order customers must need the same reassurance. At least such a need would help to explain why the catalogues are saturated with "personalized" objects. Or it may be that this almost frightening craze for repeated self-identification is part of the neurotic pattern David Riesman describes in *The Lonely Crowd*. Perhaps in a world sodden with people, anonymity is something to be fought even on the doodad level. At any rate one can buy cheaply from the catalogues a thousand reassurances of one's own identity: personalized tie bars, tie tacks, cuff links, television program covers. One can buy a personalized denture dish with the standard cute saying. One can buy a sensational bullfight cover featuring one's own name as the matador. The very dogs get into the act: Fido may now muse over the sight of his name emblazoned on his towel and his mat.

On the other hand the explorer of Cataloguia will soon remark a curious tendency to strip the objects *themselves* of their proper identity. This passion for metamorphosis, for the distortion of reality, recalls Dali's universe of melting watches, or perhaps the fantastic protean pantheon of the Hindus. A record album holds eight records—but they are really coasters. Open a miniature sewing machine and it produces salt and pepper shakers. A pair of binoculars holds two half-pints of liquor. An ash tray stands on a coil suggesting the Indian rope trick. A small cart holds lipsticks and earrings. And, if an object cannot be changed

into something else, it may be inverted: thus you can buy a
clock that keeps perfect time but whose numerals are reversed
and whose hands turn backward. Some catalogues are so rich in
these aberrations that reading them gives one many of the
sensations of a nightmare: *Alice in Wonderland* passed through
the mind of a merchandiser.

The final impression left by Cataloguia is that here lies the
collective answer to Thoreau. Here is anti-Walden, crying "Complicate, complicate!" The energy, the earnestness, the sincerity
of the message are awe-inspiring. Salvation is to be found
neither in faith nor in works. It is to be found in objects. Look
not to the Everlasting Arms. Look to the ever-increasing inven-
tory. For what comes in the mail is more than a piece of plastic;
it is the full, it is the good life.

To the owner of a pair of shoes Cataloguia cries: "You are
missing what shoes have to give you unless you place them in a
special See-Thru box, unless you place them on a special Extens-
ible Shelf, unless you widen them with a special widener, unless
you keep them fragrant with Sweet-Shu Spray."

Are you content with squeezing your tooth paste on your
brush? Raise yourself from your barbarous condition: use a
Squeeze-Rite Tooth Paste and Toothbrush Holder which *automatically* squeezes out just the amount of tooth paste you need.

Why fill your pipe archaically when you can enrich the experience by pressing the plunger of a Phil-O-Matic? Shine your
shoes with an electric brush. Own a battery-powered Santa
Claus whose head turns, whose eyes light up, whose bell rings
cheerfully. Why stick in the mud of Walden Pond when you
can so easily ascend to the crowded heights of Cataloguia?

Someday I should like to write an essay patterned after De
Quincey's *Confessions of an English Opium Eater*. It would
describe in the most ornate possible prose the visions that have
often overcome me after a solitary orgy of catalogue reading.
Such a vision I had only the other night. I dreamed of what
my car would look like if I could only manage to install a
few Cataloguian accessories.

My car is not a large one. Indeed it is a Volkswagen. In my vision this tiny mechanism, normally a dull tool used for getting me from one place to another, emerged in all the glittering beauty of the most baroque complication. It shone, it glittered, it sang aloud with its battery charger, its six-lane car mirror, its vacuum cleaner, its portable carport, its wind silencer, its portable broom, its extra storage compartment, its emergency blinker, its back rest, its electronic bump alarm, its gas-pedal cushion, its snack bar, its tire caddie, its map measurer, its magnetic sunglass case, its personalized magnetic driving gloves, its antiwindshield-ice-sprayer, its plastic windshield protector, its emergency sandbag, its parking-meter reminder, its sponge mitt car washer, its plastic car tote (Holds Everything), its double seat cushion, its leather visor valet, its magnetic car-key container, its magnetic dashboard tray, its air-conditioned car seat with electric blower, its blinking trouble light, its traveling litter basket, its Grip-Sno treads, its snow-and-ice melter, its tire grips, its tow pulls, its traction mats, its trunk-lid holder, its auto compass, its "Huge Wind-up Key" (for laughs), and finally its dazzling ownership plaque:

THIS CAR MADE ESPECIALLY FOR CLIFTON FADIMAN

A Kind Word

for American Autumn

> Where are the songs of Spring? Ay, where are they?
> Think not of them, thou hast thy music too. . . .
> KEATS, *To Autumn*

As PRODUCTS OF CLIMATE we are all parochial. My parish pump lies in the North Temperate Zone. Probably yours does too. Thus the gossip you and I exchange all our lives, gossip of wind and weather, gossip of the passings and resurrections of the seasons, is but local news. Translate it into Penguin, Polar Bear, or Kangaroo, and it would mean nothing to these distant cousins. Though all perched on one globe we more truly live on different invisible Main Streets. My Main Street is congruent with a brief segment of an imaginary line known as North Latitude 41 degrees plus a few minutes. From birth to death my latitudinal blinders obscure all springs and summers, falls and winters but my own. We live by special suns, and pinpoint our whereabouts by stars that shine otherwhere for Bushman and for Eskimo.

So autumn is only our own limited autumn, our fall, and not, so to speak, the Fall of Man. But, however straitened, it offers excellent matter for wonder and delight; and it may be that, though it has paid us roughly the same annual visit since the last Ice Age, we have not yet viewed it justly.

When we consider the seasons, we see them not only through our own eyes but through the eyes of those powerful persuaders, the poets. Our response to Nature is partly natural, partly

89

learned. The poets have taught us to link spring with joy,
autumn with melancholy. James Thomson in *The Seasons* (herewith nominated as the most unreadable well-thought-of long
poem in English) contemplates autumn and suggests glumly
that

> In every breeze the Power
> Of Philosophic Melancholy comes!

I question this insidious, capital-lettered propaganda. All
seasons are good of their kind, just as all the decades of our
life would show themselves to be, could we once learn to regard
ourselves as unique incidents in Nature rather than as machines
subject only to the law of attrition and decay. Through the
alteration of the seasons we are supplied free of charge with
four personalities. Though the name and address remain un-
changed, April man and December man are somewhat different
fellows.

But let us now stand up for autumn. With us it begins more
or less with Labor Day and runs through October and November. Should we not think of fall as the start rather than the fag
end of the year? Does there not come, with the vivid turning of
the leaves, a heightened color to the life of man, deepening with
the passage of the autumn days, rising with the onset of the
Christmas season to a chromatic crescendo? You are about to
tell me that spring is the time when the sap starts running, when
the leaves make their first brave show? But we are neither sap
nor leaves, and, though I welcome spring as gladly as any
sonneteer, I also remember that it is the season in which blooms
the Bureau of Internal Revenue. I seem to gather my own internal revenue with the onset of fall rather than of spring, and
believe the same to be true of many of my neighbors.

Are we so wrong to call it the time of beginningness? Not
for Nature as a whole, perhaps, but surely for Nature's most
interesting subdivision—men, women, and children. After Labor
Day along invisible flightways we fly back, with some wistfulness
but more anticipation, from our carefully organized Arcadias of
hill or wood or seashore, back to the busy rookeries of social re-

lations. We may not move a physical inch, but our minds all migrate after Labor Day has come and gone. In the deeper sense as well as the trivial one the social season begins. We discover ourselves as political animals, as parts of a *polis,* a city; and perhaps it is no accident that our Election Day should be a ritual of autumn.

After Labor Day the basic national rhythm, that of industry, intensifies. During the summer we throttle down, sometimes to the point of stalling, our competitive thrusts and urges; but the first winds of autumn seem to revive in us our native keen passion for buying and selling, making and exchanging. Men feel this, of course, more than women do. Indeed, I think it is fair to say that the linkage of melancholy and fall is more natural to women than to men; it may have some subtle connection with fertility rhythms from which the male consciousness is excluded.

Yet for all of us, men and women, old and young, autumn is a clarion call. We have done with loafing and inviting our souls. Now the time has come to invite other souls. The barbecue pit and the picnic basket are laid by for a sunny day. Once again the pleasures of the table and the drawing room beckon us with formal gestures elaborated over three millennia of polite living. The artificial simplicities of summer clothing give way to the no more artificial complexities of the fall wardrobe. We dress ourselves, like the peacocks we are, less for Nature's sun and boundless airs than for our own man-made sun that we have forced through copper wires, and for our man-made constricted cubes of enclosed space. The house itself, one of our oldest inventions, is rediscovered. We refurbish and redecorate and trick it up, and feel again the pleasures of what is cozy— the hearth, the lamp, the closed door. Or we rush to replace the shells in which we live: Moving Day too is for the most part autumnal.

Researchers into these curious matters tell us it is in the autumn that we dream least. Perhaps it is not entirely fanciful to suggest that the iceberg of consciousness floats highest out of the water in the fall. Reverie attracts us less than activity; it is no season for dreams, whether of the day or of the night.

The very air, charged by an invisible generator, crackles with new business—new business in the popular arts, in fashions and gardening, in food and sport, in books and travel.

This business is for us grownups, or those on the point of becoming grown-up. But there is new business also for the most important part of our population, the children. It is a mistake to nod our heads in uncritical agreement with Shakespeare's vivid but stereotyped picture of

> the whining school-boy, with his satchel
> And shining morning face, creeping like snail
> Unwillingly to school.

It is only our national sentimentality that makes us assume that all children are so many Huckleberry Finns, and that the boy who plays hooky and goes fishin' is more apt to succeed than the one who is willing to learn what his teacher is willing to teach. It is true that we have done what we can to turn education in some instances into either a bore or a nine-to-three taffy-pull; but children still look forward to the opening, at least, of school, to the new and more important grade, the new teacher, the new desk, the new textbook, the new map on the new wall. Whatever its defects, school is still the main, sometimes the only, chart to the most glamorous of all Treasure Islands—the child's own mind. Agreed, he is reluctant to surrender summer's freedoms; but it is only the little appetitive animal in him that demurs. To the other part of him, the little rational animal, the opening of school is a real experience, not necessarily happy, but deeply interesting. It is interesting precisely because it is serious. Those educators who are trying to keep the classroom windows permanently open to the mindless airs of summer freedom are depriving the child of one of his deepest satisfactions—the satisfaction of considering, on his own proper level, serious matters in an atmosphere of order and discipline. For the child, the autumnal opening of the school door marks the beginning of real rather than play life. And in that grave pleasure we may share vicariously.

And so I would suggest to Congress that we change our

calendar to conform to what is psychologically true, and that the day following Labor Day be termed New Year's Day. I know this cannot be done in legal fact, but for us who live in the North Temperate Zone and who feel, like the instinctive animals we are, the invigorating breath of autumn's first brisk winds, it has already been accomplished in the calendar of the spirit.

'Tis well an old age is out
And time to begin a new.

Men, Books, and a Pianist

A Visit With the Bedroom Boys

IN AN OPEN LETTER to his publishers Ben Hecht sums up his novel *The Sensualists* as "a scientific look into our Renaissance of sex peculiarities and erotic phantasy; a sort of 19th Century novel minus the asterisks." One of the episodes that improves on the asterisks shows us a police sergeant off duty. The sergeant half stuns a woman with his club. Then, using surgical knives and scissors, he cuts out and trims her intestines, kidneys, and other neighboring organs. Then he blows off the top of his own head.

You can't call this drab. Yet, for us old erotic phantasists, is it enough? Literature these days is so sex-happy that I can't always keep my perversions straight, but I seem to remember a Tennessee Williams story in which a giant Negro masseur massages a highly co-operative smaller white man to death and then, in an access of affection, bit by bit, over a twenty-four-hour period, eats him. *Desire and the Black Masseur* quite puts in the shade the abdominal collage, the three murders, the suicide, the standard seductions, and the Lesbianism which are really, when you come right down to it, about all *The Sensualists* has to offer. Oh, there's dope addiction, of course, but *that* any normal decent sexual phantasist has a right to expect. I'm not saying Mr. Hecht is niggardly; but perhaps he's a smidgen —shall we say mealy-minded?

97

We are, true enough, in the very middle of a literary "Renaissance of sex peculiarities and erotic phantasy," with no Reformation in sight. It's almost too easy to demonstrate Mr. Hecht's thesis. By chance, as this is written, I've been reading advance editorial reports on some books soon to be published. Their titles and authors don't matter. What is interesting is that out of a random score I should encounter at least four by dedicated Bedroom Boys or Bedroom Girls. Here is a biography of a pre-World War I European political figure who, fortunately for the author, doubled as a homosexual; the biographer "fairly revels in his depiction of sexual activity between males and between males and females." Here's a novelist who "almost audibly slobbers over some of the adventitious sexual episodes he includes." The theme of still another work of fiction is "only an excuse for a variety of sexual exercises." And the prize exhibit is a product of creative imagination involving infidelity (that's for the Sunday school crowd), Lesbianism, impotence, voyeurism, and satyriasis. In this one the heroine, asked for a donation to the school bazaar, offers a hand-painted diaphragm.

Now in these matters one reader's cantharides is another man's saltpeter. Hence no generally acceptable formula characterizes our Renaissance. For example, I have before me six novels, all part of the contemporary Rebirth of Candor: Mr. Hecht's book, John O'Hara's *From the Terrace*, Vladimir Nabokov's *Lolita*, J. P. Donleavy's *The Ginger Man*, Pietro di Donato's *This Woman*, and Grace Metalious' *Peyton Place*. In literary value they differ widely. *Lolita*, though minor, is a work of art. *From the Terrace* is an expert, knowledgeable, realistic novel which would be thoroughly interesting even with the franker passages omitted. *The Ginger Man* is streaky with a wild beat talent quite unsustained by common sense. *The Sensualists* is a high-grade shocker set in a series of actual and symbolical bedrooms. *This Woman* is to the art of narrative what the dance of a crazed dervish is to the art of ballet. *Peyton Place* is laborious trash.

And while all six novels depend for their partial or total effect on the delineation of some kind of erotic behavior, the authors, as they contemplate Eros, strike quite different attitudes. Mr.

Hecht sees himself as a sardonic clinician of the neuroses. Mr. Nabokov is an art-for-art's-saker who happens to have chosen a statistically rare sex obsession as a theme peculiarly suited to his elegant talents, just as Flaubert once chose third-century B.C. Carthage as suited to his. Mr. Donleavy is a bright Joyceling who specializes in images of lust and excrement as the most forcible expression of his hero's distaste for a subject on which the said hero does not appear to have done much homework, to wit human life. Mr. di Donato is a kind of D. H. Lawrence unencumbered by a cerebral cortex, eager to transpose sexual excitement, with a minimum of modification, from the alcove to the printed page, and a bit baffled to discover that English prose, however tumid, still insists on being made not with orgasms but with words and sentences. Mr. O'Hara is, among other more important talents, an able, honest, vigorous reporter, not to say photographer, of what he believes to be the sexual mores of the American upper class; and simply takes legitimate advantage of our new Renaissance freedom of speech. Mrs. Metalious is a village *voyeuse* looking through a back-fence peephole and passing the juiciest bits on to the neighbors.

For all their diversity, however, these writers have one thing in common. Twenty-five years ago either they could not have been published at all, or they would have collided with that paragon of pure-mindedness, the American cop. Since the days when *Tobacco Road* carried enough shock value to make a fortune for its author, the national sense of sin, once our pride and joy, has grown more and more sluggish. *The Ginger Man,* for instance, is a literary sex kit with a complete stock, even including fellatio. Yet *The Ginger Man,* selling moderately well, particularly to the late Mr. Carnegie's libraries, hasn't had a bit of trouble, except Down Under where the sensitive Australians have banned it. In Paris the gendarmes imposed a semiban on the Olympia Press edition of *Lolita.* Over here it's virtually required reading in the women's clubs.

For this latter by-passing of our lofty moral standards we may assign at least two reasons. Our virtuous indignation is more often excited by the label than by the poison. Not that

Lolita, though strong medicine, is poison. But it contains no bad words. Furthermore it is so subtly written that the well-rinsed mind can work straight through some rather surprising passages in bland unconsciousness of just what is going on. However, even where the vocabulary is, as with Mr. O'Hara, notable for its single *entendre,* censorship risk is much lighter than in 1933 when Judge Woolsey handed down his classic decision in favor of *Ulysses.*

These novels then, all contributory to Mr. Hecht's Renaissance, have so far enjoyed a socially approved public career. In an effort to distinguish additional features of the Renaissance, it is worth considering such books carefully, along with others. I am thinking of such kith and kin as James Jones and his successful experiment in logorrhea, *Some Came Running;* Norman Mailer and his sex-freak waxworks, *The Deer Park;* Tennessee Williams with his highly regarded application of lyric tenderness to what used to be called degeneracy; and even— though here I tread on sacred ground—the Dixie Dante, Mr. William Faulkner, and his subtropical libidinal infernos.

The first thing to note about the current Bedroom Boys is that, unlike their predecessors of a generation or two ago, they are not rebels against Puritanism. Dreiser, Anderson, Lawrence, even the early Hemingway were conscious (and brave) enemies of fake gentility and genuine prudery. The new crop write as victors in a battle fought and won so long ago that it bores them even to mention it. They are not crusaders for freedom of speech and conduct. They take both for granted; or sometimes seem to operate in a world of their own whose values do not impinge on the dull recognizable American environment in which most of us live.

Their foe is not the moral hypocrite—that stuff is for squares like Dickens or Sinclair Lewis. Their foe is the normally sexed human being—for the normally sexed human being is precisely the one who, because he defeats their peculiar talents, represents a real threat. Poor old Dreiser implored people to face the facts of life. Our chaps will settle for facing the fantasies of abnormality. The nineteenth-century decadent sighed for a new sin. The modernist sighs for a new perversion.

Just as he is no rebel, so is he no pornographer. Pornography is one of the most restricted of the literary arts; I was even about to say, one of the purest. It is strictly a job for professionals. Its aim is single: to supply that peculiar and ineradicably human pleasure arising from the vicarious contemplation of lewd images. The good pornographer works exclusively to achieve this aim. Thus the classic in the field, *Memoirs of the Life of Fanny Hill*, has for over two centuries been an underground best-seller. Why? Because its author, John Cleland, knew precisely what he was after. He works at his pornography with the single-mindedness of a salesman selling you a vacuum cleaner. By the way, there is not an indecent word in *Fanny Hill*, any more than there is in *Lolita*, a book it in no other way resembles.

Cleland is a successful pornographer. William Shakespeare is not. In *Venus and Adonis* Shakespeare tried to write a pornographic poem. He failed because his genius kept breaking in. The reader, seeking in *Venus and Adonis* the pleasures of the lewd, is continually disappointed. Alien matter—rhythm, classical allusions and, worst of all, sheer beauty of language—interrupt the train of sensual reverie. The poem, from the viewpoint of the eager adolescent, is a bust.

Now the Bedroom Boys are not pornographers, as Cleland was one. The best of them are not in the least interested in arousing the pleasure derived from the vicarious contemplation of lewd images. All Mr. Nabokov wants to do, for example, is to get inside the mind of a monomaniac. He is no more pornographic than Proust or Joyce or Mann or any other first-class writer who illustrates his private vision of life with a dramatization of some sexual abnormality. The same is true of Mr. Faulkner. Whether or not you are moved by his work, you cannot accuse him of pandering to lust. For such trivialities he is too serious, even too solemn, a man.

But even if it could be shown that some of the Bedroom Boys would *like* to be pornographers, I fear we must, however sorrowfully, deny them the title. For they do not succeed in supplying the pleasure arising from the contemplation of lewd images. A work such as *The Deer Park* may both shock and disgust; but shock and disgust are not pleasures. The plain fact is that most of these writers are really not interested at all in sexual activity considered as a pleasure, which is the orthodox, traditional view. Some are interested in it as a disease; others as a torment; others as a substitute for religion. And there are some for whom it is simply a King Charles' head; they cannot write about anything else because they cannot think about anything else. In all these cases the erotic passages may be interesting for other reasons, but they cannot be interesting as pornography.

Their books are angry or gloomy or frenzied or (as with Mr. Nabokov) even witty. But they are not naughty; and they are not gay; and they are not, by ordinary standards, even erotic in the sense of dealing sensually with the amorous in men and women. A great many of them not only do not celebrate sexuality; they seem to be sore at it, as if it had done their authors, an injury that could be requited only by the writing of a novel.

One thinks of other Bedroom Boys of the past. I don't mean professional pornographers, who work in such a narrow groove that they cannot long interest any reasonably reflective mind. I mean a novelist like Choderlos de Laclos, whose *Dangerous Relations* is a truly delicious erotic romance, naughty and gay and sensual. I mean Chaucer and Dunbar and Burns and Aristophanes and Gautier and Béroalde de Verville and Casanova and Ovid. These are writers of unequal merit and with quite diverse views of lovemaking. But they agree in one thing: they're for it. Many of them were, by strict standards, immoral men; but they at least managed to make immorality colorful, interesting, even seductive. They may have praised *l'amour* too extravagantly. But at least they praised it. They found it funny and beautiful and tender and grotesque and moving and sentimental and farcical; and it is all these things. Above all they found it joyful, which had been the general experience of mankind until the present generation of Bedroom Boys took over.

I cannot believe that, even in our doom-threatened world, the erotic relation between men and women (or if we must be broad-minded, between human beings of the same sex) is quite as morbid, perverse, complicated, frenzied, revengeful, introverted, frustrated, or accompanied by so damn much *talk* as would appear to be the case if we are to accept the alcove reports of Mr. di Donato, Mr. Hecht, Mr. Mailer, Mr. Jones, and their literary cousins and their sisters and their aunts.

> Oh! Somewhere in this favored land
>   the sun is shining bright;
> The band is playing somewhere, and
>   somewhere hearts are light;
> And somewhere men are laughing
>   and somewhere children shout,
> But there is no joy in Sexville, where
>   the novelists hang out.

Professionals and Confessionals:

Dr. Seuss and Kenneth Grahame

I'VE BEEN THINKING LATELY about two writers of children's books who, both first-rate, are interestingly contrastable. One, Kenneth Grahame, who wrote *The Wind in the Willows,* was born in 1859. His centenary was fittingly marked by an excellent book by Peter Green: *Kenneth Grahame: A Biography.* The other is Dr. Seuss, 1951 winner of an Academy Award for the screenplay of the now-classic animated cartoon *Gerald McBoing-Boing,* and perhaps the most successful current writer of juvenile literature.

I learn from the new Grahame biography that since its first appearance in 1908 *The Wind in the Willows* has sold an average of 80,000 copies a year. I find this figure difficult to believe. I suspect, though I would enjoy being refuted, that today it is read mainly by grownups. Perhaps it also pleases that small minority of American children in whom reflection is not too severely discouraged—for it is a most thoughtful book.

Not only is it thoughtful. It is even in its dulcet way polemical. And above all it is confessional. Like Andersen, Louisa Alcott, and Mark Twain, Kenneth Grahame put into what he claimed was a children's book his deepest sense of the meaning of his own adult life. Dr. Seuss on the other hand is not in the least confessional; he is professional. He writes and draws his books, not as envelopes of covert or unconscious self-revelation, but to please and entertain himself and his young readers.

I believe that into one of these two classes—the confessional or the professional—any notable children's classic is apt to fall.

Kenneth Grahame, born a Scot in 1859, lived most of his life in England, dying in 1932. He was reared by his maternal grandmother. The older Grahame (the mother had died) coolly abandoned the four little Grahames, an action which was forever after to influence Kenneth's views on the character of grownups. The young Grahame, had he been properly educated, would have made an excellent backwater don, and we should probably be minus *The Wind in the Willows*. But his heavy-Victorian uncle would not pay the fees for Oxford and instead arranged for Kenneth to take a post in the Bank of England. His charm, natural intelligence, and physical attractiveness helped the dreamy young man to rise in the Bank until in 1898 he became its Secretary, and his financial future was assured.

Like many men he possessed no talent for that most exacting of professions, marriage; and like most men he married. (Someday, ten thousand years from now, the race will have advanced to the point where it will perhaps be one-tenth as exigent before granting a marriage license as it is today before granting a plumber's license.) Mrs. Grahame was an impossible creature, affected, demanding, at bottom a fool. They had one child, Alastair, an unhappy, physically handicapped boy, who, the evidence is now virtually all in, committed suicide at twenty by arranging to have a train run over him. There is no reason to suppose that the Grahames had any more ability at child rearing than at making a harmonious marriage.

As was the case with so many eminent Victorians and Edwardians, Grahame led two lives. The first was imposed on him by his class: the Bank of England job, marriage, money getting, paternity, respectability. The second was his dream life, the long, sad, halfhearted flight from what is called responsibility. This dream life was his redress for many things: his father's cruelty; his dissatisfaction not so much with the Bank of

England as with the England the Bank stood for; his unhealthy relationship with his wife; his bohemian detestation of "progress," industry, and trade; his aversion from the whole adult world, finding expression in a courteous misanthropy, an excessive love of nature, and an excessive idealization of animals.

Out of the conflict between the imposed life and the buried life came four slim books. One, *Pagan Papers,* is Stevenson-and-water, arty, wistful essays, perfectly in the *fin de siècle* mood of the nineties. *The Golden Age* and *Dream Days* are re-creations of the life of childhood, oddly mingling an affectionate sympathy for the young and a restrained bitterness toward grown-ups, the "Olympians," as he ironically termed them.

The only one of Grahame's books that will last is *The Wind in the Willows*. This story of the riverside adventures of the Mole, the Water Rat, the Badger, and the Toad is generally received as a delightful animal fantasy. Indeed it can be so read, particularly by children. But many readers have often vaguely felt it to be more than that, just as they know *Gulliver* to be more than a story about little people and big people. Some of us perhaps find ourselves wondering about the conceited Mr. Toad, in many ways an odd character for a child's book. By making Mr. Toad a rich man was not Grahame quietly expressing his opinion of his money-making era, as Dickens did more explicitly? By making Mr. Toad motor-mad was he not suggesting that the nineteenth century was to its own cost abandoning a life lived simply and naturally?

And then the book is not of one piece. Part of it seems simple and pleasant enough: the conversion of Mole to the delights of river life; the dangers Mole and Rat run in the Wild Wood and their rescue by Badger; Toad's transgressions; and his final rehabilitation by the sorely tried but loyal friends. But other parts of the book are allegorical, even philosophical, and young readers will almost surely pass over them lightly. With the chapter called *The Piper at the Gates of Dawn* and at several other points the tone alters. What was a humorous fancy about talking animals turns into a pagan hymn or a sly but not trivial commentary on the inferiority of humans to beasts.

All these matters are at last fully illuminated in the pages of Mr. Green's biography. I found it admirable, if a mite solemn— for occasionally the author loses sight of the fact that after all Grahame is a one-book author, and a minor one at that. He is almost overperceptive. Poring over Grahame with a magnifying lens he discovers more than a few things not open to the natural vision. What remains, once these qualifications are registered, is a fascinating exploration of a life that was a fiasco, in which all the major problems were side-stepped, the life of a charming, talented but essentially weak man. Yet out of his very failure, his hidden resentments, his reluctance to face up to the demands of his hard century, Grahame drew *The Wind in the Willows*. The sources of the little masterpiece are traced by Mr. Green in his subject's conscious and unconscious life, much as John Livingston Lowes, that supreme literary sleuth, tracked down in *The Road to Xanadu* the operations of the mind that produced *The Ancient Mariner*.

Mr. Green's conclusions are subtle and various, but one can sum them up by saying that in all his work, and particularly in *The Wind in the Willows*, Kenneth Grahame was revenging himself on the adult world which he had been forced to join, and on the century whose materialism his sensibility could not accept. He said once that he was "not a professional writer." It is true; he was a confessional one. The book that he stoutly protested he wrote for children was a letter written in invisible ink to himself.

On the other hand there is Dr. Seuss. I have known Ted Geisel for many years. (The "Seuss" is his mother's maiden name, the "Dr." represents the Ph.D. he never quite managed to collect.) I do not care to infuriate him by suggesting that he has no unconscious and that those extraordinary animals he draws are not symbolic but merely the consequence of his liking to draw extraordinary animals. He may have a complete set of private despairs that he fondles lovingly in the dark—I would be the last man to deprive him of them. He may have a dandy buried life. I wish to state, however, that if he has one it is not reflected in any of the delightful children's books he has written and drawn during the last twenty-five years. While it may not be quite the decent thing these days to say of a friend, I believe Dr. Seuss has not only added to the general store of happiness but that he is himself a happy man.

He is also—which such greater artists as Kenneth Grahame were not—a professional writer of juveniles. I do not mean that he writes with cold calculation for a shrewdly gauged market. On the contrary, he writes and draws as he does because he feels that way. But he knows exactly what he is doing. He aims to create nothing more than what meets the eye or ear. He is not *using* his books for any purpose beyond entertaining himself and his readers. *The Wind in the Willows* is a dream. But *On Beyond Zebra* (which deals with the letters of the alphabet after Z, such as YUZZ, UM, and HUMPF) and *Horton Hears a Who!*, though far more extravagant, are not dreams. They are ingenious solutions, exploited with unique humor and slyness and absurdity, of the standing problem of the juvenile-fantasy writer: how to find, not another Alice, but another rabbit hole.

The Geisels have no children ("You make 'em—I amuse 'em," says Dr. Seuss) and while he likes youngsters well enough, he does not claim any transcendental understanding of the juvenile mind. (Grahame, it might be noted, did not particularly care for *real* children, only for his dream children, just as Lewis Carroll detested boys and didn't care much for girls once they got beyond Lolita's age.) The sordid fact is that to be a good writer of juveniles you don't have to love children, any more than you have to love criminals to write *Crime and Punishment*.

Ted Geisel turned into Dr. Seuss more or less accidentally. Early in his career his absurd animals began to brighten the pages of the old *Judge*. But they did not pay dividends until they were transferred to the world of the Flit advertisements. He might have pursued his career of extermination indefinitely had it not been for his wife, who has all the qualities Elspeth Grahame lacked. Once, returning from Europe on the *Kungsholm*, Mr. Geisel, like the man in Mark Twain's story (Punch in the presence of the passenjare!) found himself mumbling over and over to the beat of the ship's engines:

> And that is a story that no one can beat,
> And to think that I saw it on Mulberry Street.

In order to prevent their lives from being darkened by the continued repetition of this couplet, Mrs. Geisel persuaded him to invent a story in which it might reasonably appear. The result was his first book, *And To Think That I Saw It on Mulberry Street*. It was rejected by twenty-seven publishers, on four grounds:

1. Fantasy doesn't sell.
2. Verse doesn't sell.
3. It had no "pattern," whatever that meant.
4. It wasn't "practical"—that is, it didn't teach the child how to become a better child, or grownup, or mortician.

The twenty-eighth publisher was densely ignorant of the juvenile market. He published the book for a fantastic reason—he liked it. Since then Dr. Seuss's books (according to my calculations there are twenty of them) have sold something in the neighborhood of four million copies. His *The Cat in the Hat* should be within sight of the million mark. It is probably the most influential first-grade reader since McGuffey. Using only 223 different words, it manages to tell a story that for the first time in the history of beginners'-grade education actually amuses the tot, and so persuades him that reading is a worth-while experience.

Dr. Seuss is a craftsman, not an allegorist, or a satirist in disguise. He modestly ascribes much of his success to the fact that he is his own illustrator, permitting him to make every page pull double weight. In his own way he is as mad about language as Flaubert was. Once he spent five hours in his publisher's office working over a single line of verse until he had removed an extra beat that bothered his ear. In the next room he overheard the editor trying to persuade a lady novelist, whose talents tend to the copious, to remove 75,000 words from her new book. (The editor lost.)

Dr. Seuss also believes that children (and grownups too—there's quite a serious Seuss cult) like him because he *bucks* the trend in children's books, supplying oddity instead of wholesome instruction, wild humor instead of mere pleasantness, and the unbelievable instead of a duplication of the child's familiar environment. Whatever may be the good Doctor's secret there is no doubt that he is the most successful writer in his field today, and a true professional. Whether his work will last, as *The Wind in the Willows* has lasted, is another matter. Possibly the absence of that very ambiguous element you find in Kenneth Grahame, that teasing sense of other meanings and under-meanings, destine it to a shorter life than children's classics saturated with the confessional element. At the moment Dr. Seuss is single-handedly changing the reading habits of hundreds of thousands of American children. That's enough for any one man. Somebody ought to give him that Ph.D. he's always hankered after.

Children, Books, and a List

THOUGH WEAKENING, our informal fun education still reigns. One of its minor consequences is that frequently writers are called upon to supply ideas to high school students who are assigned "themes." (While this procedure does not teach the student how to write or think, it does teach him how to interview people. This is how part of your tax money is spent.) The other day a neighbor of mine, a bright-faced, intelligent teen-age girl, was sent to interview me. Subject: children's reading. Among her questions was the inevitable, How do you get children to like books? No less inevitable was my reply: Start them two generations before they're born.

Obvious? Yet anxious parents of stubborn nonreaders are often bewildered when I ask two questions: How many books and linear feet of book shelving does your house contain? How many hours a week can your children actually observe *you* reading?

It is in the classroom that the child is *taught* to read (and I may as well invite some bitter correspondence from the experts by stating that he is often taught two to three years later than is needful*). But his acceptance of the *idea* of reading takes

---

* "During the year, Omar K. Moore, the Yale sociologist, has dealt the sacred dogma of reading readiness a mortal blow by showing that normal children of two, three, four, and five years of age can learn to read, write, and typewrite with ease."—*Council for Basic Education Bulletin*, June, 1961.

place, usually at the age of about eighteen months, in the home
—that is, in a home where books seem, like plumbing, to be a part
of life and where the child's parents are visible habitual readers.
I might add that having scads of books around is more important than having any *special* books around, including the
ones recommended in the lists attached to these comments.

A friend of mine once asked the English novelist Joyce Cary,
an Oxford man, whether he had observed any difference between
the performances of red-brick university scholars and those
attending Oxford and Cambridge. None whatsoever, was the
answer, and then Cary added casually that in both groups
students from families who had books around the house did all
right; the others ran into trouble.

An early familiarity with books unconsciously introduces the
child to a fundamental, liberating truth: that the largest part of
the entire universe of space and time can never be apprehended
by direct firsthand experience. The child who has never really
understood this truth is permitted by our Constitution to become President. But he remains, in the most literal sense, mentally unbalanced. So, if you want your children to read, the
first commandment, as trite as true, is: Go thou and do likewise.

I would suggest that reading, especially at an early age, should
be an integral part of life, like eating and loving and playing,
indeed almost like breathing. None the less, informal and unregi-
mented as this activity should be, we parents might keep a few
simple notions in mind.

I offer two quotations.

I know a highly reputable publisher who has issued many fine
children's books, indeed some of the finest. But the educational
psychologists and statisticians have finally got to him, as witness
a recent announcement that his firm is organizing a plan "for
fitting children's books into high school curricula and . . . building an entire reading program for grades 1 through 12." For this
publisher's lock-step scheme, which assumes that children are
not souls but quanta, I predict financial success.

The second quotation has a slightly Tory flavor. It assumes
that human beings are not neatly gradable but wildly unequal

in their powers. "I am persuaded that both children and the lower class of readers hate books that are written down to their capacity. They love those that are composed for their olders and betters." The author of this sentiment wrote books for grownups that were popular with children for over a century until mass communication taught them that words, ideas, and images should be so constructed as to pass through the brain without encountering any resistance.

Between our publisher, influenced by age-level statistics, and Sir Walter Scott, moved by his insight into the human heart, I prefer Scott. In other words, let the child read above his capacity. Ignore (obviously within reason) the neat age-level indications with which the experts provide us. The experts mean well, but they have never met your child, and you have. Look first at the book, then at your child's mind. If the book is perhaps a little too hard for him, it's a candidate for purchase. There is only one way to enlarge a rubber band and that is to stretch it.

But difficulty is not enough. The book must have quality too. A good book, such as *The Wizard of Oz*, employs a simple vocabulary; it is just about on the level of my eight-year-old daughter's word sense. But its imaginative and even moral content is sufficiently sophisticated to make her reach. That is to say, it has true literary quality. The story of Terry and his dog Spot, on the other hand, can only confront her with ideas and experiences to which she is already superior. What the child-mind measurers call a feeling of mastery is often only a feeling of boredom. Virtue lies in a little frustration.

What we should watch out for in much contemporary children's literature is an excess of one kind of talent, the talent for simplification. As I once put it, many authors are too much interested in children and insufficiently interested in themselves. They know all too well how to adapt to their clear idea of the average child in a given age bracket. Now this skill Mark Twain and Robert Louis Stevenson never possessed. They wrote out of themselves, out of their own sense of the surprisingness of life, never once asking whether they were overstepping the young reader's "experience." Defoe neglected all his own children but one—the child inside himself who helped to write *Robinson Crusoe*. Their books do not *match* the child's experience. Their books *are* an experience, "something," says Arthur Ransome, "that he lives."

Do these names seem too dusty to be convincing? I refer you to our contemporary, E. B. White, author of *Charlotte's Web*, one of the few classic children's works of our day. "What am I saying to my readers?" he asks. "Well, I never know. Writing to me is not an exercise in addressing readers, it is more as though I were talking to myself while shaving. . . . All that I ever hope to say in books is that I love the world. I guess you can find that in there, if you dig around." Dig around in the 1,628 new books for children published in 1960 and see in how many "you can find that in there."

Literature for children is not inferior literature; it is merely another kind of literature. Tolstoy is not "greater" than Lewis Carroll; the two men are working entirely different streets, indeed different universes. "Only the rarest kind of best in anything can be good enough for the young," says Walter de la Mare, and the admonition is as true as it is stern.

The best book about children's books ever written, *Books, Children and Men,* by Paul Hazard (one which I entreat my adult readers to study), contains a long and sympathetic summary of an authoritative manual entitled *Writing for Children.* Hazard concludes: "And genius, that touch of genius, without which a lasting work could not be composed, either for little or big folk? How to acquire it? The manual does not say; it did not think of that."

It did not think of that. But we must think of it. Children have just as much right of access to genius as to swimming pools and hot lunches. More. Infinitely more.

Let the child read above himself. Let him read, if not the best, at least the good. To these two counsels I would add a third: Let him travel farther in the realms of gold than in the realms of lead.

The realms of gold are crowded with works of the imagination, with what De Quincey, in his essay on Pope, called the lit-

erature of *power*. The realms of lead are crowded with what he
called the literature of *knowledge*, such literature as Lamb must
have had in mind when he spoke of "things in books' clothing."

Two flourishing divisions of today's juvenile-book output belong to the realms of lead. The lead is often very good lead—but
it is lead all the same. These two divisions are "real-life" stories
and fact books of all kinds. I wish they were less flourishing, not
because they are bad in themselves but because they are so easy
to multiply by mass-production methods that they tend to swamp
the genuine children's literature of the realms of gold, the literature which must be hand- and mind-crafted.

Real-life stories are based on the premise that children like to
read about experiences they have had or can easily recognize.
Fact books are based on the premise that children will devour
any kind of information whether or not it is of the slightest interest or importance. Both kinds of books are proper to an epoch
convinced that reality is what you read about in the newspapers.

The child brought up on an exclusive diet of real-life stories
is handicapped to the extent that he will find it difficult to step
into the realms of gold, just as the confirmed newspaper reader,
though he may be quite intelligent, is puzzled to think what
others can possibly see in such erratic fellows as Dostoevski or
Yeats. I am not pleading for fantasy, for a fairy-tale literature.
I am pleading for imagination. *Mr. Popper's Penguins* is about
an ordinary American family; it has plenty of "real life" which
Richard and Florence Atwater have transformed by humor and
tenderness, and it is this transformation that delights the children, and not a mechanical recognition of some dull one-to-one
correspondence with their own jog-trot environment. A thousand
imitators of Louisa May Alcott have made the error of supposing
that the popularity of *Little Women* lay in the fact that it was
a wholesome story about an ordinary American family when
the truth is that it is a masterpiece because its author was an
extraordinary American woman who could not help making
poetry out of her childhood memories. Such writers are rare; but
even in our own time many writers of juveniles exist who know
how to handle the familiar world without cutting the roots of

wonder. I have cited the Atwaters. I would add Oliver Butterworth and the late Eric Knight—and there are others.

Nor am I opposed to fact books as such. *Kon-Tiki* is a record of a factual adventure, but there is an interesting mind behind the facts and the adventures; and the child, though he may not know it, is reacting to the tension created by that mind as well as to the tension created by a thrilling narrative. In my lists I recommend a book of science called *Cosmic View*, not because by reading it the child may learn half a hundred facts about the two large universes outside and inside himself, but because it cannot fail to stimulate in him the amazement which is one of the components of true scientific curiosity. *Madame Curie* is recommended not because it teaches the child how radium was discovered but because it shows all of us, including the child, a rare and beautiful mind striving and suffering for truth.

And so I sorely doubt that it is worth giving your child *Einstein: Boy Mathematician* (a title which all by itself reveals a miscomprehension of Einstein, boys, and mathematics); or *Michael Gets the Measles;* or *Our Neighbors in India;* or *Getting To Know Liberia.* The years of childhood are too important to be wasted in learning the facts about measles and Liberia. They are too important to be spent mainly in the realms of lead.

In *Back to Methuselah* Shaw said, "Imagination is the beginning of creation. You imagine what you desire; you will what you imagine; and at last you create what you will." If, as we say, we are trying to make our children into creative human beings, we must see that this chain from imagination to creation is forged for them. Will imagination be stimulated by a book described thus: "To go to college, or court his girl in a convertible—that's the problem confronting the appealing hero of this true-to-life novel. (Girls 12 to 15)"? These are hardly the terms in which to present to young girls life's grave and fascinating alternatives.

To put it in Irish bull form, we must stop treating our children as though they were children. All I mean is that there is no child so dull that he can possibly react with more than weary ac-

ceptance to a book called *Let's Take a Trip to a Cement Plant.*
(Just as no child has ever been taught much by a teacher-
chaperoned trip to a dairy, except that it's a place where you
get a glass of milk free.)

I do not know what makes a children's classic, but I would
guess that some of the factors that go into any classic go into
it: passion and imagination and intelligence and the felt pressure of an individual mind, that of the author. It is not in the nature of things that passion, intelligence, imagination, and pressure
can possibly be present in a book for children about a cement
plant, or in one which tries to persuade them to accept the idea
that they should get to know Liberia. I should add that it is
equally against nature that such books should ever be well
written. Their themes almost demand bad or at least flat and
prosaic writing; and that is the kind of writing found in most
fact books, with some honorable exceptions.

If the reader is still with me, he will now understand the lists
that follow.

I have called the first one "Only Yesteryear" to suggest that a
child's classic may be "old-fashioned" but still retain perennial
appeal. It is a good thing for a child to read old-fashioned books.
Let him realize that there is more than one way of telling a
story, and that monosyllabic prose and machine-gun action are
not the only tricks in a writer's kit. Give him a peephole into
the past, for his school does not in all cases provide it. Let him
discover for himself that the myths and epics of ancient Greece
remain far more important and interesting than the setup of his
town's fire department.

"Only Yesteryear" is a traditional list with few surprises in it.
The pre-1920 classics are pretty well established, and there aren't
many of them. But I have kept to the tradition partly *because*
it is a tradition, because the child should have some notion of
the best that has been written for him by men and women now
dead, just as the grownup should have some notion of the vaster
adult intellectual tradition which has produced him. These fifty
items (and others you will want to add from among your own
favorites) do not talk down. The authors *meant* them, and the

child who likes to read will feel that they meant them. The result will be the mental and imaginative enlargement that we all say we are seeking for our children.

"Only Yesterday" consists of books published during the last forty years. Some, such as *Mr. Popper's Penguins, Hitty, Johnny Tremain, Lassie Come Home, The Story of Dr. Dolittle,* and the books of A. A. Milne, Dr. Seuss, P. L. Travers, and E. B. White, have already won out in the classics sweepstakes. It is the children themselves who have made these books classics, for in the long run publishers can fool us but not the youngsters.

Some of the more modern titles are open to argument. Some represent special favorites of my own or my family; some represent wild bets on the future; and one or two, such as Kees Boeke's *Cosmic View,* call attention to books I think undeservedly neglected, and which youngsters will go for if they're given a chance.

The lists are neither "authoritative" nor whimsical. All the items, in my opinion, have excellence of some sort. Several have greatness. Lists such as these are legion, and no atmosphere of Holy Writ surrounds any of them. Children's librarians and others knowledgeable in the subject would probably agree with about 60 per cent of the selections and amiably question the remainder in favor of beloved favorites of their own, particularly in the contemporary field.

There are a hundred authors, but the total number of books involved runs to something like 125 to 150 individual titles. There might have been more or fewer; but as you ransack the field, a curious fact emerges: fifty authors seem to exhaust the recognized older classics. I discovered also that the same number, more or less, covered all the post-1920 items about which I had definite, positive feelings. One hundred is a pleasant, round, easily rememberable number; so I left it at that. Don't take it too seriously—perhaps I'm merely a prisoner of the decimal system.

A starred item (*) indicates that the title is either the first or the best known of a series. In the case of the *Oz* books, I have found excellence only in those written by L. Frank Baum; his successors have done their best, but their best is not good enough. In all other cases, the entire series may be recommended with confidence.

Before drawing up this list I examined or read more than four hundred books, kindly sent me by many generous publishers. As these books represented the publishers' own estimate of their finest offerings, I do not feel that I would have done much better if I had read a thousand. Among the post-1920 items I have had to make many hairline decisions. Limitations both of space and my own taste have doubtless excluded many works of merit. This is inevitable; and I can only beg the indulgence of those authors and publishers who may feel themselves slighted.

With respect to illustrations I confess a bias toward the old-fashioned. I am all for the color, the dash, and—out with the dreadful word—the literalness of the N. C. Wyeth school. Just as the text itself should not read too easily, so I think illustrations should be more than a few modernistic scratches. I am for detail; let the small reader pore over the picture and learn what there is to be learned from skillful representation. (He can absorb High Art through his finger-painting class.)

As to that bugaboo: Age Level. In a few cases I have indicated that a book is more likely to appeal to either the younger or the older end of our eight-to-fifteen gamut; but for the most part I prefer not to declare myself. Clearly the average eight-year-old is not going to get much out of *The Red Badge of Courage;* and equally clearly the world-weary teen-ager will turn up his nose at the sweet and simple books of Laura Wilder. The point to stress is that if a book is good enough it makes hay of age levels; when my daughter was five, my son was seven and I was fifty-four—and we all enjoyed *Mary Poppins* about equally. (Of course our children are as brilliant as their father may be retarded.)

Always, as I have said, let the child read above himself. If his reading is exactly suited to his mental ability, nothing will happen inside his mind. Of course, one must use common sense; if the book is really so hard as to discourage the child, you simply

point out how enjoyable it will be next year, and supply him
with another book.

In these lists you will find a fair but not large number of books
written for adults. One of the most interesting phenomena in the
history of literature is that involved in the gradual (or sometimes sudden) juvenilization of certain grown-up books. We are
familiar with this process in the classic instances of *Gulliver,
Robinson Crusoe,* and *Jane Eyre.* But it is going on at this moment. *Gone With the Wind* was a great success with the general
public; but in the course of the last few years it has become the
special property of the young adolescent. The same transformation is noticeable with *Cress Delahanty* and *National Velvet* and
The Yearling, all written by conscious, subtle, sophisticated artists. The most recent example is *Born Free.* I predict (and this
is not a criticism of Mrs. Adamson's delightful account of her
tame lioness) that in ten years few grownups will read it, but
that children's librarians will have to be vigilant if they are to
keep it on the shelves.

I am no champion of predigested classics. But in four cases
I have had to modify my stand. These are the Bible, the Arabian
Nights, and the legendry of Greece (including Homer) and the
Norse myths.

The child should be familiar with the Bible, but there is no
use denying that to him it is, particularly in the magnificent but
difficult King James version, a forbidding book. Let him start,
I think, with Walter de la Mare's beautiful retellings; and in
time he will find his way to the original. The point is not that
simplifications are in themselves to be condemned; they are
only to be condemned if they are (as is usually the case) examples of bad or dishonest writing. De la Mare is an artist; he
respects his audience. The Arabian Nights I have always thought
pretty dull, but the child should nevertheless make friends with
Ali Baba and Sinbad, and an edited version that cuts out some
of the dreariness of the original is all to the good. There is a
time to read first-rate translations of the Greek epics, but if
they're insisted upon too early in the child's reading life, Homer
may lose a reader forever. I suggest Gustav Schwab's scholarly

but fluently written compendium of all the Greek myths and legends, including the *Odyssey* and the *Iliad*. So with the wonderful Norse myths, beautifully handled in Padraic Colum's *The Children of Odin.*

The lists are as accurate as I could make them. A few of these titles (such as Enid Blyton's *Valley of Adventure*) are easy enough to find in a good public library but may, if asked for in a bookstore, upset the average clerk. Do the best you can; I've chosen the best I know.

Only Yesteryear (Before 1920)

Louisa May Alcott, *Little Women.*＊

Thomas Bailey Aldrich, *The Story of a Bad Boy.*

Hans Christian Andersen, *Fairy Tales and Legends.*

Arabian Nights, edited by Kate Douglas Wiggin and Nora A. Smith.

Jane Austen, *Pride and Prejudice.*

James Barrie, *Peter Pan and Wendy.*

L. Frank Baum, *The Wizard of Oz* ＊; *The Wizard of Oz and The Land of Oz* (one volume).＊

Stories From the Bible, retold by Walter de la Mare.

Charlotte Brontë, *Jane Eyre.*

Emily Brontë, *Wuthering Heights.*

Frances Hodgson Burnett, *The Secret Garden.*

Lewis Carroll, *Alice's Adventures in Wonderland* and *Through the Looking-Glass.*

Carlo Collodi, *Pinocchio.*

Joseph Conrad, *The Portable Conrad,* including *Typhoon, The Nigger of the Narcissus,* and *Heart of Darkness.*

James Fenimore Cooper, *The Leatherstocking Saga.*

Stephen Crane, *The Red Badge of Courage.*

Daniel Defoe, *Robinson Crusoe.*

Walter de la Mare, *The Three Royal Monkeys.*

Charles Dickens, *David Copperfield; Great Expectations.*

Mary Mapes Dodge, *Hans Brinker.*

Arthur Conan Doyle, *The Complete Sherlock Holmes.*

Alexandre Dumas, *The Three Musketeers; The Count of Monte Cristo.*

Kenneth Grahame, *The Wind in the Willows.*

Grimm Brothers, *Grimms' Fairy Tales.*

W. H. Hudson, *A Little Boy Lost.*

Victor Hugo, *Les Misérables.*

Washington Irving, *Rip Van Winkle* and *The Legend of Sleepy Hollow.*

The Story of King Arthur and His Knights, written and illustrated by Howard Pyle.

Charles Kingsley, *Westward Ho!*

Rudyard Kipling, *The Jungle Books; Kim; Just-So Stories; Captains Courageous.*

Selma Lagerlöf, *The Wonderful Adventures of Nils.**

Edward Lear, *The Complete Nonsense Book.*

Jack London, *The Call of the Wild.*

Herman Melville, *Moby Dick.*

E. Nesbit, *Five Children and It.**

(Norse Myths) Padraic Colum, *The Children of Odin.*

Edgar Allan Poe, *Tales.*

Howard Pyle, *The Merry Adventures of Robin Hood.*

Charles Reade, *The Cloister and the Hearth.*

Gustav Schwab, *Gods and Heroes: Myths and Epics of Ancient Greece.*

Johanna Spyri, *Heidi.*

James Stephens, *The Crock of Gold.*

Robert Louis Stevenson, *Kidnapped; Treasure Island; The Black Arrow.*

Jonathan Swift, *Gulliver's Travels.*

Booth Tarkington, *Penrod.*

William Makepeace Thackeray, *Vanity Fair.*

Mark Twain, *The Adventures of Tom Sawyer* and *The Adventures of Huckleberry Finn.*

Jules Verne, *The Mysterious Island; Twenty Thousand Leagues Under the Sea.*

H. G. Wells, *Seven Science Fiction Novels.*

Oscar Wilde, *The Complete Fairy Tales of Oscar Wilde.*

Only Yesterday (1920-1960)

Joy Adamson, *Born Free*. Written originally for adults, this recent story of a tame lion cub has already been claimed by the young.

Richard T. and Florence H. Atwater, *Mr. Popper's Penguins*. What happened when the Popper family found themselves the owners of some penguins; sly and humorous.

Enid Bagnold, *National Velvet*. A fourteen-year-old girl, a horse, and the Grand National; subtle writing which youngsters take in their stride.

Hilaire Belloc, *Cautionary Verses*. Some of these wonderful nonsense rhymes were written before 1920; this is an omnibus volume.

Ludwig Bemelmans, *Madeline*.* The pictures make more enchanting this story of a little girl in Paris.

Paul Berna, *The Horse Without a Head*. First-rate French import, about a gang of vivid village kids, some dogs, and a notable collection of villains.

Enid Blyton, *The Valley of Adventure*. Four children, a romantic background, and a treasure hunt. Very English, but my ten-year-old son calls it one of the best books he has ever read.

Kees Boeke, *Cosmic View: The Universe in Forty Jumps*. One of my own enthusiasms. A book of drawings and charts of the microcosm and the macrocosm which truly enlarges the imagination of young and old.

James Boyd, *Drums*. Fine, solid, *long* story of the American Revolution.

Ben Lucien Burman, *High Water at Catfish Bend*. Delicious talking-animal yarn set against a background of the lower Mississippi. Good sequel: *The Owl Hoots Twice at Catfish Bend*.

Oliver Butterworth, *The Trouble With Jenny's Ear*. A favorite in our house; funny real-life yarn involving some of the wonders and absurdities of modern communications technology.

Eve Curie, *Madame Curie*. I'm taking a chance on this splendid biography of the great woman scientist—it's for grownups, but I think older boys and girls can handle it easily.

Walter de la Mare, *Come Hither.* Incomparably the best anthology in existence of fine poetry suitable for children; with magical notes and commentary.

Walter D. Edmonds, *The Matchlock Gun.* Short, exciting story of a heroic ten-year-old of colonial days.

Eleanor Farjeon, *The Little Bookroom.* Twenty-seven of this distinguished Englishwoman's best tales of fantasy and real life.

Rachel Field, *Hitty: Her First Hundred Years.* About a doll, and in its way a classic.

Esther Forbes, *Johnny Tremain.* First-rate historical novel, its hero an apprentice boy of Revolutionary Boston.

C. S. Forester, *Captain Horatio Hornblower.** The best of the grand Hornblower yarns; for older boys.

Marguerite Henry, *King of the Wind; Misty of Chincoteague.* Deservedly popular horse stories for the younger set.

Hergé, *The Adventures of Tintin.** Enormously successful on the Continent, this amusing and well-drawn series represents one of the few sets of comics I would care to place in the hands of an intelligent child.

Thor Heyerdahl, *Kon-Tiki.* A modern classic of extraordinary real-life adventure, this appeals to older boys and girls. There's a fine special edition in color for younger ones.

Will James, *Smoky, the Cow Horse.* A fine horse-and-cowboy story, told in authentic but not obtrusive lingo.

John F. Kennedy, *Profiles in Courage.* I think intelligent older boys and girls can take this; there is some sort of juvenile version available too.

Eric Knight, *Lassie Come Home.* This, about a faithful Yorkshire collie, is quite simply one of the best dog stories ever written.

C. S. Lewis, *The Lion, the Witch and the Wardrobe.** One of a series of beautifully written fantasies, by an English don.

Charles Lindbergh, *The Spirit of St. Louis.* Written for grownups, but fine for older boys.

Astrid Lindgren, *Pippi Longstocking.** Absurd and matter-of-fact, this series, translated from the Swedish, is greatly liked by younger children.

Hugh Lofting, *The Story of Dr. Dolittle.** Dr. Dolittle goes rolling right along; hard to beat for the eight-to-ten crowd.

David McCord, *Far and Few.* There are many excellent books of children's verse by contemporary poets; I happen to like this best.

John Masefield, *The Bird of Dawning.* A fine yarn about the days of sail.

A. A. Milne, *The World of Pooh; The World of Christopher Robin.* Handy and handsome omnibus volumes.

Margaret Mitchell, *Gone With the Wind.* Older boys and girls take naturally to this, just as their Victorian similars took to Scott and Cooper.

Charles Nordhoff and James Norman Hall, *The Bounty Trilogy.* This classic sea story is just right, as is Forester, for older boys.

Mary Norton, *The Borrowers.** About some miniature people who live in an old English country house; Mrs. Norton is the real thing.

Mary O'Hara, *My Friend Flicka.** One of the best horse stories of its period, and enormously popular.

Arthur Ransome, *Swallows and Amazons.** About a group of English Lake Country children and their sailing and camping adventures. Superior writing and full of technical detail children love as long as it's not pushed down their throats.

Marjorie Kinnan Rawlings, *The Yearling.* The children have taken over this beautiful story of a lad and his pet deer.

Kenneth Roberts, *Northwest Passage.* First-rate historical, about Major Robert Rogers, his Rangers, and the French and Indian War. Long, thank heaven.

Antoine de St. Exupéry, *The Little Prince.* One of the few absolute modern successes in the field of the traditional fairy tale. Exquisitely written.

Felix Salten, *Bambi.* A mild but pleasing tale about a deer in the woods around Vienna.

Carl Sandburg, *Rootabaga Stories.* Home-made folk tales that retain their freshness. *Abe Lincoln Grows Up.* The relevant sections from Sandburg's famous biography.

Elizabeth Seeman, *The Talking Dog and the Barking Man.* A personal favorite, about a spotted dog and a Mexican pitchman, and, to my taste, wonderfully funny and charming.

Dr. Seuss. Any but preferably all of his numerous books.

John Steinbeck, *The Red Pony.* Not intended for children, this moving tale of a boy and a pony is fine for older boys and girls.

J. R. R. Tolkien, *The Hobbit.* Written by a learned Oxford don, this beautifully composed fantasy about a tiny dwarflike creature appeals to the exceptionally imaginative and literate child.

P. L. Travers, *Mary Poppins.** This story of a nursemaid with magical powers is now an undoubted classic.

Jessamyn West, *Cress Delahanty.* Tenderly written story of a teen-age girl, written for grownups, but which has proved increasingly popular with other teen-age girls.

E. B. White, *Charlotte's Web; Stuart Little.* Animal tales lit with unique fantasy and humor. Literature with a capital L.

Laura Wilder, *Little House in the Big Woods.** Charming, simple re-creation of the world of the pioneers; for young readers.

Henry Williamson, *Tarka the Otter.* A masterpiece of its kind, a remarkable evocation of the life of an otter; originally written for grownups, and suitable for youngsters with some feeling for style.

They Have Their Exits and
Their Entrances

IT MUST BE A MARK of an unscholarly nature that the parts of
history that interest me most involve beginnings and endings.

The real student is of course attracted to the meat of the sandwich. But to stir the sense of wonder nothing serves like a
contemplation of beginnings, as to stir the sense of philosophy
nothing equals a rumination upon endings.

It is the story of the first Ford, not the millionth, that thrills.
It is to little David, not the sensible young Copperfield, that the
magic clings. It is not sentiment alone, but the breath of poetry
itself, that makes mothers enclose in lockets the first curling
tendrils of baby hair. And as for oyster eating, its development
moves me not, yet that proverbial hero who first ate the bivalve
still beckons my imagination.

The spell of endings has a different quality. It is tied up with
the pleasure of illumination, the recognition of the moment of
final truth. Tristan and Isolde, Romeo and Juliet have fastened
themselves forever in our fancy precisely because their legends
end in death: we could not forgive them had they lived happily
ever after. The man or the bull must die, and there is a sinister
artist in us who prefers the man.

For most writers the beginning is a torment. So much (in modern journalism too much) turns on it. It can attract the unknown, unknowable reader, or repel him, or leave him cold. Beyond this it may have a baleful effect on the writer. Often it is a Gorgon's head, turning him to stone, a basilisk fascinating him to immobility. Or it may act like rails, determining too rigidly the tone and content of what is to follow. The lead, not the writer, becomes boss.

And so even the hardened professional is nervous when he first puts pen to paper. He feels that same tense, stomach-tightening quiver that grips the actor as the curtain rises, even though he can correct, and the actor cannot.

Each writer has his own difficulty. To take a handy example, I have never, in these essays, been able to master the approved contemporary opening—direct, attention-getting, and square on the subject. My inclination is to start with a wide, and often windy, generalization and then to work up and away from it.

There was once a Victorian traveler and writer, William Winwood Reade, nephew of the man who wrote *The Cloister and the Hearth*. He set out to write a book on the sources of the Nile. He wound up with a best-seller called *The Martyrdom of Man* (1872). He found he could not talk about the African interior without sketching in the story of the whole world first, which he did, producing as a matter of fact a work of philosophical history that is still highly readable. My trouble is the same as Reade's, however dissimilar the result.

Because I take little pride in my own beginnings and endings, I am perhaps all the more interested to discover how my superiors turn the trick.

For some years I have been a collector of beginnings and endings. No album, no cabinet is needed. My specimens lie silent on the pages of the books on my shelves, as they do on yours, waiting to be classified and labeled. They are the beginnings and endings of certain cut-off lengths of imagination—novels, poems, stories. It is curious to note how much one may learn from contemplating them, almost without reference to the works they introduce or conclude.

The Beginning of Beginnings is to be found where you would expect to find it.

> In the beginning God created the heaven and the earth.

You cannot beat that for concision, curiosity-exciting power, and what I hope it is not irreverent to call self-assurance. It names and introduces the Hero. It suggests His most important quality, omnipotence. It sets time and place. It narrates the absolute maximum of action in the absolute minimum of words.

Nothing in my collection can match it. But I have a close second. This too derives its magnitude from the fact that it is not merely a beginning but the beginning of a beginning. Our literature is commonly thought to start with *Beowulf*. How does the starter, *Beowulf*, itself start? With two words (in the translation I prefer) that by a happy accident seem to herald the onset of English literature as with the sound of trumpets:

> What ho!

Allied to such primal openings are those we may call Keynoters. The books they introduce are to the literature that is to follow as the keynote speech is to the other speeches at a national Presidential convention. Take this one:

> You don't know about me without you have read a book by the name of *The Adventures of Tom Sawyer;* but that ain't no matter. That book was made by Mr. Mark Twain, and he told the truth, mainly. There was things which he stretched, but mainly he told the truth.

These two sentences announce not only *Huckleberry Finn* but the fact that a marriage has been arranged between the American novel and the American vernacular, just as the opening lines of *The Canterbury Tales* announce that from now on the literature of England will be written in English, and not in Norman French or Latin. As Mr. Hemingway has stated, he (which includes his school) took off from *Huckleberry Finn;* so that the

reading of these two sentences is akin to the emotion one might
feel at being present at a birth you know will turn out to be the
fountainhead of a dynasty.

This seminal quality is shared by other American opening
lines. One is the quiet haunting first sentence of "The Open
Boat" by Stephen Crane.

> None of them knew the colour of the sky.

It is hard to say why these nine words announced the start of a
whole army of naturalistic writers, daring to found their art on
exact, ruthless observation. They are nine daggers plunged into
the body of the genteel tradition.

Such keynotes may be major, as with Crane and Mark Twain.
They may be minor. I offer a minor one, suggested by the novelist Jerome Weidman, who is something of an expert in beginnings and endings, and who has supplied me with several
excellent specimens for my collection.

> They threw me off the hay truck about noon.

You may not remember that one—it's the opening of James M.
Cain's *The Postman Always Rings Twice*—but it created quite a
furor in its time. It epitomized the hard-boiled school that
flourished in the thirties. Such opening lines are interesting precisely because they are so pat to their period. They are the anti-
macassars or clouded canes of their epoch, their decade, sometimes
their very year or season.

I rummage in my collection for two perfect examples that will
light up the deep chasm between one period and another; and
I think I have them. Both the subjoined openings are by first-
rate writers, and both introduce first-rate stories. In time they
are only thirty-five years apart. But in outlook, in phrasing, in
rhythm they are worlds apart.

Here's the first:

> Among the few features of agricultural England which retain
> an appearance but little modified by the lapse of centuries, may
> be reckoned the high, grassy and furzy downs, coombs, or ewe-
> leases, as they are indifferently called, that fill a large area of

certain counties in the south and south-west. If any mark of human occupation is met with hereon, it usually takes the form of the solitary cottage of some shepherd.

Here's the second:

> I guess looking at it, now, my old man was cut out for a fat guy, one of those regular little roly fat guys you see around, but he sure never got that way, except a little toward the last, and then it wasn't his fault, he was riding over the jumps only and he could afford to carry plenty of weight then.

Probably you have already spotted these. (One opens Thomas Hardy's "The Three Strangers," the other Hemingway's "My Old Man.") But I will wager that even if you had never read a word of either Hardy or Hemingway, you would have been able to tell me which is which. One is of our time, the other not. These men feel differently. They even *breathe* differently, and they declare that difference with the first breaths their stories draw.

It is a received idea that a writer must interest the reader at once, either by enticing him into the narrative, or by shocking him—the "Hell!-said-the-Duchess" technique. This notion is only half true; as we shall see, many storytellers prefer to open their narratives as if they were essays. But just as many do believe in taking the reader by the buttonhole so that, like the Wedding Guest, he cannot choose but hear.

From my collection I select five good Buttonholers.

> Please, God, let him telephone me now.

That is the first line of Dorothy Parker's almost intolerably heart-breaking short story "A Telephone Call." It is effective. It hooks the reader by letting him in at once on a situation whose resolution he is anxious to experience.

> It began with an advertisement in the Agony Column of The Times.

Caught? Of course you are. This might be the opening of a detective story, or a crime thriller. It doesn't matter: you want to know what "it" may be and you want to read that advertisement. In fact, these are the first words of Peter Fleming's *Brazilian Adventure,* the only travel book funny enough to rank with Mark Twain's *Innocents Abroad*—and twice as well written.

> Scarlett O'Hara was not beautiful. . . .

Shock tactics, of course, and completely successful ones. Does there exist a first reader of Miss Mitchell's wily first sentence who wouldn't want to learn more about the not-beautiful Scarlett?

> It was a bright cold day in April, and the clocks were striking thirteen.

Shock tactics, too, more aggressive than Miss Mitchell's. The reader, arrested by the terminal word, soon realizes the aptness of this numeral of disaster—for the sentence opens one of the most terrible of modern satires, George Orwell's *Nineteen Eighty-Four.*

> Call me Ishmael.

These three words, launching Melville's *Moby Dick,* probably rate as the greatest Buttonholer in our literature. Their curtness, their abruptness, and their assumption that the reader will understand them without extended explanation—all make them peculiarly effective with us moderns. They are completely at variance with the typical openings of the Victorian novel. They hook the reader by suggestion. You feel at once that you have been plumped down into the middle of a man's life and that that life is going to be interestingly tragic. The Biblical overtones (Ishmael) of course play their part. On the whole this opening does about as much work as you can well demand from three words.

As we have noted, they are not typical of their time. Most of Melville's contemporaries preferred a long windup before the pitch. Here's a fair sample:

> Whether I shall turn out to be the hero of my own life, or whether that station will be held by anybody else, these pages must show.

The sentence precedes three leisurely paragraphs. Paragraph four, however, opens thus:

> I was born with a caul, which was advertised for sale, in the newspapers, at the low price of fifteen guineas.

Most modern writers would seize upon this marvelous bit of detail as the lead; but Dickens (we're talking, of course, about *David Copperfield*) does not care; he knows there's plenty more where that came from. Or—equally possible—in his haste and overweening self-confidence he may simply have made a mistake in judgment.

His beginnings are almost always atmospheric rather than narrative. He assumes that his readers have plenty of time. He seems to be saying to them, "I have a long, complicated tale to tell. Settle down, make yourselves comfortable." The brilliant opening of *A Tale of Two Cities* ("It was the best of times, it was the worst of times . . .") is an oration, the kind of thing the modern novelist would laugh at as impossibly corny. But it works, even today.

Barnaby Conrad, eminent tauromachist, writer, and restaurateur, sends me a Buttonholer that is top drawer:

> Early one June morning, in 1872, I murdered my father—an act that made a deep impression on me at the time.

That gem starts Ambrose Bierce's *An Imperfect Conflagration.*

The Commentator's opening, as opposed to the Buttonholer's, depends not on pricking our curiosity but on stimulating our minds. It is more flattering to the reader. I select two famous examples. The first is from *Anna Karenina:*

> Happy families are all alike; every unhappy family is unhappy in its own way.

So broad an abstract statement would not seem a good opening; yet it is, simply because it is so interesting. The second example is even better.

It is a truth universally acknowledged, that a single man in possession of a good fortune must be in want of a wife.

This is more than an amusing generalization, though it is that too. Its twenty-three simple words do the following jobs: foreshadow the plot; spotlight a major character; place the social level of the characters; and key us to the irony of the author's mind. This last is what is most important in *Pride and Prejudice;* Miss Austen knows that a good introduction to her novel should include an introduction to her most valuable commodity, herself.

The Commentator's generalization, however, need not be thoughtful. It may be designedly trivial, as if to stand in sly contrast to the depths into which the author intends to lead you. *The Portrait of a Lady* is one of Henry James's most serious and complex studies. The Master, smiling, begins it thus:

> Under certain circumstances there are few hours in life more agreeable than the hour dedicated to the ceremony known as afternoon tea.

Some openings are conceived along classic journalistic lines; they plunge *in medias res* and supply all the crucial facts (where? when? who? what?) at once. A perfect example is to be found in Thornton Wilder's *The Bridge of San Luis Rey:*

> On Friday noon, July the twentieth, 1714, the finest bridge in all Peru broke and precipitated five travelers into the gulf below.

Others employ the conversational gambit: "They order, said I, this matter better in France," the opening of Sterne's *Sentimental Journey;* or the seemingly casual one, as in Norman Douglas' *South Wind:* "The bishop was feeling rather sea-sick"; or the advertising headline: "A spectre is haunting Europe—the spectre of Communism," from *The Communist Manifesto*—just as arresting (and just as exaggerated) as any good advertising headline is apt to be.

A minor subdivision of my collection is labeled Concealed Entrances. I offer an example of this from one of the most famous books in the world, Rousseau's *Social Contract*. From it most of us remember only one line, among the most telling single lines ever written:

Man is born free; and everywhere he is in chains.

For years I had assumed that this was how Rousseau began his masterpiece. He *should* have done so; but, on looking it up, I discovered that in fact this wonderful opening is preceded and concealed by three deadly dull introductory paragraphs.

I hesitate to conclude these remarks on a note of ingratitude to Mr. Weidman, who so courteously supplied me with several additions to my collection. But truth must be served. For several decades Mr. Weidman has been hugging to his breast a brilliant personal discovery. This consists of the opening of O. Henry's most famous story, "The Gift of the Magi." It runs as follows:

One dollar and eighty-seven cents. That was all. And sixty cents of it was in pennies.

Now, argues Mr. Weidman, if you deduct the sixty pennies you get one dollar and twenty-seven cents. Of this a dollar and a quarter must have been *not* in pennies. In that case you are left with two odd pennies. In other words O. Henry should have said, "And sixty-*two* cents of it was in pennies." For fifty years, Mr. Weidman declares gleefully, O. Henry's arithmetical error has been piously preserved in edition after edition.

I have long admired Mr. Weidman's prize curio. To tell the truth, I am heartily sorry that by sheer accident I recently came across a fact that rehabilitates O. Henry's numismatics. A two-cent bronze piece was minted from 1864 to 1873 and was undoubtedly in circulation around the turn of the century, the period of the story. Not only that, but if you come across one today, remember it's still good legal tender.

As a matter of fact I bought one the other day for fifty cents and presented it to Mr. Weidman as a lucky piece.

II

We have now considered the ways in which writers, according to their temperaments or the fashion of their time, dive, slither, or sidle into their stories. No less interesting are the ways in which they get themselves out of their self-made jams. Says Longfellow: "Great is the art of beginning, but greater the art is of ending"; and it is true that first-rate exits are harder to contrive than first-rate entrances.

As the basket is topped by the best-looking apples, so a writer will often put into his opening pages, even his opening paragraph, the very heart of the impulse that birthed his story. If what follows is forced or scanty, the weakness, no matter how crafty he may be, is apt to show through in the conclusion. It corresponds to the bullfight's moment of truth. Just as it is almost impossible to die insincerely (though it has been done) so is it hard for the writer, approaching his conclusion, to conceal, camouflage, or seemingly magnify the exact content of his mind. Thus many modern short stories, ingenious elaborations of little, dispense with any conclusion whatever. With nothing to wrap, no string is needed.

I confess to a partiality for the old-fashioned, full-dress ending, satisfactory in its explicitness, leaving you confident that the author has understood and properly valued his own material. I have searched my collection for the greatest master—that is, one whose endings are almost always matchless—and tentatively select Joseph Conrad. No one will accuse Conrad of lack of subtlety, and his modernity is evidenced by the fact that there are dozens of current novelists living off his innovations and discoveries in the art of the novel. But his endings have that glowing summatory quality, like a resolution in music, that our contemporaries, preferring the oblique or the ironical, would rather avoid. They are signatures, all showing a striking family resemblance, as recognizable as the conclusions of Mozart's late symphonies.

It is in the long short story that Conrad is flawless, achieving his end without strain, producing in the reader precisely the right degree of the right emotion. A large part of this success turns often on the closing lines. I offer a familiar example.

This, cunning in its use of rhythm to hypnotize the reader, is from *Youth*, the tale of the romantic East that Marlow evokes

out of his radiant young manhood and tells in late middle age
to a group of lifeworn contemporaries:

> And we all nodded at him: the man of finance, the man of
> accounts, the man of law, we all nodded at him over the polished
> table that like a still sheet of brown water reflected our faces,
> lined, wrinkled; our faces marked by toil, by deceptions, by suc-
> cess, by love; our weary eyes looking still, looking always, look-
> ing anxiously for something out of life, that while it is expected
> is already gone—has passed unseen, in a sigh, in a flash—together
> with the youth, with the strength, with the romance of illusions.

Here the effect is achieved not by statement but by incanta-
tion. Note that it is all one long sentence, developing inexorably
like the slow decay of our lives, but that its incremental effect
depends on the careful handling of five related series of short
phrases set off by commas: the group beginning with "the man
of finance"; that beginning with "by toil"; that beginning with
"looking still"; that beginning with "unseen"; that beginning with
"with the youth." It is impossible to read this crafty sentence
aloud without making the pauses Conrad wishes you to make;
his marks of punctuation exert on you precisely the influence
that the conductor's baton wields over his orchestra. The magical
result is that a platitude (for all that Conrad is saying is that we
cannot retain the illusions of youth) moves us like a revelation.
And it's all done with a few commas and a few ordinary words.
If you care to note how literature differs from mere writing,
there you have it.

The full-dress closing *à la* Conrad is not popular today. Writers
are fearful of using the full resources of the orchestra of language
lest they be accused of rhetoric. The typical ending of the novels
and short stories now most in favor is low-toned, diminuendo,
downbeat, and artfully simple. The model was supplied by
Ernest Hemingway in 1929 in *A Farewell to Arms.*

> But after I had got them out and shut the door and turned
> off the light it wasn't any good. It was like saying good-by to a
> statue. After a while I went out and left the hospital and walked
> back to the hotel in the rain.

That famous rain still drizzles drearily in the final chapters of a thousand stories by lesser writers over whom Hemingway still exerts dominance. It did its job well for *A Farewell to Arms*. One wishes it would stop working overtime.

Both the Conrad story and the Hemingway novel end on a note of sadness. But the difference is profound. Conrad's endings seem to open a door, beyond which, it is true, one may view nothing but the mysterious tragedy of all human life; whereas Hemingway closes that same door. Conrad works toward reverberation, Hemingway toward silence. They achieve their effect with equal art. It comes down simply to the question, which effect moves you more deeply?

I believe the difference is not merely one of temperament, but of time. Our writers feel ill at ease with the idea of total perspective; they will endure to be called anything but philosophical. Earlier, to illustrate the difference between one period and another, I quoted the openings of Hemingway's "My Old Man" and Hardy's "The Three Strangers," which are only thirty-five years apart. Here are the closings of the stories, Hemingway's first:

> And George Gardner looked at me to see if I'd heard and I had all right and he said, "Don't you listen to what those bums said, Joe. Your old man was one swell guy."
>
> But I don't know. Seems like when they get started they don't leave a guy nothing.

Here's Hardy's:

> The grass has long been green on the graves of Shepherd Fennel and his frugal wife; the guests who made up the christening party have mainly followed their entertainers to the tomb; the baby in whose honour they had all met is a matron in the sere and yellow leaf. But the arrival of the three strangers at the shepherd's that night, and the details connected therewith, is a story as well known as ever in the country about Higher Crowstairs.

Both are fine stories, but the endings seem to open into different worlds. For all its "stilted" phrasing, Hardy's quiet, leisurely exit is an exit into time, giving us a corner-of-the-eye glance at the procession of the generations of men. Hemingway exits into nothingness, and takes the reader with him. Those brought up on the first kind of story will never quite feel all there is to be felt by those brought up on the second kind of story; and vice versa.

The Hemingway ending, in which the curtain falls, not on a lighted stage but on a gray abyss, belongs to the twenties. In 1925 it was given its most memorable poetic expression by T. S. Eliot, whose *The Hollow Men* fades out thus:

> This is the way the world ends
> This is the way the world ends
> This is the way the world ends
> Not with a bang but a whimper

The effect here is secured by marrying this statement of despair to the gay, childlike lilt of a nursery rhyme, and by terminating with a word almost silly in its flatness. As an ending it may be said to be also a beginning, the beginning of a whole school of writers who have echoed the manner and the matter of Eliot and Hemingway.

Some endings open outward; they draw up a window in the mind. Take the artfully simple words that close *Walden:*

> Only that day dawns to which we are awake. There is more day to dawn. The sun is but a morning star.

Other endings point backward; they recapitulate the book. An excellent example is from *Treasure Island:*

> Oxen and wain-ropes would not bring me back again to that accursed island; and the worst dreams that ever I have are when I hear the surf booming about its coasts, or start upright in bed, with the sharp voice of Captain Flint still ringing in my ears: "Pieces of eight! pieces of eight!"

But the perfect bravura specimen of the recapitulative ending is the 175-word sentence that brings to a dying fall Lytton Strachey's masterpiece and the life of the blind, silent, and ancient Queen Victoria.

Admitted that this is pure performance, a little like the perfectly executed legerdemain of the parlor magician—yet what beautiful trickery it is, what small miracles are performed with the mere conjunction *and*, how much of a whole vast, imposing, preposterous era is caught in these suave, minor violin rhythms!

> Perhaps her fading mind called up once more the shadows of the past to float before it, and retraced, for the last time, the vanished visions of that long history—passing back and back, through the cloud of years, to older and ever older memories— to the spring woods at Osborne, so full of primroses for Lord Beaconsfield—to Lord Palmerston's queer clothes and high demeanour, and Albert's face under the green lamp, and Albert's first stag at Balmoral, and Albert in his blue-and-silver uniform, and the Baron coming in through a doorway, and Lord M. dreaming at Windsor with the rooks cawing in the elm trees, and the Archbishop of Canterbury on his knees in the dawn, and the old King's turkey cock ejaculations, and Uncle Leopold's soft voice at Claremont, and Lehzen with the globes, and her mother's feathers sweeping down towards her, and a great old repeater watch of her father's in its tortoise-shell case, and a yellow rug, and some friendly flounces of sprigged muslin, and the trees and the grass at Kensington.

In contrast to the summing-up ending, which frankly repeats in memorable form what we have already learned from the book, is the concealed-clue close. Here the author makes a final appearance with a revelatory sentence that seems to throw a novel flood of light on his characters but which, had we been more perceptive, we should have ourselves anticipated. At the end of Somerset Maugham's *Cakes and Ale* the narrator and Rosie are looking at a portrait of the vulgar blatant Lord George, to whom Rosie, much to everyone's surprise, had long ago lost her heart; and he asks her out of sheer curiosity what she had ever seen in him; and she replies with devastating innocence, "I'll tell you. He was always such a perfect gentleman."

This is irony so delicate that it does not pall on rereading. When I was an undergraduate it was the kind of thing that sent us into raptures, but, being young, we preferred the lesser subtlety of the famous end of Anatole France's *The Procurator of Judaea.* You will perhaps recall it. In his latter years Pontius Pilate is being idly questioned about certain events that had occurred during his earlier reign:

> Pontius Pilate contracted his brows, and his hand rose to his forehead in the attitude of one who probes the deeps of memory. Then after a silence of some seconds—
> "Jesus?" he murmured, "Jesus—of Nazareth? I cannot call him to mind."

Today this seems silly stuff to me. But it is perfect for rebellious youth, for then it seems to point up depths of cynical wisdom which it takes some time to realize are not actually there. The same kind of ironic blasphemy, handled with a more cunning art, marks the ending of Flaubert's *Herodias,* in which after the wildly sensual dance and the terrible decapitation of John, Flaubert tells us, with elaborate offhandedness:

> And all three of them took the head of Iaokanaan and went towards Galilee. As it was very heavy, they carried it alternately.

The French original, and particularly the final *alternativement,* renders to a marvel the sense of a rather heavy burden being transferred rhythmically from the hand of one person to that of another.

Among my collection are a few oddities. One is the close of *Vanity Fair*—"Come, children, let us shut up the box and the puppets, for our play is played out." This is the only example I know in which the author gives away at the end his own view, in this case a mean one, of his profession. Most closings aim at an effect of some kind; this one aims to neutralize any effect at all. It does not succeed in its aim, for though much of Thackeray *is* puppetry, for over a hundred years now we have accepted Becky Sharp as a person somewhat realer than most of our acquaintances.

Then there is the ending of *A Tale of Two Cities:*

> It is a far, far better thing that I do, than I have ever done; it is a far, far better rest that I go to, than I have ever known.

This is a curious ending, not in itself, but because nine out of ten who have read the book misremember it. Most of us, if challenged, would say that these are the words Sidney Carton utters on the scaffold, just before being guillotined. But they are not. The execution is never described, though Dickens' art is such that we imagine it to have been. Actually Dickens assumes that these are the thoughts that *would* have passed through Carton's mind; they are not actually uttered.

Another rare bird is the ending whose full meaning is disclosed only in connection with the opening. It is part of a frame. Here, for example, is the first sentence of Maugham's *Of Human Bondage:* "The day broke gray and dull." Here is the last: "Cabs and omnibuses hurried to and fro, and crowds passed, hastening in every direction, and the sun was shining." In between these two sentences a life has passed from a condition of human bondage to one of qualified human freedom. The passage is symbolized by a pair of contrasting weather reports.

I shall end these considerations on endings by citing two examples by supreme artists, one perhaps the greatest manipulator of the plain style in English, the other perhaps the greatest master of prose who has ever lived.

Jonathan Swift's *A Modest Proposal* is constantly and deservedly cited as an unrivaled piece of savage dead-pan irony. In it Swift suggests that the best way to relieve Ireland's misery is by selling off the children at the age of a year, so that they may be served up at the tables of persons of quality, particularly landlords who "as they have already devoured most of the parents, seem to have the best title to the children." Sentence by plausible sentence Swift builds up his fiendish proposal until you think you can stand no more. Then, in the last two sentences, and particularly in the last five words, he reaches an apex of horrible persuasiveness, and turns your blood to ice:

> I profess, in the sincerity of my heart, that I have not the least personal interest in endeavouring to promote this necessary work, having no other motive than the public good of my country, by advancing our trade, providing for infants, relieving the poor, and giving some pleasure to the rich. I have no children

by which I can propose to get a single penny, the youngest being nine years old, and my wife past childbearing.

My final example is in utter contrast. It is simple as the Lord's Prayer and has the same capacity to move the heart. It is from Plato. Phaedo is narrating to Echecrates the last hours of Socrates, condemned to death by drinking hemlock.

After carefully recalling Socrates' final words and describing in almost emotionless detail the exact manner of his dying, he is made by Plato to utter a sentence which in its pure and absolute simplicity, free of all pretention to effect, almost, one might say, free of artistry, quietly tears your heart in two:

> Such was the end, Echecrates, of our friend; concerning whom I may truly say, that of all the men of his time whom I have known, he was the wisest and justest and best.

I do not think that has ever been beaten.

Ah! The Literary Life

THE WRITER IN AMERICA likes to write about the position of the writer in America. Or, with such work delayers as pipe cleaning and pencil sharpening exhausted, he may even rout out a fellow pro with whom to *talk* about the position of the writer in America. What gives the theme perennial freshness is that his position is indefinable. The writer, somewhat like Mahomet's coffin, oscillates between overvaluation and undervaluation, both on his own part and that of his public.

It all depends on circumstances. In 1953, Mr. Humphrey, then Secretary of the Treasury, snatched the (jamless) bread from book reviewers' mouths when he diposed of Mr. Hemingway's *The Old Man and the Sea* with "Why would anybody be interested in some old man who was a failure?" But only a little over a decade before, some of the President's speeches were being written by Robert Sherwood, a mere playwright.

This shaky situation is by no means bad for the writer. As a lower-echelon sample of the breed, I for one would not wish it changed. For most men life is a search for the proper manila folder in which to get themselves filed. But if the writer were given fixed status, so that he knew exactly where he fitted, he might stop writing.

His uncertainty is a reflection of the public's view of him, a curious, unstable mixture.

One ingredient is a residue from a primitive era. At one time the tribal intellectual (shaman, medicine man, prophet, bard, storyteller) was a being set apart. He was presumed to be in touch with a world to which the average man in the cave had no access. As we shall see, this superstitious image of the writer as the wielder of semimagical powers persists even in our commonsensical world.

On the other hand, two factors have joined to produce a very different kind of public view of the writer, varying from tolerant contempt to active suspicion. The two factors are our passion for the production and exchange of consumable goods, and our passion for mass literacy.

The writer does not produce consumable goods. He produces nonconsumable, useless goods such as the Declaration of Independence. Hence he is looked upon rather uneasily, viewed unconsciously as a kind of second-class citizen, as are his kinsmen, the teacher and the preacher, the artist and the pure scientist.

Because the writer feels that in a way this second-class citizenship is not entirely a figment, he frequently seeks animal reassurance by herding with his own kind. He forms local polities within which he may declare himself the superior caste. Hence the growth of such creative ghettos as Westport or New City or Greenwich Village. Like all ghettos, these are self-defeating: they increase the evil from which the ghetto dwellers are trying to escape.

Writers should try to live cheek by jowl with definitely first-class citizens such as plumbers and bank presidents. In the course of time this should help the plumbers and bank presidents to get used to the writers, and vice versa. The writer's position will not be any more clearly established but he may at least neutralize the suspicion that he is somehow subversive.

During the past fifty years the writer's status has been further confused by our passion for literacy. Once the writer enjoyed the small prestige accruing from the possession of talents not generally possessed. Today, though the real writer is still numerically rare, he does not seem to be. Universal literacy has made him appear as pervasive as light and air.

Universal literacy is an American passion with serious, almost religious overtones, like golf, fishing, wall-to-wall carpeting, and hot lunch for school children. This passion has been so fervently cultivated that now everybody can "read" and "write." What were formerly activities whose essential connection was with thinking have now become universally practiced small-muscle movements of the eyes and fingers, movements into which thought may or may not enter.

We have all become "readers" and "writers" in that we are all proficient in these small-muscle gestures. Hence the writer and the "writer" are confused in the public mind. At one time I assisted in the preparation of dialogue for a television show. I was called a "writer," when in fact no real writing, that is, thinking, was involved. In this sense there are literally millions of American "writers" engaged in the transmission of signals that are not true messages, statements conveyed from one active mind to another active mind. Most screenplays, advertisements, government speeches, and so forth are merely more or less complex word carpentry.

Amid this roar of wholesale small-muscle activity, the voice of the old-fashioned writer, who works with real emotions and real ideas and struggles with most exacting techniques, may be lost. His value depreciates because he seems to be doing only what everybody else is doing.

His value is further depreciated by the inevitable consequence of mass literacy—easy printability. Everything gets into print; and physically all print looks much alike. Thus a gutter-press editorial and a poem by W. H. Auden *seem* to be similar products, though actually they are in no way connected except that both employ words and are printed by the same kind of machine.

We have thus a curious mixed-up climate of opinion within which the writer, a hardy soul, nevertheless manages to survive to flourish, and to enjoy himself. On the one hand he is valued as a kind of seer: his opinions are requested on every subject, they are respectfully printed, and no attention is paid to them. On the other hand he is viewed as a harmless, somewhat eccentric nonproducer or merely as one who does a little better or more visibly what all of us feel we can do pretty well ourselves.

This incapacity of the writer to make clear what he's really up to reflects itself in the official attitude toward his income. A novelist may educate himself for twenty years, starve for another ten, and then hit the jack pot with a best-seller. By law he must pay in taxes the larger part of the money he makes during his one, two, or three good years. He is then free to starve again.

I consider this perfectly reasonable on the government's part. It is a representative government—that is, it represents the unconscious feelings, as well as the conscious desires, of most of us. Among these unconscious feelings is the sense that the writer is a specialized being whose rewards are other than monetary, and who therefore is not entitled to exceptional protection, as for instance the holders of oil leases are so entitled.

This feeling applies also to teachers, preachers, scientists, and other producers of intangible goods. It is only when it can be shown that a producer of intangible goods can also produce something really useful like a flying piece of metal with a dying dog in it that a public demand arises that he be given a little extra compensation.

On the one hand it is felt that the writer doesn't do any real work. On the other it is felt that the unreal work he does is the spontaneous overflow of some magical energy. Hence if the writer is a magician there is no reason why we should not call upon him whenever we wish for a display of his inexhaustible magic.

This explains why every writer who has achieved a little notoriety is constantly called upon to write gratis. If there is a leak in the plumbing of the White House, a plumber is paid to fix it. But any number of government agencies constantly call upon writers to "knock off" (the term is an exact reflection of the view of the writer-as-magician) a few hundred or a few thousand words to be used in some undeniably excellent governmental project.

The writer is regarded as a kind of public utility. Here are some of the requests I have received, all courteously worded and all from good citizens who would never think of asking the plumber for free service:

1. From a schoolteacher: please suggest six books for outside reading for my class.

2. From a high school student: please send material on Sinclair Lewis; I have to write a theme.

3. From an organization: please come and talk to us about your work. (One of the corollaries of the magician theory is the conviction that all writers can talk in public, though actually there is not the slightest link between the two abilities, and indeed some evidence to the contrary.)

4. From a charitable institution (which, however, pays the stenographer who types the letter): please judge a writing contest, herewith described.

5. From a government agency: please write and record your opinion of Dostoevski, which we will broadcast to the Soviet Union.

6. From a reader: please list, with reasons, the ten greatest books you have read.

7. From a fellow writer: please read my unpublished manuscript and tell me why it remains unpublished.

Back of these requests lie two assumptions. The first is that the writer is a wonder worker, and can therefore produce his petty miracles without labor. The second is that, inasmuch as everybody can "read" and "write," we are not asking him to do anything we ourselves couldn't do, if we merely put our minds to it. These two assumptions of course contradict each other.

One of the interesting consequences of the magician theory is the notion not only that the writer is omniscient but that he *owes* it to his public to be omniscient. Every mail brings me letters from stern readers of my articles pointing out that I "neglected" to mention such-and-such, or indicating shock that

I should have "forgotten" or "overlooked" such-and-such. The plain fact, of course, is that I didn't *know* such-and-such.

But the tone of the letters, while perfectly friendly, is obviously admonishing: I have been derelict in my duty because I didn't mention a fact which happens to be the correspondent's favorite nugget of knowledge. It is curious that when the plumber makes a mistake he charges you for it. But when the writer makes a mistake there's a feeling that he has betrayed the community.

Would I change my job? No more than I would change my country.

I may be parochial but I consider both job and country the most interesting in existence. And they are interesting for the same reason: they elude definition, they refuse to stay put, they may lead to anything.

Samuel Johnson couldn't have been wronger when he remarked that no man but a blockhead ever wrote except for money. A writer wants to make as much money as is possible *with the kind of writing he wants to do.* But that is not the same thing as writing *for* money.

The final attractions of writing, and its final rewards, are two. The first is the absolutely inexhaustible pleasure of exploring the content of your own mind, so that when you die you will not suddenly at the last moment exclaim in panic, "Who am I, and what have I done with my life?"

The second is the secret thrill of feeling that you are actually, even if in only the slightest degree, touching another mind, changing it, possibly even helping it.

Reader's Roulette

LET US TALK about random reading. By random reading I mean little more than reading for no clearly definable reason. To defend it is to defend aimlessness itself. This I do, not endorsing it as a major goal, but suggesting that it merits a minor place in our highly organized lives. The overdetermined mind, like the overdetermined muscle, is subject to charley horse.

That mode of time-wasting (not to be confused with time-killing) known as random reading presupposes a kind of amorality of the intellect. We must blank out all considerations of improvement, instruction, retention. We must float free, divorced from any concern with the fashionable, the current, the generally respected. Random reading is as purposeless as a casual stroll through a flower garden.

Yet it is not so easy as it sounds. As with much frivolity it requires management. There are fewer books than one might think that are open to the random reader. For one thing, there are not many whose looseness of structure matches one's vagueness of mood. A novel cannot be read at random: either swallow it whole or, after tasting, reject it. So with histories, biographies, serious treatises of all sorts, and any volume, such as a travel book, threaded on a connected series of events. The ideal book for random reading is usually made up of short turns distinguished for their disorganization.

Anthologies, then? Some, but not most. On my shelves are about three hundred anthologies. All but a few cater to specific needs. Their readers are at once set on rails. They service insomniacs, erotomaniacs, aelurophiles, armchair adventurers, ghost buffs, and so on. They automatically sieve out all but one kind of reader, reminding one of those curious institutions, men's clubs, invented so that we may meet ourselves under other names.

Years ago I put together an anthology that continues to attract readers, largely I think because its title, *Reading I've Liked,* suggests disorder, lack of system—randomness. Sometimes, however, this same quality may mark a collection that is quite organically constructed. I am thinking of the finest general anthology I know, *The Limits of Art,* edited by Huntington Cairns. It contains almost fifteen hundred pages of selections, many very brief, in prose and verse, from Homer to Joyce, from many languages. Where the original is not English, that original plus a fine translation is given. But these selections are unusual in that each one, in the judgment of some responsible critic, is superlative, touching "the limits of art"; and in each case that judgment is appended. The result is a book of endless fascination, perfect for any random reader interested in touching only the peaks, offering nothing to the earnest student.

A contemporary anthologist with the true ragbag mind is the English critic Daniel George. To the tramp reader I recommend his two collections, *A Peck of Troubles* and *A Book of Anecdotes.* The first is quite agreeably absurd: it contains brief accounts of some of life's minor harassments and embarrassments, griefs and miseries, as equably endured and gravely recorded by historical personages. I open the book at random to "Delusions" and encounter this passage from Caroline Fox's *Journal* of June 6, 1842:

> Swedenborg was a thoroughly practical, mechanical man, and was in England learning shipbuilding. He went into a little inn in Bishopsgate Street, and was eating his dinner very fast, when he thought he saw in the corner of the room a vision of Jesus Christ, who said to him, "Eat slower." This was the beginning of all his visions and communications.

The discovery that we owe Swedenborgianism to a Fletcher-
izing Deity is an example of that serendipity continually rewarding the random reader.

Mr. George's *A Book of Anecdotes,* a more ambitious affair, is
even more entertaining. The latest (and surely not the last)
of such collections, it is more scholarly than most, and a boon
to skeptical souls who would determine the exact amount of
truth lying behind classic references like those of Columbus and
the egg, Newton and the apple, King Alfred and the cakes. A
half-hour with it brings home the fact that modern gossip
columnists are doing their best to murder the art of the anecdote.
Their weary wisecracks, emitted by efficiently publicized non-
minds, are a long way from the kind of thing Mr. George deals
in. I open him at random and come upon Balzac who, according
to the *Goncourt Journals,* once expressed his ultimate ambition
—to be "so celebrated, so famous, that it would permit me to
break wind in society and society would think it a most natural
thing."

Do you have time for one more? Mr. George tells us that in
The Story of My Life (1896) Augustus Hare relates a remarkable incident of somnambulism:

> A lady was awoke in the night with the disagreeable sense of
> not being alone in the room, and soon felt a thud upon her bed.
> There was no doubt that someone was moving to and fro in the
> room, and that hands were constantly moving upon her bed.
> She was so dreadfully frightened, that at last she fainted. When
> she came to herself, it was broad daylight, and she found that
> the butler had walked in his sleep and had laid the table for
> fourteen upon her bed.

In making up my list of books that marry well to the random
mood, I found few by contemporaries. Random reading is disengaged reading, and we are never quite disengaged from our
coevals. We read them to hiss or to boo, or at least to judge;
and judgment mixes ill with random reading.

Moreover our contemporaries do not write many dippable
books. Just as there are natural poets and natural novelists, so

there are natural miscellanists, men of wayward and digressive temper. To such temperaments the climate of the English seventeenth (and also nineteenth) century was kind. Ours is less so. For example, millions at one time enjoyed newspaper columnists such as F.P.A., Don Marquis, Christopher Morley. Their stock in trade was a blend of topical comment, occasional verse, and unabashedly personal philosophy, all flavored with a kind of literary wit. Where are their similars today?

No, American literature is not rich in the randomly readable. English literature, however, is all awash with it, a circumstance perhaps linked to the Englishman's distrust of system, his suspicion of all rigid intellectual forms, and (at least among the leisured classes) a keen sense of the necessity to cultivate the non-useful. This last helps to explain why the English are among the best gardeners in the world.

From the seventeenth century I name two standard classics; I might name two dozen. Who today reads for pleasure Thomas Fuller's *Worthies of England,* a vast and curious work recently reprinted after having languished for over a century on the shelves of scholars? County by county the Reverend Fuller reports on the commodities, manufacturers, "medicinal waters," buildings, "wonders," proverbs, and, best of all, "worthies" or distinguished citizens, living or dead, of England. It is a true medley, though doubtless Fuller thought of himself as a most systematic writer. The "facts" are no longer of much importance, except to antiquarians. The Fullerisms are the thing, and there are thousands of them. I learn on page 165, for example, that Essex was once noted for the production of gunpowder, which "is the emblem of politic revenge, for it biteth first, and barketh afterwards, the bullet being at the mark before the report is heard; so that it maketh a noise, not by way of warning, but triumph." You can learn the formula for the velocity of sound anywhere. Nowhere but in Fuller will you find it so interpreted. Such a mind should be preserved in the Smithsonian of our affection.

This is even truer of John Aubrey whose *Brief Lives* of some of his predecessors and seventeenth-century contemporaries has the same interest that attaches to observing odd faces and figures in the street. A few of his subjects (Ben Jonson, Descartes, Shakespeare) are the world's property; most are quite obscure. But it is an obscurity lit on every page by flashes of wonderful absurdity. Sir Jonas Moore, the mathematician, is a mere name. Yet Aubrey rescues him for us with a single line: "Sciatica: he cured it by boyling his Buttock."

Benjamin Disraeli's father, Isaac, had what he called "a fragmentary mind." A few generations ago his *Curiosities of Literature* and *Amenities of Literature* attracted random readers. But, though you can encounter almost anything in these literary sideshows, from "Jocular Preachers" to the "Secret History of Authors Who Have Ruined Their Booksellers," Isaac's style is so prolix and so musty with dried-up library paste that he can no longer be generally recommended. Yet there are plums lying in his dust.

Fuller was a great favorite of that tedious nineteenth-century poet, the friend of Coleridge and Wordsworth, Robert Southey. Something of Fuller's comfortable amble paces Southey's own fantastic masterpiece of long-windedness, *The Doctor. The Doctor*, originally published in seven volumes from 1834 to 1847, is almost impossible to describe, and, except for really expert time-wasters, almost impossible to read. Presumably an account of the life and opinions of a Yorkshire physician, it is actually a vast hash of everything that happened to be in Southey's lumber-filled head when he set pen to paper. It may outlast Shakespeare, but only because it contains a story most of us assume dropped out of nowhere: that of The Three Bears, which is generally credited to Southey, though a learned correspondent informs me that in its original form it is by one Eleanor Mure whose version preceded Southey's by a few years.

Southey, I admit, offers the random reader a certain amount of resistance. My other nineteenth-century nominee, Samuel Butler, is open to any lively mind whose only aim is to shake hands with another and livelier one. Butler left Bernard Shaw not only his ideas but a good deal of his crotchetiness. Among his other legacies to the world are his *Notebooks*. On the whole I think Butler's casual notes and opinions represent about the most rewarding single mine of random reading in English. He combines oddness and acuity; and he is incapable of writing an edgeless sentence. The only test, again, is to open him at random (I guarantee I am playing this game fairly). I read: "Man is a jelly which quivers so much as to run about." There is a dreadful truth in this: "It does not matter what a man hates provided he hates something." And a wry charm in this: "The great pleasure of a dog is that you may make a fool of yourself with him and not only will he not scold you but he will make a fool of himself too."

I pass by, as already well known to random readers, standards like Fowler's *Modern English Usage* and Ivor Brown's series of eight delightful treatises on odd English words. But there must be many hobos of the reading lamp still to acquaint themselves with four volumes that have appeared during the last few years and are again testimony to the persistent English talent for making a work of art out of the miscellaneous. These four volumes, edited by Geoffrey Grigson and Charles Gibbs-Smith, all resplendently illustrated in color and black and white (first-rate Christmas gifts, by the way) are entitled: *People, Places, Things,* and *Ideas*. In the brief, saltily written essays that make up these hefty tomes, nothing is "covered," no proper "representation" is attempted. All the editors are after is to give the browsing reader a constantly deepening sense of the infinite diversity of that piece of work that is a man. Insofar as reading can jerk us into a momentary consciousness of what Henry James called the Thickness of Things, these four mixed bags can be confidently recommended. *People* opens with Lord Acton, ends with Brigham Young. *Places* begins with Abbasanta, ends with Yosemite Falls. *Things* begins with the Aeolian harp, ends with Zippers. *Ideas* begins with the Absolute, ends with Yoga. In between these alphas and omegas lie four varicolored worlds of probably useless information. Again and again, dipping into *People, Places, Things,* or *Ideas,* I have been surprised, rewarded, and stimulated, usually all at the same time. Perfect random reading—a small art, sirs, and yet there are those who love it.

Books Mentioned

The Limits of Art, collected and edited by Huntington Cairns.

A Peck of Troubles, collected by Daniel George.

A Book of Anecdotes, selected and edited by Daniel George.

The Worthies of England, by Thomas Fuller, edited with an introduction and notes by John Freeman.

Aubrey's Brief Lives, edited from the Original Manuscripts and with an introduction by Oliver Lawson Dick.

Curiosities of Literature, by Isaac Disraeli. (Many editions— mine is the excellent one in three volumes, edited by his son.)

Amenities of Literature, by Isaac Disraeli. (Hard to find; mine is again an edition edited by his son.)

The Doctor, by Robert Southey. (Editions are hard to come by: mine is dated 1848.)

Samuel Butler's Notebooks.

A Dictionary of Modern English Usage, by H. W. Fowler.

Ivor Brown's word books. The best of these is *Chosen Words*.

People; Places; Things; Ideas. Four volumes, fully illustrated, edited by Geoffrey Grigson and Charles Harvard Gibbs-Smith.

My Unfavorite Classics

I HAVE LONG FELT that every college curriculum should include a course called *The Nonappreciation of Literature*. Here the student would be encouraged to figure out which books bore him, and for what reasons. The writing of a well-argued term paper on "Why I Can't Stand *Paradise Lost*" might very well lead to a finer enjoyment of other kinds of poetry. For we learn by what we reject as well as by what we accept. No man can "like" literature as a whole any more than he can like all the people he meets. You can force a man into Philistinism by insisting that he do the first just as you can force him into misanthropy by insisting that he do the second.

For almost half a century literature has meant a great deal to me. Not as a "subject," for it is not a subject as geometry or Sanskrit is a subject. But as a mode (a good one, but only one) of enhancing, clarifying, and concentrating whatever fugitive sense I have of my own existence. Experience has taught me that this sense is strengthened rather than weakened by the cheerful admission that certain books are closed books to me— or at any rate no more than half open. I am not currently on their wave length. Perhaps I never shall be. In the hope that my readers may be heartened to make candid confession of their own aversions I here list a few of mine.

157

Let's start with a drugstore classic: Boccaccio's *Decameron.*
This collection of traditional European and Oriental tales appeared in 1353. These hundred stories are represented as narrated
by ten Florentine ladies and gentlemen who have withdrawn to
a country house to escape the plague of 1348. To the grown-up
reader of today, encountering the book for the first time and
unawed by its reputation, I pose the question: would the plague
have been preferable to the *Decameron?*

For six hundred years the *Decameron* has led two lives, one
aboveboard, the other underground. The literary historian has
kept it going as a classic. You and I have sustained it as erotica.
I know not what course others may take, but I do not think
it defensible on either count.

True enough, it was the first highly successful assemblage of
tales produced in Europe since Ovid's *Metamorphoses.* Its
framework has been imitated. Its plots have been borrowed.
As a fountainhead Boccaccio gets full marks. But a fountainhead
is not a taleteller. As taleteller Boccaccio belongs in the dead
files. He wrote to entertain, and I can well believe he did entertain. That is, he entertained a society with plenty of time on its
hands, that reacted freshly to narrative devices that have since
staled, that was fond of moralizing. But in the mere matter
of *mechanics,* we have learned how to tell a tale better than
Boccaccio could (though not as well as Homer could). I find
him longwinded, unable to handle time sequences, simple-
minded as to characterization, and about as lively as the *Elsie*
books.

His popular fame, however, does not rest on his literary qualities but on his presumed power to titillate. Now I am as game
for titillation as the next man. But the mid-twentieth-century
reader who has had to assimilate the assorted candors of a
James Jones, a Tennessee Williams, a Grace Metalious, or a
Norman Mailer (not to mention a great writer such as James
Joyce) has developed a shock threshold too high for Boccaccio
to assault. One of his narrators speaks of these "gay tales, perhaps conducive to lasciviousness." Perhaps they conduced easier
in Boccaccio's time. I neither attack nor defend our moral climate,

but it seems to me of a nature such that Boccaccio's spiciest anecdotes now appear poorly told, overelaborate, stag-party yarns that harp on a very few strings. The ideal age at which to read them is fourteen, when we will devour a lot of literary starch for a little paprika. This has nothing to do with taste or morals, and everything to do with puberty. As a boys' classic something may be said for the *Decameron*. To the young teenager it may very well bring a delighted guilty blush of pleasure. But, alas, I am no barefoot boy with cheek of red.

Nor am I any better fitted to enjoy that other treasury of marvels, the Arabian Nights. This may be great stuff in the Arabic, but whether in the English versions of Lane, Payne, or Burton, or in the famous French translation by Galland, the Princess Shahrazad emerges as a supreme mistress of barbiturate prose. I sympathize with the lady in her predicament. I can well understand that any narrator who can retain her head only by extending her tale will tell a story as if she were being paid by the word. But sympathy is not the same as interest.

It's not that the adventures of Sinbad and Aladdin and Ali Baba don't make good yarns. They do—although note that we've named the best of them. But we must distinguish between a plot and a story. The plots of many of the Arabian Nights are first-rate. The stories are tedious, overornamented, involved. Too many of them make clumsy use of the Chinese-box technique—the story within a story—which is precarious enough even in the hands of a master like Conrad. And, sluggish as they are, their movement is still further impeded by the interpolated verse which in its English dress no vanity press would publish even if generously bribed. As for the so-called licentiousness, it is monotonous and unimaginative. I prefer a good daydream any time.

My trouble may be that, as far as concerns the art of narrative, I believe that East is East and West is West and never the twain shall meet. I've tackled classics like the Japanese *Tale of Genji* and the Chinese *All Men Are Brothers* and the Indian *Ramayana*. I've tried translations of Persian poetry only to be licked by the bulbuls and the gazelles. I've conscientiously read a few contemporary Chinese and Japanese novelists and short-

story writers. In all cases I have been thrown for a loss. Once
the international date line, going westward from our country,
is crossed, storytelling seems to undergo a sea change to which
I cannot adapt. The "orientalism" of the Arabian Nights in particular does not affect me as it did a marveling eighteenth-century Europe. It is not "exotic" but merely cloying—about as
interesting as a meal of Turkish delight topped off with Seconal.

Boccaccio and the Arabian Nights are of course pretty remote.
The great French novelist Gustave Flaubert (1821-1880), however, is a true modern. His detached, thoroughgoing disillusion-
ment is part of the complex mood of our own day. No one who
studies his dedicated life or reads his eloquent correspondence
can fail to admire Flaubert, even to like him. Some of his output
—I think of the dazzling *Three Tales*—seems quite untouched by
the hand of time.

But to his best-known novel, *Madame Bovary*, I lack the key.
Clearly this is not Flaubert's fault. Any of the tales of the
Decameron or the Arabian Nights could be improved in two
hours with a blue pencil. Not so *Madame Bovary*. Flaubert took
five years to write it, and it is on its own terms perfect.

However, I do not think my insensibility is entirely my fault
either. Put my difficulty this way: *Bovary* may be a perfect novel
—but it is also a perfect period novel.

I find (I've made four attempts) that I cannot be moved by
poor Emma's troubles unless by an effort of will I transport myself in fancy back to the provincial life of France in the 1840s.
This effort of will—which I need not make for other nineteenth-
century novelists, Dickens or Tolstoy—blunts my reading pleasure.

Emma Bovary, you recall, is ruined by her frustrated passion
to escape the dull middle-class existence of her little Norman
village and the company of her amiable clod of a husband. She
dies of Bovarysme, the same disease of the imagination from
which Sinclair Lewis' Carol Kennicott, if less dramatically, also
suffered. She is the pioneer example of the revolt from the village, Main Street's first outstanding literary victim.

The first. But not the last. And there may lie my trouble. Since

Emma's day her story has been too often rewritten, and often quite skillfully. The analysis of provincial manners, of bourgeois Philistinism, of the neurosis of erotic romanticism—all this has been carried so much further and worked out in so much greater detail that Flaubert's novel, though accurate and truthful, has the accuracy and truthfulness of a blueprint. We cannot easily react freshly to Emma's struggles and fantasies and adulteries. The tale has been told too many times; the poor lady is almost too easy to understand. In a sense we understand her better than her creator did—and that is fatal.

Like that of many French masterpieces, from Racine to Mauriac, the novel's psychology is exact; but, also like them, it seems, when compared with the tumultuous richness and "thickness" of a work by Dickens or Dostoevski, thin and schematic. It is clear but cold. There can be an excess of detachment as well as of commitment.

Nor do I find Flaubert's highly praised pictures of middle-class provincial life particularly striking. Homais, the small-minded rationalist, for example, seems a one-note creation. Dickens would have tossed him off with a negligent flick of the pen, whereas Flaubert works over this petty satirical portrait with the anxious care of a medieval miniaturist.

Finally the long-drawn-out suicide scene, followed by the death of Charles Bovary, strikes me each time I read it as a set piece of relentless lugubriousness rather than as a tragedy of classic dimensions.

No, even in so exquisitely sensitive a translation as that of Francis Steegmuller (which I honestly believe preserves 90 per cent of Flaubert's famous style), I will probably never learn to like *Madame Bovary*.

Flaubert worshiped form, Thomas Wolfe worshiped spontaneity. The first delicately tracked down the one exact word, the second rioted in a welter of vocabulary. Flaubert knew precisely what he thought of human life (not much). Wolfe up to his all-too-early death sought furiously for meanings.

A distaste for *Bovary* might argue a liking for the novels of Thomas Wolfe. Yet I am even less comfortable with Wolfe than

I am with Flaubert, which, admitted, makes me look rather foolish.

I was twenty-five when I read Wolfe's first novel, thirty-six when I read his fourth and last. I admired each of the last three less than I had admired its predecessor, though I am convinced that one is about as good as the next, indeed that they are all part of the same book. Today, trying them for the second time, I find I cannot read them at all. All of which is hardly conclusive evidence that Wolfe is essentially a young man's writer; but that's what I believe.

Wolfe's chaos answers the chaos within the young man. His alternate frenzied acceptances and rejections reflect and confirm the pendulum swing of the emotions when one is under thirty.

Some writers have a way with words. With others words have a way. Hemingway is an example of the first case, Wolfe of the second. Doubtless the second has its attractions. Many people in the eighteenth century were mad for Ossian, that Ossian of whom Samuel Johnson remarked, "A man might write such stuff forever, if he would *abandon* his mind to it." Wolfe certainly had a kind of Ossianic genius, a genius, like Whitman's, of abandonment. Though not impossible, it is difficult to like equally well both kinds of genius, that of control and that of abandonment. As I age I find myself responding more to the first kind than to the second. It is perfectly possible that my inability to reread Thomas Wolfe with any pleasure is connected less with maturing taste than with hardening arteries. I have little doubt that we read with our bodies as well as with our minds.

To add to this list of my unfavorite classics would be profitless. There is little sense in the mere recitation of one's aversions —though I would, if space permitted, enjoy putting in a bad word for Goethe's *Wilhelm Meister*, Manzoni's *Betrothed*, Romain Rolland's *Jean-Christophe*, George Eliot's *Silas Marner*, Oliver Goldsmith's *Vicar of Wakefield*, and any version whatsoever of the Paul Bunyan legends. In one way or another each of these is hallowed ground. One of them, *Wilhelm Meister*, is by a very great writer, among the greatest. Two of them (*Silas*

Marner and *The Vicar of Wakefield*) are held in such pious respect that they have created in millions of school children an active distaste for reading. All of them seem to me dull and/or foolish.

The essential thing is to admit that each of us possesses certain anesthetic areas in his mental and emotional make-up. To be fearful of confessing one's dislike of certain books that happen to evoke mechanical reverence (or which of course may be genuinely enjoyed by readers of a different temper) is to roil and muddy the wellspring of our pleasure in literature in general. To hate books is to be forever a kind of child. But to be blind and deaf to certain of these books is simply an admission that we are, being human, limited beings.

The Red and the Black

I. The Mind of Stendhal

To BEGIN with, that was not his name, Stendhal being merely the most publicly acknowledged of the over 150 pseudonyms he used for purposes of largely unnecessary deception.

This odd creature—he was christened Marie-Henri Beyle—led two simultaneous lives: one chronological, one posthumous. The seeming paradox is characteristic of him in general.

Stendhal's chronological existence extended from 1783, when he was born in Grenoble, to 1842, when he died in Paris. We know a great deal about him, for he set down his thoughts and actions in exhaustive detail, scribbling on his fingernails when paper was unavailable. The record is interesting but hardly spectacular: Hollywood will never base a film on his life.

His outward career may be described as a succession of almosts. A fairly good mathematician, he almost entered the Ecole Polytechnique but found the preparations for the entrance examinations too troublesome. Through his influential cousin Pierre Daru (whose wife he seduced, almost) he obtained a commission in Napoleon's army. During the second Italian campaign he almost saw combat. Back in Paris, living on money from his hated father, he almost wrote several plays. In Marseilles he almost became a businessman. During the Russian campaign, serving as a noncombatant officer, he almost succeeded in mildly distinguishing himself.

From 1814 to 1821 he lived in his beloved Italy but did not quite manage to succeed even as an expatriate. Suspected of liberal tendencies by the Austrian police, he decamped to Paris. In 1830 he was appointed French consul at Civitavecchia. This minor post he almost contrived to fill adequately, except during his many periods of leave. (Stendhal was a great success at wangling vacations.) In 1841 he returned to Paris on legitimate sick leave and on March 22, 1842, died of a stroke.

During his lifetime he almost gained a high reputation as wit, lover, and writer. But not quite. His writing career was managed with almost infallible negligence. He never published anything under his own name; much of his work remained in manuscript at his death; some of it is still unpublished. His many books, articles, compilations netted him hardly a pittance. Today his fame rests largely on his novels, but his first one, *Armance*, did not appear until he was forty-four; *The Red and the Black* until he was forty-seven; and *The Charterhouse of Parma* (written in fifty-three days, and it shows it) until three years before his death.

Stendhal was a smallish, fattish man, fond of dandiacal costume, conversation, ladies, and almost-ladies. He pursued his many love affairs as if never quite certain whether he were Casanova making conquests or a psychologist making notes. As Casanova he was not always successful. His diaries record his fiascos with the same detail that others devote to an account of their triumphs. He admired and visited England and in the course of several decades of assiduous study almost succeeded in mastering the language to the degree that a second-year American high school student masters French.

At first glance, then, a rather undistinguished figure, a rather undistinguished life.

But this was merely the one presented to the world. This life was merely his chronological life. His real life was posthumous, and a complete triumph. By posthumous I do not mean merely that since his death his reputation has steadily grown, so that today his is one of the half-dozen greatest names in the development of the European novel. I mean that in a real sense he himself lived posthumously, that is, in the future. The greater part of his imaginative life was enacted in front of an audience he was never to encounter, those "happy few" of the coming generations for whom he wrote and thought.

The life for which he was unfitted—that of a would-be popular playwright, soldier, businessman, civil servant—he lived unsuccessfully. The life for which he was fitted—that spent grasping the history of his time in terms of the perspective of the future —he lived successfully. Thus Stendhal is something of an oddity. Perhaps part of his fascination for us springs from the fact that he was odd without being minor.

We usually think of a contemplative as one who spends his life in a meditation upon God. Stendhal spent his life, an active and worldly one, in a meditation upon men. He was that rare bird, a lay contemplative. In a period during which all men seemed to be scrabbling for "careers"—that is, money—Stendhal too went through the motions of scrabbling, though he never sought a job if a sinecure was available. Essentially, however, he remained that oddity, an unfixed man, attached only to his own thought. "I am but a passenger on this boat," he loved to say; and, as his epitaph, suggested *Visse, amo, scrisse.*

As a young man of twenty-eight he chose *nosce te ipsum* as his device; and to know himself was his profession. His whole life resembled one of those Grand Tours taken by the young English milords to acquaint them with human nature. To be "an observer of the human heart" and to portray it was his overarching ambition. One way of portraying it, he thought, was through "egotism provided it be sincere." This is one of the basic principles of Beylist philosophy, if we understand by egotism what is today called introspection. The medium of his egotism was his books. In a sense all of them, even the novels, are part of an interminable, formless diary. Everything he wrote contributed to his self-analysis; he remained throughout his life, as someone has remarked about Henry James, on very good terms with himself. Had he had any religion, his work might have been entitled "Spiritual Exercises."

Contemplation plus self-contemplation sum up Stendhal's real life. Emerson put it this way: "Living is what a man thinks about all day." Stendhal neither worked nor idled. He thought all day.

He thought almost for thought's sake. It was for him a metaphysical necessity: "If I am not clear, my whole universe crumbles into nothingness." He believed that the mind could be formed and developed by study and will power. At times he sounds almost like Dale Carnegie with genius: "The Abbé Hélie has swift and complete transitions. That's very good and should be imitated." As one would expect, he thought there was a "logic of happiness," and tried all his life to refine his formulas.

But this was only one side of Stendhal, the part he called "logique," a word he was fond of intoning with a kind of ecclesiastical preciseness. Stendhal was bipolar: part of him went back to Descartes and the rationality of the eighteenth century; part of him had an affinity with the romanticism of the early part of his own century. The interplay of forces between these poles created the tension and made Stendhal an artist as well as an observer; and it is this same interplay that he transfers to the hero of *The Red and the Black*, who is both an icy intellectual and a furious romantic. In Stendhal the bipolarity extended into almost every field. For example, he thought of himself as a champion of the democratic age to come; yet the whole bias of his temperament is aristocratic. He championed the spontaneity of Shakespeare against the frigidity of Racine; but his psychology, when it is not dazzlingly modern, is far more Racinian than Shakespearean. He combined a passion for exact analysis with a delight in the unexpected—*l'imprévu* is one of his favorite words.

Volumes have been written about the contradictions in Stendhal's personality, contradictions which, instead of tearing him apart, generated his whole intellectual life and career. What I here stress is the essential, underlying contradiction, that between what was present-minded in Stendhal, his unusual capacity to enjoy, analyze, and enjoy through analysis his day-to-day experience; and what was future-minded, his equally unusual capacity to think of himself constantly as a citizen of a culture still in time's womb.

The interesting thing about Stendhal is not that he has been rediscovered by every generation since his death, but that he foresaw that discovery with absolute clairvoyance. He seems to have felt, and not out of the simple vanity that afflicts many unsuccessful scribblers, that he was a writer with a brilliant future. In the 1830s he was already a great novelist, but there were few to recognize the fact. "I shall be understood about 1880," he remarked casually, and that turned out to be true. Again he said, "I have drawn a lottery ticket whose winning number is: to be read in 1935"; and that has also turned out to be true. This prescience derived not from his *espagnolisme,* his passionate temperament, but from his *logique.* He based his claim to the attention of the future not on his sense of the *absolute* value of his work (as Shakespeare does, or Horace), but on his clear insight into the form that future was to take, a form for which he knew his special genius had a lively affinity.

Again and again, notably in his diaries, he makes statements about society which he prophesies will be commonplaces "in the days to come when my babblings may perhaps be heard." His sense of the future was sharpened by his effortless ability to see through his own time. In a way his "century in which everything can be bought" bored him, so that almost in self-defense his active intelligence went to work on the less transparent problems of the future. Like Julien Sorel, he felt deeply at odds with his period. As early as 1803 we find him saying, "In the present order of society lofty souls must nearly always be unhappy." As a very young man he had already marked out for himself his noncontemporary role: "I must go entirely out of my century and consider myself to be beneath the eyes of the great men of the century of Louis XIV. I must always work for the twentieth century."

One must, however, distinguish his outsiderism from the *Weltschmerz* of Werther and other romantic heroes. It sprang not from a deficiency but from an excess of mind. There is no self-pity in Stendhal. Though he rejected most of the dominant moral and political doctrines of his time, he did not feel aggrieved, much less revengeful. "I do not believe that society owes me anything in the least." Stendhal would be as scornful of our Welfare State as he was of the bourgeois monarchy of Louis-Philippe. All he really wanted from his time was the leisure and opportunity to study it, and these were granted him.

This study was unsystematic, for Stendhal's scholarship was slipshod, and though he possessed high energy his organizing abilities were limited. But he had a certain power of divination, difficult to explain; and, by actually rubbing elbows with a great variety of men and women he derived insights often denied to the most profound student of history. Thus in 1826 he was able quite casually to set a date for the Italian struggle for unification. He chose 1845, which is near enough. His clairvoyance extended even to relatively trivial matters: "What," he once speculated, "will become of the capital invested in the railroads if a carriage is invented that can run on ordinary roads?" He doesn't hedge on his prophecies: in 1813, when Chateaubriand was as much the rage as Faulkner is today, he remarked bluntly, "In 1913 people will no longer be concerned with his writings." Like most of his predictions, that one came true right on time.

Like Tocqueville, he is a Great Ancestor; that is, we are continually tracing back to him the origin, or at least the first energetic formulation, of many of our commonly received ideas and art forms. The psychological novel, for example, can claim a number of rather misty grandfathers, Diderot and Sterne and Richardson among them; but its father, as we shall see when we discuss *The Red and the Black*, would appear to be Stendhal.

Stendhal's heroes anticipate Nietzsche's superman. They anticipate Dostoevski's, too, even though their struggle is with men, whereas the Myshkins and Raskolnikovs engage God.

The idea of therapy by confession is as old as recorded history, but it is developed *consciously* in Stendhal's half-absurd, half-brilliant *On Love*.

In his novels Stendhal lays down the main lines of at least

a dozen motifs which have engrossed novelists since his day: the revolt from the village, the struggle against the father, the sense of social inferiority, the position of the intellectual, the declassed man, the realistic description of war, emotional ambivalence, the nonparty revolutionary.

His formula—"A novel is a mirror carried along a road"—contains the seed of Zola and the naturalistic school. It would be difficult to believe that Flaubert and Proust did not learn from him. Just because he constantly wrote against the grain of the novels of his time, he engendered a thousand novels of a future time. Novels of physical description, costume fiction, the triumphant romances of Scott—these dominated his era. He was bored with them, not necessarily because they were bad (some were first-rate of their kind) but because he felt in his bones that they had no future. And so it was not until he was forty-four that he started his first novel *Armance*, anticipating by thirty years the victory (Flaubert's *Madame Bovary*) of psychological realism.

A whole book could easily be written about any one of a dozen aspects of Stendhal's mind, so rich is it, so various, so free. I have chosen to stress mainly its future-ranging character. It is what gives Stendhal his extraordinary contemporaneity: he is not merely a live classic but, if one ignores the trivial fact that he is dead, a classic of our own day. Also, it is singled out again and again by Stendhal's peers, by men with minds proportioned to Stendhal's own mind. It was Nietzsche who called him "that remarkable anticipatory and forerunning man who with Napoleonic tempo traversed his Europe, in fact several centuries of the European soul, as a . . . discoverer thereof." His own contemporary Balzac was one of the few who understood at once what Stendhal was up to and distinguished him from his rivals as "one of the most eminent masters of the literature of ideas." And it was Paul Valéry who summed it up: "We should never be finished with Stendhal. I can think of no greater praise than that."

II. The Red and the Black

All this praise may be quite justifiable, but it does not alter the fact that to the American reader living in the second half of the twentieh century *The Red and the Black* interposes certain seemingly solid obstacles.

There are some novels (*War and Peace,* for example) that give much, but not all, on the very first reading. There are some novels (*Look Homeward, Angel,* for example) that give all on the first reading, and little on the second. And there are some novels that give little—or even nothing—on the first reading but reveal more and more of themselves with each successive attempt.

The Red and the Black falls, I think, into the third category. The great French critic Hippolyte Taine declared that he had read it more than eighty-four times. While such assiduity suggests a repetition compulsion rather than pure enthusiasm, the reader who is unwilling to give *The Red and the Black* at least a second reading and preferably a third may never quite see what all the shouting is about. Stendhal is an acquired taste.

Before a relish for *The Red and the Black* can be formed several obstacles must be faced.

First, there is the title itself. The Red refers to the color of the uniform of Napoleon's soldiers. The Black refers to the cassock of the clergy. The hero Julien Sorel wears this cassock but in his heart belongs to the Napoleonic period of glory immediately preceding him. It is too late in the day for great actions. Now the road to power, for one born poor and obscure, lies through the Church. Julien therefore adopts hypocrisy as his mode of being; and the consequent war in his breast between what he professes and what he is partly precipitates his ruin.

Now this particular conflict of social forces can interest us only mildly today. We are no longer taken in by Napoleon's supposed "liberalism" and, unless we are Frenchmen, can hardly be moved by the myth of *la gloire.* Nor can we share Stendhal's hatred of clerical reaction, or fear, as he does, the sinister power of the "Congregation," an arm of the Jesuits. These are old, unhappy, far-off things, and battles long ago. The very title of the book, then, connotes something dusty and remote.

Second, there is the plot. At first reading the book smacks of opera rather than literature. The ingredients are a bit ridiculous: the poor boy who seduces the wife of his rich employer; anonymous letters; midnight assignations, followed by jumps out of windows; the aristocratic heiress who falls in love with the poor seminarist, and is willing to sacrifice all for her passion; more midnight assignations and narrow escapes; and a denouement involving an attempt at murder, a series of highly melodramatic prison scenes, and a lurid final tableau that recalls Salome and the severed head of John the Baptist.

Third, there is the dialogue. The translation by Lowell Bair is the first complete, modern American translation in thirty years. It is an excellent one, rapid, plain, clear. It is faithful to the original, yet manages to avoid almost completely any suggestion of Gallicism. Nevertheless it cannot (nor should it) make of Stendhal's dialogue anything other than what it is. And what it is seems to us formal, marmoreal, unreal. There are interchanges, particularly between Julien and Mathilde, that sound almost like Racine—a master Stendhal disowned but whose influence he never shook off. There are soliloquies that recall Shakespeare. The beginning reader may well ask, If Stendhal is as modern as you say he is, why doesn't he write like a modern?

These are merely three obstacles, selected from many. They are real; they cannot be waved aside.

I suggest that we do not wave them aside, then, but accept them, and seek for other qualities that more than compensate for them.

Stendhal, of course, for all his future-mindedness, was a man of his time: he wrote of what surrounded him. And what surrounded him in the 1830s was, among other things, the Napoleonic legend and the power of the Jesuits. *The Red and the Black* must be read in part as a historical novel. But only in part, and that the least part.

We must also accept the fact that Stendhal was not a master of plot; he was a master of ideas and feelings.

And we must accept the fact that people in the 1830s *did* talk rather more like books than we do today, and furthermore that the phonographic rendition of actual conversation is a recent development in the novel.

On a second or third reading these obstacles, and others akin to them, diminish in importance; and the virtues of *The Red and the Black* correspondingly move into the forefront of our consciousness.

Of these virtues the most salient is the one already noted in connection with Stendhal's temperament in general. *The Red and the Black* (far more remarkably than Stendhal's other major novel, *The Charterhouse of Parma*) is a precursor. It sets the tone, the angle of attack, and much of the actual content for a hundred post-Stendhalian writers of fiction. It is possible to argue that it is not one of the world's greatest novels. It lacks Tolstoy's broad humanity, Fielding's humor, Dickens' power of characterization, Dostoevski's tragic penetration. But it is possible to argue that if any single work deserves to be called the father of the modern novel, that work is the anticipatory compendium known as *The Red and the Black*.

Almost a century before *Main Street*, Stendhal, speaking of Julien's birthplace, writes: "The tyranny of public opinion—and what public opinion!—is as stupid in the small towns of France as it is in the United States of America." In this sentence he not only announces one of the book's major themes, but one of the major themes of the realistic novel of our century—and as a kind of extra throws in a judgment of our country that perhaps only a handful of Europeans of his time would have had sufficient intuition to make.

In Lionel Trilling's brilliant essay on Henry James's *The Princess Casamassima* the reader will find a commentary on the kind of novel that turns on the fortunes of what Mr. Trilling calls The Young Man from the Provinces. Our publishers' lists are rich in such novels; apparently there is still pay dirt in this well-worked mine. The best recent examples are perhaps the post-*Look Homeward, Angel* series of Thomas Wolfe. Back of these is Fitzgerald's *The Great Gatsby*. Mr. Trilling lists the entire genealogy, involving *The Princess Casamassima,* Flaubert's *Sentimental Education,* Dickens' *Great Expectations,* Balzac's *Lost Illusions* and *Père Goriot.* But back of all these stands *The Red and the Black,* just as back of that stand two real-life Young Men from the Provinces, Napoleon and Rousseau. *The Red and the Black* is not only the first novel to announce the theme explicitly; it is also the first to give it classic formulation. "For Julien, achieving success meant first of all leaving Verrières." That does not seem a particularly exciting sentence, until you reflect on the number and wide distribution of its progeny.

The Red and the Black, with its pitiless portrait of an empty society, bored because, as Count Altamira says, "there are no true passions left in the nineteenth century," anticipates another school of novelists, from the early Aldous Huxley to the latest duodecimo existentialist. Mathilde de la Mole, yearning for the cruelties and valors of the Wars of the League, heralds a thousand dissatisfied heroines, of whom Emma Bovary and Carol Kennicott are merely the most renowned.

In Julien's development of the theme, "Was Danton right to steal?" lies the germ of all the novels that have since debated the problem of ends and means. In Julien himself we have the first classic portrait of the Hero as Intellectual, a portrait to be eclipsed in power and clarity almost a century later by Joyce's Stephen Dedalus.

The one point upon which virtually all critics agree is that Stendhal was the first to suffuse the novel with a systematic psychology. There were great psychologists before him—Cervantes pre-eminently, Richardson, Sterne—but they do not watch the movements of their characters' minds with Stendhal's hawklike intentness. There is nothing unconscious about the variety and pattern of his insights. He knows precisely what he is up to. Though he wrote long before the term had passed into the vulgar tongue, he was quite aware that Julien is a study of an Oedipus complex. When we first see him, Julien is sitting astride a rafter in the paternal sawmill, symbolically high above his father—until his father brutally knocks him down. And the affair with Madame de Rênal is almost too clearly tinged with the morbid coloring of unconscious mother-incest.

D. H. Lawrence and a dozen other modern writers have accustomed us to recognize as true the fact that men are not so much ruled by a single passion as by the oscillation from one passion to its opposite. Stendhal assumes this seemingly modern viewpoint as if it were to be taken for granted. "Sure that he loved her, Mathilde utterly despised him"—and yet a little later on there is nothing she more desires than to be Julien's slave. This is not carelessness on Stendhal's part, but one of the root doctrines of his psychological system.

The most saliently modern trait of Julien's complex mind is his self-consciousness. Not only does Stendhal watch Julien; Julien watches himself. When Madame de Rênal, the first of his two great loves, withdraws her hand from his accidental contact, Julien "decided it was his *duty* to make Madame de Rênal leave it in place when he touched it." But this very consciousness of duty "immediately removed all pleasure from his heart." Before Stendhal, who ever described a love scene in terms of such cold, almost mathematical introspection?

But, in order first to be struck by, then to delight in, finally to marvel at *The Red and the Black*, one need not be a literary historian, curious about origins and connections. Had it been as infertile as a mule, it would still remain a remarkable work.

Stendhal based his plot (perhaps that is why it sounds so improbable) on a real crime of his day, a newspaper account of a French peasant who was convicted of shooting his mistress, and executed. Into this tabloid melodrama Stendhal injected virtually an entire literature of ideas.

He has no grace, little charm, less humor. His wit is so dry that it evaporates on the mind as a dry sherry does on the palate. He is not really a good storyteller. He does not know much about plausibility. He introduces people, drops them, picks them up two hundred pages later. He repeats himself. His exposition is often bald. At times his characters sound as if they belonged in the libretto of a second-rate Italian opera. (It is hard to keep a straight face when Mathilde cries out "The voice of honour speaks . . . I must obey at once.")

As a matter of fact a good case could be made for the proposition that Stendhal is not really a first-rate novelist at all. But he is something just as interesting and in some respects better—a first-rate intelligence who happens to be using the novel as a medium. Unless the reader keeps this simple fact in mind he may be bored or baffled. If he does keep it in mind he will be neither.

Julien Sorel is for many reasons a lost soul. He is lost because no man can live by hypocrisy. He is lost because the tension between his passions and his rationality tears him to pieces. He is lost because he does not know how to love, but only how to observe the process of lovemaking. Because he attaches his passion for Mathilde to the chariot of his ambition, it has no power to enlarge him; it becomes merely a tactical move in a war against society. He is lost because his enjoyment of the fashionable world is continually vitiated by an uncontrollable clairvoyance that forces him to see through its shams and corruptions. He is lost because no one can really become his friend: "Other people could not help Julien; he was too different." He is lost because he has the intelligence to overcome his peasant background, but not the humor to place it in proper perspective. He is lost because he has an image of himself as a Napoleonic hero born out of his due time: "In those days a man like me was either killed or became a general by the age of thirty-six." He is lost because he does not have the gift, as necessary in his day as in ours, of equably enduring boredom.

But it all boils down to this: he is lost because in a society that has no place for the theoretical intelligence, he is a man of brains. This does not mean he is wise; the close reader will note that Stendhal, something of a fool himself, knows that his hero is on occasion a fool also. But a man may be foolish and yet live by ideas, and die by them; and this is Julien's case.

The Red and the Black, then, a partly autobiographical novel, is a study of the intellectual forced to act in a society which has not yet developed any proper standards by which to judge the intellect. Mental agility is respected; mental adaptability is respected; success is respected. But thought is not respected.

Poor Julien is cursed with a mind so active that he cannot accept any experience without analyzing it to a point where it loses what gives it its value. Stendhal had the same kind of mind himself, but he saved himself from ruin by embracing a life of observation and reflection. If Julien had limited himself to confiding the content of his mind to a diary, he would have avoided trouble, as his creator did, and we would have had no novel.

The Red and the Black is the classic study of the outsider. Julien is an outsider because he is basely born into a class society; because he is bookish in an elegant but Philistine world; because he is spiritually an orphan, feeling himself hated by his whole family; because his mind is admired for its more trivial qualities—agility, power of memory, poll-parrot scholarship. But all this bitter sense of exclusion is brought to a head by his intellectual pride. It is this intellectual pride that wins him the love of the equally arrogant Mathilde, whose pride springs from aristocracy rather than brains: "He despises others, and that's why I don't despise him."

Stendhal sees through Julien, but he respects him too. Above all he selects Julien as his hero-villain because only through a mind like Julien's can Stendhal filter his own spate of ideas about society and the human heart. A simpler-minded character, a more virtuous character, a more charming character would have been valueless to him. He needed Julien to express his own view of a world which, like ours, had not evolved sufficiently to make proper use of a mind like Julien's. He needed Julien to project his idea of the classless man, of the man who, by virtue of his intellect, should be relieved of the obligations of class affiliation and class loyalty. And finally he needed Julien because Julien was at bottom not a lover, not a Napoleon *manqué,* not an ambitious cleric, but what Stendhal himself was—a psychologist.

The difference between them is that Julien, though he succeeded as a psychologist, failed as a man; whereas Stendhal succeeded both as man and psychologist. And, should you ask in what Stendhal's success lies, I would reply—in the creation of Julien Sorel.

Typee

ON JANUARY 3, 1841, twenty-one-year-old Herman Melville shipped out of New Bedford, Massachusetts, as a member of the crew of the whaler *Acushnet*, Valentine Pease master. There was little reason for anyone to wager that the voyage would prove any less pointless than young Melville's earlier random stabs at a career. Scion of a respectable New York family, Herman had thus far grasped only the wrong end of the stick. He had worked as a clerk at the New York State Bank; on his uncle Thomas' farm at Pittsfield, Massachusetts; as a clerk again in his brother Gansevoort's Albany store. Then he had briefly attended the Albany Classical School; taught in Pittsfield; studied engineering and surveying at the Lansingburgh (New York) Academy; shipped as a sailor aboard the trader *St. Lawrence* and spent five weeks in Liverpool; turned once more to schoolteaching, only to throw that up and sign articles on the *Acushnet*.

A clear case of a young man who didn't know what he wanted, and might never know; of everything our schools are spending our money to head off: the Ill-Adjusted, Non-All-Around Man. And yet this abortive *Acushnet* voyage, rooted in restlessness and uncertainty, was to steer Melville on to his proper path. It would inspire *Typee*, his first book. It would lay a long powder train of thought that a decade later was to explode in *Moby Dick*.

It began the education that continued inside Melville's brooding head to the day of his death, September 28, 1891.

The external events back of *Typee* are quickly summarized. On July 9, 1842, after a year and a half aboard the *Acushnet,* Melville, chafing under unpleasant shipboard conditions or merely hankering for adventure, or perhaps both, jumped ship at Nuku Hiva in the Marquesas. His fellow deserter was one Richard Tobias Greene, the "Toby" of *Typee.* Melville's sketch of Toby sounds like an anticipatory boys' book version of Captain Ahab: "He was one of that class of rovers you sometimes meet at sea, who never reveal their origin, never allude to home, and go rambling over the world as if pursued by some mysterious fate they cannot elude." Following a number of near disasters and narrow escapes, in the course of which Melville suffered a severe leg injury, they reached the interior valley of Typee, reputedly the dwelling place of fierce cannibals ("Typee" means a fancier of human flesh). Toby escaped but Melville "was detained in an indulgent captivity for about the space of four months."

Melville was drawing the longbow here. Actually he stayed with the Typees for only three weeks and five days. In circumstances still rather obscure he was rescued from his fearsome-friendly hosts, and on August 9 shipped aboard the Australian whaling bark *Lucy Ann* as able seaman, being put down for a 120th lay or share of the proceeds of the catch. Some of his experiences and observations on the voyage provided the material for *Omoo,* the sequel to *Typee.*

As for *Typee* itself, it arose in this manner. On October 14, 1844, Melville, following a series of short voyages, was discharged from the U. S. Navy. He rejoined his mother at Lansingburgh. He had now reached his twenty-fifth year without forming any aim in life. Some friend, or possibly a member of the family, happened to say to him: "Why don't you put in book form that story of your South Sea adventures which we all enjoy so much?" And that fateful winter Melville worked on *Typee.*

Many years later, in a letter to his friend Hawthorne, Melville was to write: "Until I was twenty-five, I had no development at all. From my twenty-fifth year I date my life. Three weeks have scarcely past, at any time between then and now, that I have not unfolded within myself."

The twenty-fifth year, from which Melville dated his life, was the year of the composition of *Typee*. There lies its first, perhaps its greatest, importance: *Typee* discovered Melville to himself. He found out that he was more than a man. He was a mind. Concretely, we may guess that *Typee's* success determined him to become a writer. Had it failed absolutely the world might have lost *Moby Dick* and *Billy Budd*.

But it did not fail. The first volume was published in England on February 27, 1846, to the accompaniment of generally favorable notices, which were confirmed the following month with the appearance in the United States of the complete story. The more virtuous reviewers objected to what seems to us a few coy hints of carnality in the book; and others, with a vested interest in imposing trousers and Mother Hubbards on the South Sea Islanders, roared with pain at Melville's criticism of the missionary movement.

But men of intelligence in general were delighted with *Typee's* freshness, novelty of background, and narrative energy. Washington Irving prophesied success for it. Hawthorne, later to become one of Melville's closest friends, reviewed it with a touch of Puritan timorousness, but on the whole favorably. Longfellow found it "very curious and interesting." The then obscure Whitman thought it "a strange, graceful, most readable book." One English reviewer, with considerable penetration, found Melville's manner "New World all over." Even the opposition press helped to give *Typee* currency. One highly specialized periodical—it called itself *The Christian Parlor Magazine* —excommunicated the book as "An apotheosis of barbarism! A panegyric on cannibal delights!" Such a notice must have sent many amateurs of barbarism to the bookstores. In justice to Melville's Polynesian friends it should be stated that while he talks a lot about cannibalism, he never explicitly *says* that he witnessed this intimate custom among the Typees. Indeed his tact is such as to convey the impression that the Typees consisted largely of libel lawyers.

One reader, the journalist Evart Duyckinck, wrote in a letter to Hawthorne: "A lively and pleasant book, not over philosophical perhaps . . ." And that, more than a century later, seems a fair enough summary.

The obvious faults of taste and imagination in the *Venus and Adonis* of the young Shakespeare (he may have been twenty-eight when he wrote it) in no way invalidate his supremacy. So with Melville's first fruits. *Typee* is good 'prentice work. But it were vain to try to detect in it the future creator of *Moby Dick*. The adventure episodes, preluding his settling down among the savages, have vigor enough. But to our modern taste the style as a whole is circumlocutory, the movement uncertain, the humor arch or heavy. Moreover, Melville's mind was not scientific. His observation of primitive manners shows a good eye, aided by a good memory; no more.

Nor, as a record of actual experience, is it all trustworthy. Doubtless the story's major lines parallel the facts. A great deal of it—the diverting popgun episode, for example, and Melville's troubles with his would-be tattooers—has the solid smack of reality. And we may be sure of a Fayaway. Yet obviously what we have in Fayaway is a heavily idealized portrait painted with the brush of inhibition. Not quite a fake, not quite a daydream, Fayaway partakes of the qualities of both. As a character she does not exist. But as a sexual emblem she is extremely interesting. She is one of the earliest literary embodiments of the "civilized" white man's yearning for something not generally available in the home bedroom: that combination of the slavish, the passive, and the wanton which for some odd reason the Westerner believes may be found among primitive females of another pigmentation.

The best one can say for *Typee* as an adventure yarn (no faint praise) is that it should be ranged a few shelves below *Robinson Crusoe*. For all its faults it does have the central quality of suspense. Will Melville and Toby make a safe getaway from their vessel? Will they survive the perils of their preliminary exploration of the island? Will Melville discover the motive back of his detention by the Typees? Will any attempt be made to convert him literally into a Polynesian? Finally, how will he escape? Melville's handling of these excitements is skillful enough to make of *Typee* a good book for boys, and for that boy who, whatever our chronological age, lives in all of us.

But *Typee* is of course something more than a boys' book. It stands as a landmark in the literature of primitive utopias. It is an eloquent if simple presentation of the case against the hypocrisies and coercions of civilization, a case which in our day has been given a subtler, more terrifying statement in Huxley's *Brave New World*.

The ancestry of this literature is ancient and tangled. We find traces of it even as far back as Hesiod, and after him in Polybius' description of Arcadia. Dryden's famous line in *The Conquest of Granada* (1670), "When wild in woods the noble savage ran," popularized a phrase and an attitude. (On the other hand the harder-headed Hobbes tersely summed up the life of the noble savage thus: "No arts; no letters; no society; and what is worst of all, continual fear and danger of violent death.") In 1688 that curious, pitiful creature Aphra Behn, England's first professional authoress, wrote *Oroonoko,* a short novel about a couple of noble savages of Surinam. Later on in 1695 a play was made of *Oroonoko* and it became the hit of the season. The eighteenth century saw the Noble Savage reach a new high on the stock market of the imagination. Bougainville's narrative of his voyage around the world (1767-1769), with its idyllic description of Tahitian life, is a key document in the history of civilization-baiting, and should be considered a direct ancestor of *Typee*.

Typee may have started the South Sea mythology which crashed through to best-sellerdom in 1919 with Frederick O'Brien's *White Shadows in the South Seas,* and of which Stevenson, Conrad, Maugham are the great names. In our own day the vein is almost exhausted. But Melville was lucky enough to tap it at a time when it was still loaded with pay ore. He recalled, or invented, Fayaway; and with Sex finally on the scene, the South Sea romance was set up in business. It has had a lively career, finally reaching its nadir in the hula-hula advertisements of our tourist-cruise shipping lines.

Melville of course had little idea that with *Typee* he was taking his place not far from the starting point of a popular literary tradition. His pictures of Marquesan life may have sprung in part from an obscure sense of what the public wanted. But, as this sense was at no time highly developed in him, it is more probable that his praise of the Noble Savage and the Child of Nature (he actually uses these phrases) was fundamentally sincere.

The literature of the exotic, from Herodotus to Thor Heyerdahl, is partly a response to the audience's natural thirst for marvels. But it is also partly an expression of the writer's dissatisfaction, often unconscious, with his own time and place.

Baffled young men, not to mention baffled middle-aged and old men, faced with a refractory present, are apt to take refuge in a more malleable past. That past may be a fossilized one—a Marquesan island, for example. Each of us has his own private Nuku Hiva, real or imaginary. (Today's modish metaphor calls it our childhood, or the womb; there will be a different metaphor tomorrow.) Out of this Nuku Hiva the artist will fashion that part of his work which is steeped in the colors of protest and rejection. So with *Typee*. Disguised as a forecastle yarn, it is just such a work.

The young Melville, like the old Melville and the old Ahab, sought a principle of harmony not to be found in mid-nineteenth-century America. The Melville of *Typee* felt, naively, that he had discovered this principle among his happy cannibals, and that its opposite was at work in the civilization that so far had frustrated him. The thesis of *Typee* may seem stale today, as it is assuredly questionable; but Melville advanced it, one feels, with all the excitement of discovery: "The primitive state of society, the enjoyments of life, though few

and simple, are spread over a great extent, and are unalloyed;
but civilization, for every advantage she imparts, holds a
hundred evils in reserve. . . ."

Melville, however deep his thought was to dive, never quite
got over this romantic hanker after an island paradise. It is possible (his married life was not overhappy) that this wistfulness
had a sexual base. Years afterward he was to write of

> Marquesas and glenned isles that be
> Authentic Edens in a Pagan sea

as if somehow he had drifted far, too far away from a golden
land in which his natural impulses had once had their unchecked
way.

Only a very young man, and one innocent of anthropological
and psychological knowledge, could have written: "It is to this
indwelling, this universally diffused perception of what is *just*
and *noble*, that the integrity of the Marquesans in their intercourse with each other is to be attributed." We, who know more
only because a handful of great researchers and scholars have
taught us more, may smile superiorly at such simplicity. But we
should restrain that smile. Melville's perception of nobility in
his savages sprang from the nobility in his own nature, his refusal,
even at twenty-one, to accept the shibboleths of civilization
as God-ordained. Melville never joined the optimistic parade
of his century, any more than he would join ours, were he
alive today. The Typees may not have been what he thought
them, but at least, he felt, they did not resemble the hucksters
and the hypocrites he had left behind him when the *Acushnet*
cleared New Bedford harbor.

And so, in a sense, we may read this first book of Melville's
as a boyish prefiguring of Melville's life-quest for meaning. In
Typee we cannot see the artist he was to become; but we can
make out the man.

American Light Verse,
Once Over Lightly

SOME YEARS AGO, I ventured, quite seriously, to nominate
Ogden Nash for a Pulitzer Prize. There were no seconds, but the
idea of giving the prize to a first-rate light-verse writer seems to
have occurred independently to the Pulitzer Prize jury, for
in 1961 Larchmont's Sappho, Miss Phyllis McGinley, carried off
the award.

The event marked an official recognition of two related facts
of which lovers of light verse have for some time been aware:
first, that a light-verse poet *is* a poet, and may be, as in this case,
a very fine one; second, that only thin partitions today divide the
bounds of light and serious verse.

What *is* light verse? As with life, we seem to know what it is,
until we start to define it. I offer two examples.

Recently these lines relieved the good gray broker's prose of
that excellent periodical *The Wall Street Journal*.

The Product

If it is new, process exclusive,
And advertising is effusive;
If it will crackle, snap, or fizz,
And make some moppet cry, "Gee whiz!"

If movie stars proclaim its virtue,
And if it's safe (won't really hurt you);
If it's of any earthly use,
And cheap and easy to produce,
The thing will sell, and never doubt it.
What home would be complete without it?

Agreed that this is light verse and nothing but. Then how about this?

Fire and Ice

Some say the world will end in fire,
Some say in ice.
From what I've tasted of desire
I hold with those who favor fire.
But if it had to perish twice,
I think I know enough of hate
To say that for destruction ice
Is also great
And would suffice.

We can all see that "The Product" is not designed as "poetry." Equally clearly we can see that Robert Frost's creation *is* so designed. Yet its pungency, its irony, its air of casual talk, the puff of wry playfulness on which it floats—all have made it at home in anthologies of light, as well as serious, poetry.

What is the difference between the two?

The first slices an accepted notion into metered, rhymed lines. They could not say much less without saying nothing at all. Nevertheless they afford us a moment's mild satisfaction. This satisfaction springs partly from the mechanical lilt and chime of the couplets (though that first line lurches a bit), and partly from our pleased recognition of the truth, however trivial, of their content. Robert Frost, on the other hand, uses a complex, cunning rhythmic form to make a surprising, quite untrivial statement that succeeds not only in amusing us—but in moving us.

We may call the first example perfectly sound factory-made light verse. The author is not personally involved in it but is using

certain mechanical skills to cobble up ten acceptable lines intended to divert us for thirty seconds. The second example we
shall call mind-made light verse. Though the mood may be one
of mockery, the author is intensely involved in what he is saying,
and so involves us too. The first is tied to the day and the literary
market place. The second is attached to the vague floating universe of Truth. Between these two poles lies all of light verse,
from newspaper filler to Pope's *Rape of the Lock.*

At its best, light verse—mind-made light verse—flows from the
same sources as does any other fine verse. Not lack of seriousness,
but a different kind of seriousness distinguishes it from more
formal poetry. Wit, humor, satire, irony, parody, often nonsense
pervade it—and these are by no means trivial qualities, though
they may weigh less than eloquence, sublimity, or profundity.
In tone, light verse runs to the deft, the neat, the pointed, rather
than to the hauntingly associative or reverberant. When it utters "permanent truths" they are apt to be permanent commonplaces. That early light-verse writer Horace, speaking of "the
charm that waits upon common things," touches the core of his
art.

Light verse is social rather than personal. It uses a public
rather than a private language. If the poem is any good, the
poet lives in every line of it; but only a special part of him
lives there, the part not dipped in the dark dye of the unconscious—the critical, ironic, observant part. High lyric poetry is a
cry, light verse an eye. Being less subjective, light verse is more
readily checked against the hard reality on which it is a comment. It is a public art, more like oratory or caricature than like
profound lyric or dramatic poetry. Thus light verse, if in a flourishing state, as it is today among us, can tell us much about
ourselves.

Often it tells us by telling us off.

John Milton's view of the Deity is rather depressing; his mind
was about as far from that of the light versifier as can be conceived. Can the light-verse mind handle Milton's matter? Here
are two of the four stanzas comprising Phyllis McGinley's "The
Day After Sunday":

On page 27, just opposite Fashion Trends,
  One reads at a glance how He scolded the Baptists a little,
Was firm with the Catholics, practical with the Friends,
To Unitarians was pleasantly noncommital.

Always on Monday morning the press reports
  God as revealed to His vicars in various guises—
Benevolent, stormy, patient, or out of sorts.
God knows which God is the God God recognizes.

Of course these sly lines are less about God than they are about us, and the rather dubious churchgoers we turn out to be.

For over thirty years Phyllis McGinley has been scrutinizing herself, the suburb in which she lives, and the American world of which the suburb is a part. The scrutiny has been sharp but tolerant. It has never been merely polite—politeness is the curse of the nineteenth-century drawing-room verse from whose genteel bondage we have totally freed ourselves. And it has always been, without apology, the scrutiny of a woman who is glad to be one, and for whom a large part of the savor of daily life comes from the simple fact that males and females baffle each other. With almost absolute technical mastery, she writes (with some exceptions) about small matters, as most light-verse writers have done since Herrick's day; and, like Herrick, she usually contrives to say something about them not at all small.

Here are eight lines of what we have called mind-made light verse, verse whose final pair of lines quietly crumbles the wall supposed to separate light from serious poetry. Miss McGinley is offering us a "Girl's-Eye View of Relatives":

Walk in strange woods, they warn you about the snakes there.
Climb, and they fear you'll fall.
Books, angular boys, or swimming in deep water—
Fathers mistrust them all.
Men are the worriers. It is difficult for them
To learn what they must learn:
How you have a journey to take and very likely
For a while, will not return.

The Pulitzer jury did well.
And, when the time comes, let us hope they will do as well by

Ogden Nash. Mr. Nash, now in his thirty-third year of freewheel versifying, remains a phenomenon. For one thing, he is the only poet I know who makes an honest living almost entirely out of verse, without benefit of foundation grants, prizes, scholarships, or emoluments for being a Poet in Residence. For another thing, though deceptively easy to imitate, he remains a master without a school, which proves that it is his mind and not his manner that makes him a superb humorist. Finally (but this is true also of Miss McGinley), defying the old saw that American writers peter out as they age, he passes from strength to strength.

I once called Mr. Nash the laureate of an Age of Friction. Whether it be animal, vegetable, mineral, or ideological, if it annoys, if it is excessive, if it is phony, if it obtrudes or intrudes or extrudes, Mr. Nash is ready, with his double-pointed lance of uncommon rhyme and uncommon reason, to let the air out of it.

> Like the hart panteth for the water brooks I pant for a revival
>   of Shakespeare's Like You Like It.
> I can see the tense draftees relax and purr
> When the sergeant barks, "Like you were."
> —And don't try to tell me that our well has been defiled by
>   immigration;
> Like goes Madison Avenue, like so goes the nation.

But to the classical equipment of the born satirist he adds a special genius for language itself. He is a lightweight Joyce or Petronius, permanently dissatisfied with grammar and dictionary. Like certain animals, he hears sounds beyond the normal range. By deforming he creates new forms. Often these turn out to be no more than calculated nonsense. But, just as often, the verbal Indian clubs he juggles trace glittering trajectories which, pinned on paper, become lines of poetry. He once wrote some verses called "The Private Dining Room," recalling a gay incident of his salad days, in the course of which he helped entertain two young ladies named Barbara Rafferty and Lalage Cavendish. The word-trickery is magnificently funny; but behind it lie the true, the wistful *lacrimae rerum*. I quote the final stanza:

Miss Rafferty in taffeta
Grew definitely raffisher.
Miss Cavendish in lavender
Grew less and less stand-offisher.
With Lalage and Barbara
We grew a little pickereled,
We ordered Mumm and Roederer
Because the bubbles tickereled.
But lavender and taffeta
Were gone when we were soberer.
I haven't thought for thirty years
Of Lalage and Barbara.

Mr. Nash and Miss McGinley (with John Betjeman the finest
light-verse writers now using English), darting their thirty years'
worth of slings and arrows at a large part of the American scene,
always shoot from the center. That is, they feel themselves a part
of what they ridicule. They are not alienated human beings, only
detached artists.

Not so the beats, many of whom write satirical verse that I
suppose might be called "light."

Mencken once called poetry "pretty little bellyaches." The
statement could only have come from a man who had never
known real stomach trouble, the kind that produces *The Divine
Comedy*. I will admit, however, that beat poetry is ugly little
bellyaches.

It is one of the conditions of light verse that, though it may
lack other qualities, it must have the quality of control. Whitman
may be wonderful and wild at the same time; the light-verse
writer may not be. In their most nonsensical moments Edward
Lear and Lewis Carroll remain formalists. The beats, however,
not only reject their environment, which their ancestors Rimbaud
and Baudelaire also did; but they reject any controlled expression of their rejection, which Rimbaud and Baudelaire did not.
This is not because they are unskilled or lazy, for many of them
are neither; but because they feel that the imposition of any
censorship on the howlings of their unconscious is a kind of
concession to the square world.

Perhaps I can make the point clear by comparing a talented beat poet, Lawrence Ferlinghetti, with a minor Victorian poet, Arthur Hugh Clough. In the examples here given, both are troubled men, skeptical of certain aspects of the Christian religion, expressing that skepticism in parody. Here, in *Beatitude Anthology*, is Ferlinghetti:

Loud Prayer

Our father whose art's in heaven
hollow be thy name
unless things change
Thy wigdom come and gone
thy will be undone
on earth as it isn't heaven
Give us this day our daily bread
at least three times a day
and forgive us our trespasses
as we would forgive those lovelies
whom we wish would trespass
against us
And lead us not into temptation
too often on weekdays
but deliver us from evil
whose presence remains unexplained
in thy kingdom of power and glory
oh man

And here is our stuffy, non-beat, conformist Victorian:

The Latest Decalogue

Thou shalt have one God only; who
Would be at the expense of two?
No graven images may be
Worshipped, except the currency:
Swear not at all; for, for thy curse
Thine enemy is none the worse:
At church on Sunday to attend
Will serve to keep the world thy friend:
Honour thy parents; that is, all

> From whom advancement may befall:
> Thou shalt not kill; but needst not strive
> Officiously to keep alive:
> Do not adultery commit;
> Advantage rarely comes of it:
> Thou shalt not steal; an empty feat,
> When it's so lucrative to cheat:
> Bear not false witness; let the lie
> Have time on its own wings to fly:
> Thou shalt not covet; but tradition
> Approves all forms of competition.

I find Ferlinghetti inferior to Clough because indignation alone, despite the old tag, does not make verses. Ferlinghetti's emotion outruns his power of expression, whereas with Clough they are nicely graduated to each other. The first poem relies angrily on slapdash puns; the second relies coolly on beveled epigrams.

The beats, such as Ferlinghetti and Kenneth Rexroth, are way out on a limb of their own; whereas Miss McGinley and Mr. Nash represent the peak of an established hierarchy. Between the pad of the rebels and the academy of the veterans there flourishes a lively school of brilliant light versifiers. Some, like Morris Bishop, Richard Armour, and David McCord, have been working the territory for many years. Others, like John Updike, J. V. Cunningham, Robert Paul Smith, and Walker Gibson, are comparative newcomers. Many, like William Jay Smith, Robert Francis, John Ciardi, John Holmes, and Theodore Roethke, are essentially serious poets with double-barreled temperaments. Some are specialists: Helen Bevington creates the most delicious light verse year after year by exploiting the narrow field of literary reference; Edward Gorey continues to rhyme his comic sadism; Marya Mannes reworks the almost abandoned field of political satire. All I am trying to say is that our own day can hold its own against that of the preceding generation of Dorothy Parker, Hoffenstein, Newman Levy, and the early E. B. White.

This is all the more remarkable when we consider what sort of day it is. Or night: for you can hardly apply the lucent monosyllable *day* to an era in which the gas chamber, the Bomb, and the moon as a murder platform are accepted as commonplaces. Light-verse writers have had to make some odd accommodations to these obscenities, but they have not abdicated. They have even found it possible to be funny about annihilation, as is Marya Mannes in

On Limited Warfare

Don'tcha worry, honey chile,
　Don'tcha cry no more,
It's jest a li'l ole atom bomb
　In a li'l ole lim'ted war.

It's jest a bitsy warhead, chile,
　On a li'l ole tactical shell,
And all it'll do is blow us-all
　To a li'l ole lim'ted hell.

Even when the younger light poets seem to be engaged in perfect foolery, they are really shaping their witty fancies to the troubling pressures of our time. I offer a miniature satire by the dazzling John Updike, a poem which also illustrates the ability of the younger men to twist and distort the language into new and laughable shapes.

The Newlyweds

After a one-day honeymoon, the Fishers rushed off to a soft-drink-bottlers' convention, then on to a ball game, a TV rehearsal and a movie preview.   —Life

"We're married," said Eddie.
Said Debbie, "Incredi-

ble! When is our honey-
moon?" "Over and done," he

replied. "Feeling logy?
Drink Coke." "Look at Yogi

go!" Debbie cried. "Groovy!"
"Rehearsal?" "The movie."

"Some weddie," said Debbie.
Said Eddie, "Yeah, mebbe."

The hallmark of the finest current American light verse, I think, is simply that it says more, and says it more subtly, than did the masters of the nineteenth and early twentieth centuries. It encroaches continually and successfully on the traditional territory of serious poetry. The drawing-room note is dead: there is lightness without triviality and technical skill without the silly acrobatics of the artificial French forms. Only our time could produce a piece of light verse like this one by Walker Gibson, with its troubling ambiguity of tone, its heart of irony beating inside the flesh of humor:

David

Master of metaphor, at three
He's learned the language of mirage—
Sees dump trucks climbing every tree;
The sky, he says, is their garage.

And like a derrick, ducks his head;
Contrives his airplane arms like flaps;
Mother and father sleep like dead;
Behind the barn the dead cat naps.

This is no simple world. To him
Man is machine, machine is man,
And the corpse talks, the lilies swim.
Of course, we tell him what we can.

Some Follow-up Reading for Those Interested

ANTHOLOGIES, GENERAL

The Silver Treasury of Light Verse, edited by Oscar Williams.
Innocent Merriment: An Anthology of Light Verse, selected by Franklin P. Adams ("F.P.A.").
An Anthology of Light Verse, edited and with an introduction by Louis Kronenberger.

ANTHOLOGIES, FAVORITE

The Fireside Book of Humorous Poetry, edited by William Cole.
What Cheer: An Anthology of American and British Humorous
and Witty Verse Gathered, Sifted, and Salted, with an introduction by David McCord.
The Oxford Book of Light Verse, chosen by W. H. Auden.

ANTHOLOGIES, SPECIALIZED

Straw in the Hair: An Anthology of Nonsensical and Surrealist
Verse, compiled and edited by Denys Kilham Roberts.
The Worldly Muse: An Anthology of Serious Light Verse, edited
and with an introduction by A. J. M. Smith.
The Stuffed Owl: An Anthology of Bad Verse, selected and ar-
ranged by D. B. Wyndham Lewis and Charles Lee.

BOOKS BY SINGLE AUTHORS

Times Three, by Phyllis McGinley.
Verses From 1929 On, by Ogden Nash.

Artur Rubinstein: Freehand
Sketch of a Mind in Motion

THE LAST TIME I heard Artur Rubinstein play was on February 27, 1959, at Carnegie Hall. An all-Chopin recital, followed by five encores. Triumph. Afterward, with about two hundred others, we struggled backstage to shake the master's hand. The atmosphere was electric: we were not only numerous but excited —the concluding encore had been de Falla's *Ritual Fire Dance*, the musical equivalent, as Rubinstein plays it, of ten grains of Benzedrine.

At the entrance to the little anteroom the uniformed Cerberus, thinking to protect the artist from what looked like a miniature mob, kept pushing us back, letting in only a few at a time, shutting the door violently in the faces of those still to be admitted. Suddenly Rubinstein flung open the door. For two solid hours he had been playing compositions of increasing difficulty and subtlety. He was tired. He is in his seventies. But his face and body and voice were charged with almost terrifying energy. "Let them in! Do not keep them out! These are my friends! Do you hear, do you understand—*my friends!*"

There was passion in the voice. But it was not so much a passion of wrath directed at the well-intentioned if rather tactless guard. It was a positive passion, a passion *for* friendship.

To Rubinstein we were no mere autograph seekers. We were, whether he knew us or not, his *friends;* and, because we loved music, worthy of all respect and consideration.

A few weeks before, I had asked Rubinstein whether we might lunch and talk together. We—a young lady had kindly agreed to join us and take notes—awaited him in the restaurant. He entered, his stride thirty-five years his junior, sat down at the table, ordered drinks in Italian (from the eight languages he speaks he selects one as an ordinary man would a tie) and started to apologize: "So sorry to be late. For two hours I have been at my lawyer's, making a testament. What a nuisance, this business of a testament. One figures, one schemes, one arranges, and in the end—what? It is practically impossible to leave anything for yourself!" And his face, mobile as an actor's but bare of any nuance of calculation, broke apart in a smile as the three of us relished the little joke.

Little—but pure Rubinstein. It was easy to understand his limited enthusiasm for the making of wills. For the core of Rubinstein is not his passion for the piano, deep as that is. It is his passion for life.

He leaned over the table, resting on it the ten most valuable fingers in the world, and spoke, among other things, of music. Many musicians are garrulous; few have any conversation to match their brilliance as performers. Rubinstein is a startling exception. For most of us language is a blunt instrument. For him it is a pleasure to be enjoyed and exploited. Two qualities make him one of the best conversationalists I know. His ideas are clear; and they are passionate.

"It is simply my life, music. I live it, breathe it, talk with it. I am almost unconscious of it. No, I do not mean I take it for granted—one should never take for granted any of the gifts of God. But it is like an arm, a leg, part of me. On the other hand books and paintings and languages and people are passions with me, always to be cultivated. . . . Travel too. I am a lucky man to have a business which allows me to be on the road so much." He smiled. "On the train, the plane, I have time to read. There again, I am lucky to be a pianist. A splendid instrument, the piano, just the right size so that you cannot take it with you. . . . Instead of practicing I can read. A fortunate fellow, am I not?"

Rubinstein is indeed a happy man. I have met few endowed with less natural talent for suicide. Nevertheless, when he was seventeen he decided, after an unhappy love affair, to hang himself. As his fingers were less reliable then than now, the knot slipped. No sooner had he achieved this fiasco than he became vastly exhilarated. Like a hero out of Dostoevski he was reborn in joy, hope, and energy.

Since that day, despite setbacks and failures, he has neither questioned life nor tried to bargain with it. "Happiness," he likes to say, "is never a matter of conditions." His affirmative response to the world reminds one of Walt Whitman. But whereas Whitman delighted in his lack of discrimination, Rubinstein, while welcoming all sensations as interesting, orders and arranges them. He unites the young man's lust for experience with the patrician's judgment of it. With the poet he shares a constant awareness that all life is a miracle—but when he lights a cigar he prefers the miracle of an Upmann to the miracle of a stogie. At seven he was served his first lobster, tasted it, and saw that it was good. Since then he has never been finicky about food, wine, or ideas. The best is good enough for him.

Just as a combination of spontaneity and intelligence is one of the keys to his complex temperament, so is it one of the keys to his complex pianistic art. His attack may be basically "romantic" (whatever that much-abused word may mean) but he imposes upon it a technique of noble severity.

Yet one must qualify. Up to his forty-fifth year, though famous in both hemispheres, Rubinstein had not yet become Rubinstein. He relied too greatly on his *élan*. He lived on the capital of his temperament and his genius. His appetite for life was so keen it forced into a secondary role the self-discipline without which no performer can be supremely great. In his younger Paris days his disapproving colleagues would frequently encounter him breakfasting in a fashionable restaurant—at 5:30 P.M. Such habits, while pointing to unplumbed reserves of energy, hardly con-

duced to the perfecting of his technique. They explained why in
the course of some of his most successful recitals he would drop
enough notes, he says, to make up another performance.

Then—it may have been the influence of his wise and understanding wife, it may have been the power of his mind to
re-educate his will—he threw himself into a long summer of Dra-
conic self-discipline and, with the passing of the years, emerged
as the Rubinstein honored today wherever the literature of the
piano is understood.

This capacity to grow in one's middle years is in general rare
enough. Studying the biographies of musical performers, one is
struck with its infrequency among them in particular. First-rate
chess players, mathematicians, and virtuosi (there are exceptions) seem at a relatively early age to achieve the high plateau
on which they remain. Rubinstein too was a child prodigy, but
it is his Goethean growth after forty-five that is the truly pro-
digious phenomenon. Such dogged persistence in maturing is
more marked among European than among American artists. It
is possible that this may have been remotely in his mind when,
upon my mentioning the spectacular Mr. Cliburn, Rubinstein
expressed sincere admiration capped by the sympathetic comment that a certain peril is involved in being so good so young.

Yet, even after he had shed some of the Bohemian traits im-
peding his artistic development, the essential romantic Rubinstein remained unaltered. He is as deeply convinced now as ever
that life is unpackageable. His own biography is starred with
miracles: once in his youth when all seemed lost, an error in a
telegram was responsible for his receiving a thousand rubles
meant, it was later discovered, for Koussevitzky. But his belief
in miracles roots in something deeper than gratitude for strokes
of good fortune. It is part of his daily vision. It is what gives
his conversation intensity as well as sparkle. It expresses itself
around his dinner table; or at any of his fabulous nonstop parties
(there is a book to be written called *King Artur and His Noble
Nights*); or in the fond contemplation of the glowing end of his
cigar or the glowing luminescence of his Dufys and Renoirs; or
in the way his eyes kindle as he recalls the fine spirits he has

known, from the days of Paderewski, Debussy, and Henry James to our own epoch.

His sense that life cannot be crowded into a corner accompanies him to the keyboard. For what he offers one needs a word less monochrome than recital. The notes are there, of course, and they must be played, and played well. But he will do what he legitimately can to introduce into a program ostensibly on rails the characteristic Rubinstein signature of the *imprévu*. He will give recitals whose programs he decides the moment after disposing his coattails on the piano bench. He will wait for the intermission before choosing, out of the existing twenty-seven, the four Chopin *études* that are to feature the second half of the evening. He hates to play the same concerto two nights running. And, though the improvisational style of the nineteenth century is today *streng verboten,* he is constitutionally unable to repeat exactly his interpretation of any piece of music. He is sufficiently great to *permit* the flux of impromptu life, indeed the impetus of whim, to color his performance. He will even indulge in occasional musical stunting, not out of "showmanship" but to release part of the fun and fantasy of his Mercutio nature.

In the same way, the unconventionality of his spirit as a whole spills over into his judgments of music. His repertory is vast not only by virtue of his fabulous memory and his purely technical control, but by virtue of the freshness and catholicity of his appreciation. As much as any other single man he is responsible for the shift in our attitude to Chopin, so that we no longer think of this composer as the Verlaine of the keyboard, all sighs by candlelight, but as a major figure developing major musical ideas. Rubinstein, as much as anyone, "discovered" Villa-Lobos. Rubinstein, as much as anyone, delivered modern Spanish music, which is of the East, to the musical audiences of the West. It is quite appropriate that this cosmopolitan should be called Artur, one of the few first names that hardly changes its spelling as it crosses the dozens of frontiers dividing Europe. He is an internationalist in music, as he is in living, and is suspicious of boundaries in either. (Except in the case of Germany; he will not play for Germans.)

The broad spectrum of Rubinstein's interests will always prevent him from exploiting only a single virtue—the virtue of the virtuoso. He speaks with admiration of the newer American pianists, the "fingers-of-steel school"; but it is an admiration tinged with irony, as if he felt there might be danger of the steel's infiltrating the mind. His own temperament, rooted in the rich soil of European culture, finds inadequate living space in a pair of wrists and twenty-eight finger joints.

There are pianists, and admirable ones, who live in a black-and-white universe constructed of small ivory blocks. And there are, as Rubinstein has briskly remarked, many pianists today who "have the personality of bank clerks." Rubinstein is not one of them. His cosmos includes books and paintings, ideas and eccentricities, much laughter and foolery, and all the pleasures held out for us by the polychrome visible world.

It was in the thirties that I first met Rubinstein, who was an occasional guest of a radio program, *Information Please,* that I emceed. With one of his specialties Rubinstein astounded millions: he had a remarkable acquaintance with the ramifications and relationships of all the royal and near-royal families of Europe. This did not at the time seem to me a particularly rewarding field of study, but we managed to exploit it amusingly enough. Later on, pressed to account for his mastery of this peculiar subject, Rubinstein explained simply that in the old days these were the people a poor pianist had to depend on for his bread and butter. You *had* to know them if you wanted to live, just as today, one supposes, young poets and critics become connoisseurs of Grants and Foundations.

It is true that Rubinstein has on occasion tempered with his art and his conversation the tedium of the lives of sundry monarchs and grand dukes. But he reserves his real admiration for a quite different order of humanity, for those he calls, in rather touching nineteenth-century language, "free spirits." His idea of an interesting human being is not the Duke of—oh, never mind —but Norman Douglas or Picasso or his fellow Pole Joseph Conrad.

Of these free spirits he is one. That is why for half a century he has been not merely a dominating figure in the musical world, which is after all a cosmos of narrow dimensions, but a man able, like a nonspecialized character out of the Renaissance, to exchange ideas with writers, artists, statesmen, gastronomes, wine connoisseurs, taxi drivers, bankers, soldiers, actors, princes, prelates, and lovely ladies.

I have said that his roots are in the European nineteenth century, and, though he fiercely loves his adopted country, that is true. In a sense Rubinstein is a survival; but when you are with him he makes the current scene look tawdry and bloodless. His preternatural energy (he flies to Rio as others cross Times Square), the catholicity of his interests, his gallantry, his panache, his deep respect for culture, his own polyglot attainments, his receptivity to ideas, his wit, always based on the intellect—all these are the marks of the "good European" who was the product of the century from which ours is a declension.

His main concerns are three: to enjoy, to think, to make music. They coexist harmoniously within his lively spirit and there cannot be an ear so deaf as not to catch the constant vibration of their concord.

During the course of our meal (he had ordered a Latour '47—there was no finer claret on the list) he gracefully persuaded the young lady, during intervals of note taking, to try something unknown to her palate: eels. She did, declaring them delicious. His face (Is it handsome? Is it unhandsome? It is so alive that one cannot say.) lit up with pleasure. He had created a new experience for another human being. By a small fraction he had increased the vivid sum of life.

A maestro indeed. Of more than the piano.

Journeys in Time and Space

KING: The bark is ready, and the wind at help,
Th' associates tend, and everything is bent
For England.
HAMLET: For England!
KING: Ay, Hamlet.
HAMLET: Good.

(Hamlet, IV, 3)

Fond Memories of England—By
One Who Has Never Been There

NOTE TO THE READER: *The following appeared in the April 1958 issue of* Holiday, *some time before the journey described in the four essays that follow.*

I have never visited England, and, as the years pass, so pass my hopes of setting foot on British soil. That is why, when the editors of *Holiday* magazine airily bade me write something suitable for an English issue, I at once, all awash with self-pity, replied: "I can't. I've never been to England."

But the words were as false as the mood they reflected. For quite suddenly I grew aware that, though I had never been to England, in a manner of speaking I had never *not* been to England. Inside England, in John Gunther's sense, I have not been. Yet for almost half a century England has been inside me.

I have traveled, for example, through much of West Virginia. Yet pronounce the word "Wheeling," and nothing happens inside my head. Say "Canterbury," which I have never seen, and, scant as is my scholarship, I can dilate on that Kentish town for twenty minutes, with no danger, provided I talk only to myself, of boring my audience.

Not that I possess any unusual knowledge of England. It is

only that when I think of her I feel at home. The feeling may be ill-founded. It may be sentimental. Under the shock of a real visit it might vanish. But it is *there;* just as it is there for millions, of all races and complexions, who will never glimpse the chalk cliffs of Dover or shiver to the actuality of that sorcerer's phrase, the Western Approaches.

I do not believe any other country calls up quite that feeling in the outlander. Those who have lived in France never recover, nor wish to, from the experience. But—you have to have lived there. You do not have to have lived in England to have been there.

This curious sensation, almost as of *déjà vu,* has a mixed ancestry. Even to Americans of non-English blood, England remains the Mother Country: we are tightly bound to what we rebel against (hence the stability of the family as an institution). Then there is the fact that Britain, as the only successful world empire since Rome, was until recent times almost omnipresent. But a civilization does not live in men's minds for historical reasons only. Nor does it dwell there by virtue of its power of geographical expansion. (In ten years Russia may colonize the moon. If so, I will feel even more alien to Russia than I do today.)

The mainstream that feeds the imagination can only be another and superior imagination. And it is precisely here that England has constantly played in luck. From the Venerable Bede to the venerable Churchill she has benefited from the talents, largely unpaid, of the greatest unbroken succession of press agents the world has ever seen. For millions of parochials like me England lives because Englishmen have written well of her.

I think no other country can make quite this claim. Other countries have their great writers too. But these writers have not succeeded in stamping on the minds of myriads a warm, living, breathing image of their homeplace as English writers, always without trying, have done. Perhaps it is a matter of size. England is just the right size. Our own country is too big. Perhaps it has something to do with condensation; as Belloc says, "In every inch of England you can find the history of England." Perhaps it has something to do with mere age: there is a vast difference between a literature that starts with Beowulf and one that starts with a virtual contemporary, like Ben Franklin.

The genius of place, of a place small enough to admit of complete absorption into the imagination, appears to be an eminently English genius. The love of England (to quote Belloc again) "has in it the love of landscape, as has the love of no other country." The average Englishman will express his love in the religious cultivation of his tiny garden. The unaverage Englishman will express it in the chronicles of Barset or the Wessex novels, and so, for many generations to come, fix the flavor of a whole region.

In a way England seems to be owned by its writers. Our own Concord is but a town like any other, and there is no dearth of real-estate agents ready and willing to desecrate Walden. But Shakespeare *is* Stratford; he still owns and operates it by proxy. Today the city of Nottingham has legal title to Newstead Abbey, but the value of Newstead Abbey derives from its having been Byron's ancestral home, where the visitor may still see his bedroom, the plumed helmet on the bed, the sword propped against the bedstead.

Look around Nottingham. Its environs are now yielding a profit, or a loss, to coal operators. But coal cannot warm men's minds, and it is more than likely that in fifty years these industrial landscapes will have an added aura because they were once described by D. H. Lawrence.

I might even put the matter in cold commercial terms. I would defend the thesis that the greatest single asset on the credit side of England's ledger over the last 350 years has been the thirty-seven plays of one William Shakespeare.

This faithful employee's cash value is incalculable. Day and night all over the civilized world he is hard at work, winning friends and influencing people, advertising England, attracting tourists and students, or merely riveting the attention of millions of stay-at-homes or playgoers. And all free, gratis, for nothing. All without fuss or friction. And this marvelous Organization Man will continue working into the indefinite future. Should England's power dwindle to that of Liberia she would still enjoy a triple-A Dun and Bradstreet rating in the stock exchange of the human imagination—as long as Shakespeare remains on the job. Ask any large concern how much good will is worth.

It does not seem to matter, after enough years have passed, whether a writer has lit up his patch of England by living in it or by writing about it: the two merge into one. Perhaps the imagination receives a double impact when both conditions are met. The bleak, purple-moored Brontë country lies a little clearer in my mind because I know that the "sullen hollow in a livid hillside" (Charlotte's phrase) was not only part of the setting of *Wuthering Heights,* but meant, to that "tall, long-armed girl" Emily, home.

Christopher Morley, who himself had an exquisite sense of place, once wrote an essay, "The Sense of Place." In the course of it he casually ticked off a handful of literary associations attached to a few miles of Surrey with a smidgen of Hampshire thrown in. Hazlitt (Morley's King Charles's head) came into it; and Waverley Abbey, where Scott got the name for his novels; and Jane Austen; and *Westward Ho!;* and Conan Doyle. Morley could have rambled on in this way for pages without moving, as he says, from "a few square inches of map taken at random."

Alas, I am no Morley. But, unlearned as I am, a score of colored counties lead an energetic life inside my skull because a few hundred writers, all unwitting, have worked to put them there. What they have done no map can do, no manual of geography, not even the finest histories—not Hume or Macaulay or Trevelyan. It is a special trick that can be turned only by those who do not deal in facts—the novelists, the essayists, the poets.

I am not impressed by the bright, hard young men who make fun of the "Shakespeare industry" or deride modern Cornwall because, like our own Carmel, it is a little faked and arty. What if Haworth today does look like a miniature Newark trying hard to look like a literary shrine? What if its main street does boast a sign, HEATHCLIFF IRONMONGERS? Is it not better for tourists to be sold trumpery Brontë "souvenirs" than never to have heard of the Brontës at all? Might not the hardness of New York

City be infinitesimally softened by a street named after the greatest American who ever lived there, Herman Melville?

I count it wise, even shrewd, of the English to exploit their rich literary past in every way open to them. The net effect is simple. We may put it this way. The citizens of Somerset, Massachusetts, are no better and no worse than those of Somerset, England. But one cannot easily call their town to mind, whereas the English county speaks out at once, loud and clear.

Somerset? Of course. Is not Culbone in Somerset? A quarter of a mile from Culbone Church "in a sort of Reverie brought on by two grains of Opium" the fifty-three lines of "Kubla Khan" were written, and then that immortal interrupter, "a person on business from Porlock," broke in on Coleridge's fume-laden trance.

Bath is in Somerset. Even though the Germans have left their mark on its valetudinarian elegance, still it whispers the last enchantments of the pseudoclassical age. Here, in Bath's Pulteney Street, Catherine Morland (in Jane Austen's *Northanger Abbey*) settled "in comfortable lodgings." Here in the Assembly Rooms Mr. Pickwick sat at the whist table with Miss Bolo, Mrs. Colonel Wugsby, and Lady Snuphanuph.

How far back shall we bid the imagination voyage? Wells Cathedral is still Trollope's country, a kind of twin anachronism, bespeaking the spiritual graces of the Middle Ages and the mundane comforts of Victorian ecclesiasticism.

Further back? I give you Chaucer's Wife of Bath. Further still? Little may be left of the famous ruined Abbey of Glastonbury. But even these weird Dali-esque broken columns and colonnades suffice to evoke Joseph of Arimathea, supposed to have borne to this spot the Holy Grail; and King Arthur who may—who *knows?*—be buried here.

Neighboring Devon's airs, however soft, still carry the rataplan of Drake's drum, the howl of the Baskerville hound across Dartmoor's desolate moors, the brisk noises of a hundred English detective novels.

Pass to Dorset. Hardy, of course. But I think also of the Vale of Blackmore, immortalized by Britain's second greatest dialect poet, that magnificent old man William Barnes, who wrote and lived to please himself, and in whose soft and cunning rhythms the slow, beautiful speech of the Dorsetshire yeomanry is preserved for all to listen to.

Travel east again, to Hampshire. From a hundred associations choose but Winchester, once as great as London, Winchester in whose modest Itchen Izaak Walton angled for tench and loach and grayling, Winchester which was Malory's Camelot, where Jane Austen lived hard by the Cathedral and is buried there, though no one can tell from the stone's inscription that here lies a great novelist.

Move north to Kent. Here one of the fathers of our magnificent tongue was born, here "where English is spoken broad and rude" Caxton learned that English and later printed it. Kent is Dickens country, too, with Rochester the capital of that invincible land, for Rochester is the Cloisterham of *Edwin Drood.* Kent means Canterbury, and Canterbury means the Cathedral, and the Cathedral means the murdered Becket, and Chaucer's jocund company who journeyed here "the holy blissful martir for to seke," and a series of inspired writers down to our own day's T. S. Eliot.

No, I have never been to England. Yet I seem to know something of East Anglia with its low-lying Fens, an unstable, aerial country of marsh and heath, curlews and sunken hulks, wavelost towns and martello towers, crossed with dikes and canals and water alleys, a land of water and flint, domed by the sky as if it were a ship at sea. We know it well from the voluminous verse of that strange poet who should have been a novelist, George Crabbe, who wrote of unheroic lives in heroic couplets, and, though living his later life as a curate in Leicestershire, never truly moved away from his native Aldeburgh.

Say Norfolk and I see again the great prize fight that took place at North Walsham, in Borrow's *Lavengro.* But mainly Norfolk means Yarmouth and the Peggottys and the waiter at the Angel Inn who so generously helped to finish little David Copperfield's dinner. But what use to mention Dickens? His touch is on a hundred places in Essex, Surrey, Sussex, Kent, Suffolk, Yorkshire.

Did I say Yorkshire? At Hull, in the East Riding, there began the career of a man who will be remembered when the noise of the captains and the kings has faded. His name is Robinson Crusoe.

Yes, it is old stuff. These pilgrimages of the imagination have been done again and again. I know that to many who take a fearful pride in being contemporary with the Space Age (an age in which there is space to move but none in which to breathe freely) it is silly to think of Shelley in his Lakeland home, astonishing the natives with blue flames conjured up in bottles in the dead of night; or of the Romans digging clay in those same Staffordshire pits on which millennia later Arnold Bennett would found his novels of the Five Towns; or of the Thames, whose scant two hundred miles bind an unending series of readers to a noble company of writers; or of Bedford, where during his imprisonment Bunyan wrote *Pilgrim's Progress,* and near which I hope the ruins of Houghton House still stand, which was his Palace Beautiful; or of Bristol in Gloucestershire, where, in a room of the Church of St. Mary Redcliff, Chatterton claimed to have found his Rowley manuscripts, and with this lie made Bristol all the richer, as Homer's Troy is remembered when all of the forty-six real Troys exist only in the footnotes of the archaeologists.

I have no quarrel with those who find this mere faded sentiment. I am concerned only to record my gratitude to a few hundred men and women who, because they loved our English tongue, have given me a passport to their land that no State Department can ever rescind.

The Fine Art of Travel

HERE ARE the bare facts of my sentimental journey to England.
Ten days I spent in a seaborne England called the *Queen Elizabeth*. Of my thirty-two nonmarine days I spent half in London,
half in the provinces. Of England's thirty-nine counties I traversed, outside the London area, only seventeen. I did not touch
Cornwall, the industrial Midlands, the Lake Country, or the
North of England. (Wales and Scotland are different nations
entirely.) In my wanderings I motored about 2,300 miles and
walked perhaps 150, most of the latter in London.

You are doubtless thinking I should have walked the whole
2,450 miles. I deserve the reproach but, alas, we are all prisoners
of a century which has given life to the tourist only through the
death of the pilgrim. If Chaucer's people had used charabancs
the *Canterbury Tales* might never have been written. In our
hearts we know that true travel perished with the Middle Ages.

In my defense I can say only that I did not fly. The Cunard
Line, though gently, puts it well: "The human frame is not made
for constant high octane performance." But even aboard the
magnificent *Queen Elizabeth,* a machine which at least has the
good sense to advance at a reasonable rate of speed, the sensation of movement is of course diminished to a virtual zero. All
is smooth, luxurious, *interior*. On the open deck you greet with

pleasure a gust of rain. It reassures you. Your epidermis is still alive.

I suppose one measure of man's evolution is the widening gap between himself and direct experience—walking or rowing or sailing a boat. We have gone a long way from the tribal wanderings of the Ice Age to the hurtling prisons de luxe of the Jet Age; from Homer's wars, all shouts and clouts, to the ICBM which enables us to murder and die with practically patrician remoteness. Five hundred years hence only sexual intercourse, eating, and thinking may remain as direct experiences; and the latter two are being nicely eroded by frozen-food packaging and the average American school.

I admit then that for optimum experience my trip was far too comfortable. For this the British Travel Association is partly to blame. The BTA is a remarkable institution devoted to the laudable aim of seeing to it that the tourist rids himself of his filthy non-English lucre with pleasure, comfort, and spiritual profit. It took me by my trembling hand, advised me, warned me, cajoled me, wined me, dined me, scheduled me, routed me, and saw to it that I did not stumble into a disused tin mine, bury myself in a Roman ruin, or fall off Wren's Monument. The BTA is run, in London and New York, by a handful of quietly competent chaps who, if things got really sticky, could probably administer all of Great Britain.* I am grateful to the BTA.

Having no desire to strain Anglo-American relations, I did not drive. My chauffeur in East Anglia and on short sorties from London was Jimmy Hayes, a Bow Bells Cockney who looks a little like Jimmy Walker. Once, as we passed the Albert Memorial (which is the right thing to do with it), I murmured "hideous," the adjective commonly used, as we might call Times Square "busy." Jimmy bridled just a trifle, a miniature bridle. "They *do* always sye that, don't they now?" muttered Jimmy. "But I halways sye, there's a lot of work in it." Once Jimmy was telling me about a German baron he had driven around after the war. Apparently the Baron was a typical Junker, imperious,

---

* In 1847 Ralph Waldo Emerson wrote of Englishmen in general, "Each of them could at a pinch stand in the shoes of the other."

brutal, inhuman. These are my adjectives, not Jimmy's. He ruminated for a minute or so, then summed up: "Very abrupt man 'e wos—very abrupt."

On the tour through the South and Southwest I was driven by A. E. Weld-Richards, hereafter to be known as Richards. Were not his mind so lively, he might be taken for a distinguished ex-Brigadier General. To my starry-eyed Don Quixote he played the sagacious and knowledgeable Sancho Panza.

Both men became my good friends and companions; Richards also performed as court philosopher. I mention them because, often without knowing it, they taught me much about England. It would be as dishonest for me to omit their names as for a historian to omit his references.

Travel, though a minor art, is still an art and should be undertaken in the spirit of the artist. Each traveler-artist has a style proper to himself.

Richards recalled one such artist, an American who asked to be driven nonstop from London to Stratford-on-Avon, a distance of some hundred miles. Richards, to the accompaniment of complete silence, did so. Stratford attained, the traveler demanded to be shown The Birthplace. The Birthplace took three minutes to find and examine. "Okay," said the American in a tone of relief. "Got it. Now back to Portobello Road, and let's make it snappy," naming an outdoor London market to which tourists flock to pick up antiques and similar loot. They drove back the hundred miles.

I like my American because he had a clear philosophy of travel. He knew what he wanted. He wanted to cross names off a list, and he wanted to change the terrestrial position of various three-dimensional objects, in this case by shifting them from Portobello Road to his native heath. I admire him, but I cannot learn from him. Nor—and this will cause him no regret—can he learn from me. Each to his own style.

On the ship coming over I had the pleasure of meeting a quite different artist of travel. She was a lady of mature charms (and a truly excellent dancer) who announced her particular grail to be "night life." She had it all mapped out: Nice, Biarritz,

Cannes, Monte Carlo, and so forth. I respected her too because (the work of a moment) she had explored her own mind. Whatever, on a fairly varied and extensive European continent, began life after 11 P.M.—there lay the object of her travels. I may add that the lady's biography (she was alone) included this item: her husband was a night worker.

All roads do not lead to Rome. All roads lead to ten thousand Romes, one Rome to a customer. These reports then will deal only with *my* Rome, or rather my England, that is, the only England disclosable to my limited vision, straitened knowledge, imperfect sympathies, and unadventurous temperament. This England emerged as a result of the application of certain principles underlying my particular Art of Travel. To me they are as meaningful as to another traveler may be his "Check-it-off; wrap it up" or his "Europe is what starts at eleven." You may disagree with them. You may dislike them. But, once they are clear to you, you can no longer condemn me for not seeing *your* England. And so, though we may part company, we shall not quarrel.

Principles of Travel
(Warning: Good Only in Case of Fadiman)

1. *Prejudice has its points.* From afar I have for many years admired the English, and for what seems to me a sound reason: for all their sins and weaknesses they have contributed more to civilization, as I take the word, than any people since the Greeks. That's all there is to it. They may commit some evil tomorrow or next year, but that cannot alter the brute fact that they are a great people.* I landed in England full of this prejudice. I left England with that prejudice doubly confirmed. And I believe I saw more of England because I came to her wearing my heart on my sleeve than if I had come coldly, bare of all bias. No doubt Detachment is a superior chap, but many doors that are shut to him swing wide to admit his simple-minded brother, Affection.

---

* "Only a hardy and wise people could have made this small territory great."—Emerson.

2. *Judge not lest ye see nought.* Travel involves observation or discovery; reflection; finally, understanding. The total process results in full enjoyment. Enjoyment. Not judgment. The good traveler is not a moralist. He does not use travel as a yardstick by which to measure his likes and dislikes, for that is but to re-discover the old frayed self he already knows; and self-approval becomes his whole pleasure.

I knew I would find English ways different from mine, and to that degree difficult or even disagreeable for me to accept. In such cases I knew what wiser men have known before me—that I must not declare my way "better" (though it may be better, for me) but try always to discover the reasoning behind the English way, or to catch a glimpse of the total image of life of which it is a part.

A trivial illustration: in three hotels out of four, on requesting orange juice for breakfast, I was brought a doll's-house goblet containing between an ounce and an ounce and a half. Most Americans drink about six ounces; I am habituated to eight or even ten. At the outset I was annoyed. Then I rapped my knuckles: observation, reflection, understanding. There must be a *reason* for this citrus miniaturization. Frugality, born of ration-ing? No. Whenever I requested a larger or extra portion, it was brought at once, nor was I charged for it. As time went on, to tell the truth, the portions appeared, without my asking, to get bigger and bigger until at last I was given a pitcher of the stuff. I later learned how this miracle had been wrought. At each hotel Richards had quietly warned the headwaiter, probably explain-ing that I was a notorious orange juice addict, wanted back in the States, violent if offered normal English doses but quiet if given giant-sized portions.

Well, it took a little time and many dialogues with Richards, but at last all became clear. It developed that, though the Eng-lishman and the American were both drinking orange juice, the Englishman drank an *idea* of orange juice that differed from the American's idea. To the American, orange juice is food, nour-ishment, vitamins. Hence he demands a healthy portion. To the

Englishman, orange juice is a kind of *mouthwash*. For this purpose an ounce or two suffices.

3. *To feel at home, stay home.* The American who tours England looking for something to remind him of things back in the States will probably find it. But on the way he will have missed everything else. He is the one who is always ordering steak because they make it that way back in Indiana too. Yet all about him there lie not only many extremely interesting (though indigestible) English culinary novelties but also English masterpieces, from grilled Dover sole (any sensible American will eat this three times daily, if possible) to treacle tart, which, when enjoyed at the Hind's Head at Bray-on-Thames, should dispose forever of one's natural prejudice against this dismal-sounding sweet.

Remember, Fadiman, that a foreign country is not designed to make you comfortable. It is designed to make its own people comfortable. In England the designers have been working at this job for two thousand years. By now they have quite a vested interest in their own conception of what is right and proper.

4. *As between mileage and experience, choose experience.* I am rather ashamed that I covered as much territory as I did, even though it comprised only a few counties. I had intended, for example, to pass two entire days doing nothing in four hamlets mentioned in a quatrain preceding a poem by A. E. Housman. (I assume they're in Shropshire; can't find them on the map.) But I bowed my neck to the schedule. And now I shall never know whether or not it is true that

> Clunton and Clunbury,
> Clungunford and Clun
> Are the quietest places
> Under the sun.

5. *From the past choose a point of reference.* Obviously the more you have read of the history of the country you are visiting, the better. Few of us, however, are imbued with the spirit of research. I suggest something simpler. Choose *one* book, preferably a work by a creative artist, simply because artists work with the truth, fact collectors do not. From this one book

project your lines of perspective. I might have selected Chaucer, Fielding, Cobbett's *Rural Rides*. Instead I chose a fellow American, Ralph Waldo Emerson, author of *English Traits,* perhaps in its field the one classic written by a non-Englishman.

It was in 1847 that Emerson made his second voyage to England. That is 115 years ago as I write. Four generations have come and gone, England has suffered two great wars and several smaller ones. How much of what Emerson's profound mind saw is still visible to the mid-twentieth century? That was the question I put to myself.

Before setting foot on the streets of Southampton I read Emerson carefully. You may already have noticed one or two Emersonian footnotes. But, whether quoted or not, he is always stationed at the back of my mind, correcting my myopia. For England is not a television show, to be "viewed" and forgotten. England is a vast, many-scened drama, a drama still very much onstage. I shall see more of it if helped by a better observer who saw it long before me.

6. *Choose your England in advance.* This is my final principle, and it permeates the others.

Were I a genius, like Tocqueville visiting America, I would elect to see "all" of England, and the power of my mind would enable me to dominate the chaos. But I am no Tocqueville. So before I left I had to select an England. I will now sketch the England I selected, and saw.

Paul Valéry pointed out years ago that Europe was but a small cape jutting out of Asia; and the events of our century are ramming home the truth of this chilly insight. In somewhat the same way the present, though fascinating, is but the visible thin end of the vast wedge of the past. There is far more past, simple arithmetic tells us, than there is present. Hence I sought in England what there was more of rather than what there was less of.

I am aware that England is not sustained (except in a special sense I shall later speak of) by Wells Cathedral or Holbein's portraits or the mysterious lines of the Downs. It is sustained by Manchester, Birmingham, Bradford, Leeds, Wolverhampton; by

Clydeside shipwrights; by the hands and brains busy in the motor works of Sir William Rootes and Lord Nuffield. This England is a great England, but for my purposes I ignored it; and for two reasons: it is a rough duplicate of what I already know; and its form is transient.

He who knows Detroit knows the twentieth-century industrial complex, whether it be in England or India or (in a century or two) anywhere on the face of the habitable globe. I do not need to see another Detroit. This Kilroy has been there.

Also, again only in my capacity of traveler, I pass by this England because it will die, whereas the Purbeck Hills hold for me the attraction of the permanent. No one will care to preserve a Lancashire textile factory for the benefit of the curious traveler of A.D. 2500. But it is a fair bet that, by paying the future equivalent of two shillings, he will be able still to enjoy, as I did, the curiously moving sight of an excavated Roman bath; or, without payment—for to what is supremely great there is never any admission fee—the triumphant affirmation of the reversed arches of Wells Cathedral.

I knew which England I sought. I sought common things like hills, trees, meadows, streams; "conventional" tourist attractions such as cathedrals, churches, palaces, monuments, ruins, great houses. I wanted also to manage some small insight into what is permanently interesting in the contemporary Englishman—his way of speech, his tastes in food and drink and shelter and women, and especially whatever may be detected in his face, his port, his mental biases that is the consequence of 2,000 years of the richest and most complex history available to study. I did not seek his opinion of the Prime Minister, for that opinion will change tomorrow, and the Prime Minister will change the day after tomorrow.

I knew which England I did not seek: whatever in architecture, literature, industry, or mass entertainment bore the stamp of the international style. London is full of shiny steel-glass-chrome structures that echo Lever House. They are as dull as they are efficient. Why bother with these transient products of a giant Meccano set when a London that is a permanent work of art lay all about me in imposing Portland stone, Regency house fronts, Wren churches, Georgian squares of incomparable serenity, and streets and market places filled with Englishmen who, for all their absorption in the present, are human palimpsests of history?

One further point. I cannot accept the idea that England is a twentieth-century country. Part of it is, but not all. Villages exist in Devon that seem to me quite vigorous sixteenth-century communities; and men walk Sussex lanes who are pre-Norman in build, gesture, even in outlook. It is only that imagination-binding invention, the calendar, that forces us to see life under the aspect of the current. In the forgotten hamlet of Ditchling nothing seems to have happened for four hundred years. But the eyes of the men and women of Ditchling are shrewd and humorous. These folk seem to me far more alive than the "contemporary" dull-eyed teen-age youths and their sullen-raucous girls who throng the garish, up-to-date cinema palaces around Piccadilly Circus and Trafalgar Square. No man ever felt larger for walking down the Strand, but I have watched a score of men and women pause at Isaac Newton's grave and seen something quicken in their eyes.

But with this concentration on the past, the perfect, and the permanent, I ran the risk of not seeing the men for the monuments. I was no antiquarian; I hoped to flush many a real, live Englishman.

But I found out almost at once that I could not do this, could not see the England enclosed in modern times, unless I kept continually and clearly in mind three basic facts. Everybody knows them, but not all tourists are willing to interpret impressions in their light.

1. England is a "poor" country. Not starving, not depressed, not shabby. Just without any surplus. Just taxed to the bone. I heard far more talk about money in England than I have ever heard in America. Naturally, for in England money has that peculiar interest that always attaches to rarity.

So if your draft beer is not iced, that is not only because warm beer is an article of English faith but because ice costs money. And if in London your moral sensibilities are offended by the ubiquity of ladies of the evening, remember that a first-rate female confidential secretary, with high administrative ability, gets eleven pounds a week.

2. England is passing through a peaceful but extremely troublesome and above all *major* social revolution. Many Englishmen dislike intensely the dislocations attendant upon the evolution of the Welfare State and England's progress toward democracy. Being Englishmen, they obey the law. But there is plenty of tension, frustration, dissatisfaction on both sides; and many absurd ebullitions of bad temper and class resentment—the London stage is full of them. Revolutions do not march to Mozartian music. Do not listen for it. You will not hear it.

3. England is undergoing a psychological crisis of the first order. She is adjusting, like an amputated patient, to her loss of world leadership. This sense of loss, this deep stanchless wound, is felt by all, from Queen to scullery maid. It explains a certain touchiness. It accounts for the occasional hauteur toward our country—though I met not a single Englishman who did not at bottom know that his country and ours were indissolubly bound together.

Finally it explains what makes England so magnificent a place to visit. For this very wound has released an extraordinary burst of compensatory energy, felt not only in commerce and industry but in the arts—Guildford Cathedral, for example.

One morning I spent a pleasant half hour in London with the Parliamentary Secretary to the Board of Trade. This gentleman, a handsome and herculean six-feet-six, confirmed my feeling that in an odd way England was rather glad to be up against it. "Jolly good for us," said he. "Makes us more enterprising. Fine thing." As I rose to take my leave I looked up three or four feet at his strong, cheerful, competent face, and agreed.*

And so, equipped with my six principles, my three basic facts, my Emerson, and what seemed to be about nine pounds of English coinage, I was ready to start my Sentimental Journey.

---

* "I see her not dispirited, not weak, but well remembering that she has seen dark days before;—indeed, with a kind of instinct that she sees a little better in a cloudy day, and that in storm of battle and calamity, she has a second vigour and a pulse like a cannon."—Emerson.

Togetherness: English Style

Writing about the english is less writing than tracing. So much that has been said of them is true. Still worse, so much that is true of them has been said—often by themselves.

Not only do they anticipate criticism; they make a good thing of it. Indeed they can draw more satisfaction from a contemplation of their faults than I, an American, from a recital of our virtues.

I became aware of this remarkable trait one afternoon when in the course of my pilgrimage I visited the lovely manor house of Compton Wynyates, in Warwickshire. Although Comptons have occupied the site since the beginning of the thirteenth century, this serene architectural fantasy goes back only to the end of the fifteenth. We tend to think of dream castles as crowning a hill. This one, however, sleeps in the center of a deep hollow, cupped within its self-sufficient world. It glows as if each brick were cored with a small sun; its chimneys frolic with twist and gyre; its topiary gardens are a kind of game of greenery. And its interior is encrusted, inlaid, embossed with history.

Instead of approaching the house by the main road, I chose to descend the field path from the rim of the bowl enclosing Compton Wynyates. As a consequence of recent rains the mud was about six inches deep, and slippery. I reached the front gate only with a certain difficulty and, rather the worse for wear, remarked to the caretaker that it might be an idea to place at the top of the path a small notice warning adventurous visitors that in wet weather one must descend with care. He considered the suggestion courteously but not seriously. Then he said: "American lady bruk 'er leg last week a-doin' that." A slow, reminiscential smile. Then: "Bruk 'er leg, she did." Another pause. "American, she wur."

That was all. But it at once became clear to me that, although Compton Wynyates might stay in business another millennium, no notice would ever be set up at the head of that path. Furthermore I found myself muzzily convinced that the absence of a sign was a mark of good judgment; and that the American lady had, by breaking her leg, committed in every sense a faux pas. No doubt of it: the English are a superior race.

A confession of my inability to say anything new about the English will at any rate please the English. With equal composure they will accept praise or blame if the praise or blame is for traits they have themselves acknowledged over a respectable period of time. As for new accessions to the national character, the idea rouses as much fervor in them as would the idea of growing a third arm.

I shall therefore mention only well-recognized qualities. But I propose to treat them a bit unconventionally—not as isolated virtues (or, to some, faults), not indeed as virtues at all, but rather as tools of a trade.

Perhaps purpose is a better word than trade. The English have a purpose. It is not to be rich, strong, happy, and peaceful; all nations want to be rich, strong, happy, and peaceful. It is to arrange matters so that upward of 41,000,000 people can live together on a small, crowded island with a minimum of fuss, bother, and outside interference. Did not the word suggest communal wienie roasts and TV-cola orgies one might say that a major English activity has been and remains the development of techniques of Togetherness.

In *English Traits* Emerson long ago noted two seemingly contradictory aspects of the English character. He writes, "They

have solidarity, or responsibleness, and trust in each other."
But he also says, "Every one of these islanders is an island himself, safe, tranquil, incommunicable." Yet both these statements
seem to me true, and true today. The Englishman's social genius
lies in the anxious maintenance of a proper tension between
incommunicability and solidarity. When the tension is neither
too high nor too low he has achieved his goal of fussless Togetherness, his main object now becoming the preservation of
this happy state.

It's a trick he's been working at for almost two thousand years.
How is it done?
Less with mirrors than with manners.

London traffic difficulties are as frustrating as New York's,
perhaps more so. But London's manners are better. New Yorkers,
driven by London hackies who use neither horns nor four-letter
words and actually seem pleased when you tip them, miss the
spirited powder-keg atmosphere of conflict that marks a taxi
ride at home. In the course of some two thousand miles of travel
in the provinces my driver-guide Richards honked his horn three
times, gently. Only once, during the hundreds of minor motoring
inconveniences that were bound to crop up, did his impressive
military mustache quiver with irritation. When one driver extends a courtesy of the road to another, that courtesy is acknowledged with a smile and a salute, like a faint echo from the
chivalric Middle Ages through which the New World has not
passed. English motoring manners are not a sign of superior
breeding. They are a sign of good sense in a constricted land
where roads are narrow and winding, where towns have been
laid down like coral reefs, irregularly over the centuries.

The Englishman assumes his fellow will understand this mutual
need to rub along together. He has discovered that civility, in-
doctrinated from early childhood, is simply the most inexpensive
and efficient reducer of friction. And he believes that if this
general bias toward civility is catered to, fussless Togetherness
is more successfully served, and one can get on with the job.

And so his sign will read: BUSY STREETS. PLEASE BE PATIENT
AND HELPFUL—two adjectives that strike the American as be-

longing to literature rather than to life. Or HEAVY VEHICLES: LOW
GEAR ADVISED, delicately implying that the advisee is a man of
judgment. Or PLEASE HAVE THE COURTESY NOT TO PARK HERE
UNLESS YOU ARE CALLING AT THESE PREMISES—not an impersonal
command to a faceless mass (NO PARKING!) but a communication
from one thoughtful individual to another thoughtful individual,
both presumed alert to serve the national purpose.

Thus the English queue up not because their manners are better, or because they are told to do so, or because the war taught
them to do so; but because they have a deep sense that queueing
up permits them to get along more easily. They are not patient
out of lethargy. They are patient because it does not occur to
them to confuse energy with friction.

On a Saturday afternoon, when the shilling fee for general
admission is remitted, I visited the Tower of London. The plebs
in their thousands thronged the vast area. They were not sub-
dued, not notably awed by the centuries of history in stone
through which they sauntered. But—it was almost frightening—
they seemed to make almost no noise. On a Sunday night you
will see these thousands moving about Trafalgar Square, gazing
at the floodlit fountains; but if it is noise you require, you must
depend only on the thunder of the wings of the myriad
pigeons. Of a Sunday afternoon visit any of the parks, the "lungs"
of London as the Elder Pitt called them. You will view a whole
population arranging themselves on the greensward or crossing
it in attitudes whose serenity recalls Seurat's *La Grande Jatte*.

At the Bell Inn in the New Forest, Hampshire, I ate my roast
duck in a small room. Twelve young men occupied the center
table; they were celebrating the twenty-first birthday of one of
their number. Very healthy they all were, talkative, cheerful,
quite full of beer. By what miracle did they contrive not to
disturb the other diners? I do not know. But I do know that it
was an English miracle.*

English children are abnormal. They act as though their youth,
ignorance, and inexperience made them inferior to grownups,

---

* "They require a tone of voice that excites no attention in the room."
—Emerson.

whereas our doctrine is the exact contrary. In a churchyard a mother quietly admonished her small boy to stand back so that I, a grownup and a visitor, might the more easily read a tombstone inscription. The child quietly obeyed. I was indeed in another country.

Perhaps the famous English understatement has now become something of a mannerism, or is employed as conscious humor. But I believe its original function was, and its basic function still is, to reduce excitement. Is there not an exquisitely delicate difference between our NO PASSING and the English NO OVERTAKING? Their phrase perhaps stimulates just the merest speck less irritation. During the worst days of the war an American visitor asked a Kentish wheat farmer which was worse, the bombing by day or by night. "Bloody nuisances, both of them," was the reply, "but the big trouble here is the wireworm." Lack of imagination? Bravado? *Punch* humor? None of the three, I should say. Rather a sense that the war would be no better fought by too much talk of its horrors; and might even be a little better fought by concentrating on the wireworm.

I climbed the 627 winding steps that lead from the floor of St. Paul's Cathedral to the Ball at the top of the lantern. On the wall was a sign:

> The Dean and Chapter appeal to the good sense of visitors to protect these walls of this House of God from desecration by foolish scribbling. It would be painful to the Dean and Chapter to have to resort to extreme measures to protect the Cathedral, but a continuance of the present objectionable practice may compel them to do so.

I copied this because it made me smile; but, having done so, I grew a bit ashamed of myself. From the English viewpoint it is an excellent notice. The walls of course have been defaced anyway. I believe that the sign, with its fine, quiet phrasing, is more effective than any scarehead prohibition could possibly be.

(The note of the unobtrusive can be carried too far. This was borne in upon me when, on a midnight walk in Oxford, in a poignant access of nostalgia, I bought a hot dog off a barrow.

This hot dog was thoroughly English, being in its bland meat-lessness the very soul of understatement.)

Indeed it was with a wild, surprised delight that I encountered on the notice board of the village hall in Storrington, Sussex, a high-pitched political appeal urging voters to join the Conservative Party, concluding: "Captain Kerby will be pleased to help ANY constituent with ANY problem." Or was this (panicky thought) English humor? I am not sure.

Among the other mechanisms that the English have invented or elaborated to reduce social friction are such well-recognized ones as respect for privacy, conversational reserve, and the careful, even cunning, preservation of a sense of the past.

This last is a bit more complicated than may at first appear. It is usual to ascribe the Englishman's attachment to tradition to mere stodginess or fear of change. But in the first place, not all traditions *are* preserved; several, such as the nighttime Crying the Watch at Ely Place, were discontinued during the war, and have become extinct. In the second place, the many that remain are preserved, not only through the inertia common to all of us, but because they fulfill certain useful functions. The utility, however, is a subtle affair; perhaps only an Englishman can feel it fully.

Every night for several centuries they have been locking up the Tower of London. The Ceremony of the Keys takes about seven minutes. It follows a complicated and unchangeable ritual involving bear-skinned guards, a yeoman warder in a sixteenth-century hat, a candle-lit lantern, various sentry challenges, and a password known only to the Lord Mayor, resident of the Tower, and Queen Elizabeth. The whole business costs the taxpayer money; and I doubt that a taxpayer could be found who would care either to defend the ceremony on sensible grounds or urge that it be done away with by Act of Parliament.

The barristers who are members of the Middle Temple partake each week of a pudding prepared by Queen Elizabeth. I don't mean Elizabeth II. I mean Elizabeth I. About 350 years ago the queen made a pudding for her favorite Middle Templars; and ever since, every week, a new pudding has been made into which a portion of the previous week's pudding is incorporated. So today they are still eating Queen Elizabeth's pudding.

At the hospital of St. Cross at Winchester, you can go up to a grating and receive free bread and beer—a perfectly natural consequence of the fact that in 1136 the church's founder, Henry de Blois, the grandson of William the Conqueror, commanded that this be done.

In 1847 Emerson and Carlyle stopped off and got their bread and beer; and Carlyle afterward cussed out the charitable priest on the ground that the people were paying him a salary to the tune of £2,000 per annum. But of course Carlyle was a Scotsman and had stomach ulcers.

(Incidentally, when viewing Stonehenge, I recollected that Carlyle had once stopped there and lighted a cigar in a sheltered nook among the sarsens. So I too lifted a smoke ring toward the soul of the old curmudgeon-genius. I wish it had been a Havana. Unfortunately it was a Jamaican, which is what the English, unless they are filthy rich, must smoke. In fifty years, if the import duties on Havanas are retained, the ability to judge a first-rate cigar will have died out in England; and so civilization will have clambered down still another notch.)

In England, then, the cultivation of the past is as systematic as the cultivation of a fertile field, and is similarly expected to produce a harvest. That harvest may be defined as a kind of piety in which all, in greater or less degree, may join. In a sense the past is England's true Established Church.

Just as we Americans are linked by our common worship of obsolescence, so the British establish a nation-wide *entente cordiale* through their common interest in duration.* It helps things along to agree on anything, particularly if it be something as unchangeable as the past. It oils the social engine. It is part of the Togetherness machinery.

Emerson noted that the books in Merton Library at Oxford were still chained to the wall. I checked on this: they still are

---

* "This all-preserving island."—Emerson.

chained. He noted that Queen Victoria had been crowned to the accompaniment of the ceremonies of the eleventh century. So was Elizabeth II. Passing Lock's hat shop at 6 St. James's Street, the Englishman will casually glance at the two tiny windows in which the same nine ancient hats and helmets have been exhibited for several generations, and will feel that gratification that comes of having one's expectations fulfilled; and he may remember that James Lock made the eyeshade for Nelson's blind eye and feel comforted that it is preserved inside.

He may not know as he crosses Trafalgar Square that on the site once stood a small stone structure in which Queen Elizabeth I took baths, but he would expect his national historians to preserve this fact no less carefully than they preserve the facts of Waterloo or the execution of Charles I. The neat bowlered clerk, passing 20 Queen Anne's Gate twice a day will not, as I did, stop and read carefully the plaque noting that Palmerston was born there; but somehow, like subliminal advertising, that plaque is registered in his unconscious. In London there are thousands of such plaques. They were not put there by antiquarians; the social genius of England nailed them to the walls, the social genius of England keeps them there.

No fuss is made about it, but Englishmen see to it that their history is in sound working order, continually on tap; they keep the past as a good housewife keeps house. They will not let anything vanish, for they know that the past is not an illusion but bolts and rivets, mortar and cement. If you wish to study the history of the English water closet from 1870 to the present, the Parkes Museum will display it for you. When you visit the colossal new building which now houses the Board of Trade and the Air Ministry, you may also see, as I did, Henry VIII's vaulted wine cellar set deep in its foundations; and you may learn that to the Englishman there is nothing extraordinary in the fact that, to preserve the cellar, the entire structure, weighing one thousand tons, was moved laterally forty-three feet, six inches; then lowered eighteen feet, nine inches; then rolled back again thirty-three feet, ten inches.

I went to the Players' Theatre, from whose bright young

semiprofessional talents *The Boy Friend* emerged, and there, manfully pulling away at impossible beer, enjoyed *Ridgeway's Late Joys,* a potpourri of Victorian and Edwardian songs* and skits. It was presided over by a cheerful M.C. ("compère" is their term) whose every gag was well known to the audience that howled out his tag lines with a gleeful enthusiasm rather baffling to an American. But a little reflection made it all clear: the audience *liked* not being surprised. This was not a theatrical experience in the usual sense, but a communal rite evoking the emotion of familiarity.

The net effect of the English cult of tradition is not to stultify them or slow them up. It is to give them self-confidence. They lean on it. It is a kind of permanent father image. They get from it an accrual of strength.

In moods of impatience, true enough, they will speak of the gathered past reposing in Westminster Abbey as "a bit oppressive"; and I heard one Englishman refer to the moving ruins of Beaulieu as "just heaps of stones." Nevertheless, when the chips are down, they will pay to preserve that past. The National Trust, a remarkable institution devoted to precisely this aim, is able to maintain itself even though England is far from rich. My impression, for what it is worth, is that at no time in its career has England been more conscious of the value, yes the utility, of its monuments and its memories.

When you are next in London and visiting St. Paul's, poke around until you find Farringdon Street. If you look down the right manholes in Farringdon Street you will catch a glimpse of running water. It is what is left of an ancient river, the Fleet,

---

* My favorite:
    I like pickled onions,
    I like piccalilli,
    Pickled cabbage is all right
    With a bit of cold meat on Sunday night.
    I can go termatoeses,
    But what I do prefer
    Is a little bit of cucumcu-cumcu-cum
    A little bit of cucumber.

which once ran free and open in Roman times and before (hence Fleet Street).

That crypto-river flowing beneath London is like the Englishman's sense of his own past, never aggressive, often not even detectable, yet always there, sustaining him, fortifying him, and making it easier for him to live in peace with his own kind.

Fun and Games

THE OTHER DAY, looking over the memorabilia of my English trip, your Sentimental Traveler came upon this flier. It must have been handed to me at some London theater entrance.

METROPOLITAN POLICE	
C R I M E P R E V E N T I O N	The Metropolitan Police join the Management in wishing its patrons a most enjoyable performance
	To get the utmost pleasure from the occasion, patrons are reminded that . . . .
	BEFORE THE SHOW
	they should lock all windows and doors of their home and car . . . .
	AND
	AFTER THE SHOW
	they should drive carefully home
	THIEVES STEAL YOUR PLEASURE AS WELL AS YOUR PROPERTY
THANK YOU!	

I found myself reflecting that our own big-city Police Department would, in a similar instance, have employed somewhat more vigorous phrasing. The London police, on the other hand, appear to be conveying a pleasant personal message, not entirely devoid of a mild mock-courtly humor. You almost forget that they are reminding you that London is a city full of criminals, which it is.

It has been pointed out by wiser observers than your wide-eyed correspondent that in situations where we would be tense and efficient the English often seem relaxed to the point of the negligent. Like these observers I too have a profound theory to account for this phenomenon. (The ideal incubation period for profound theories is four weeks in a foreign country.) I believe that the English inject into nonplay situations an element of the play instinct; and that this tends to keep them relatively relaxed and healthy minded.

Suppose we define play as the sum of all those intellectual, artistic, erotic, or athletic activities engaged in for pleasure and without thought of self-improvement, self-advertisement, ascendancy over others, group aggrandizement, or public service, activities in which the spirit is one of frivolity and where the end to be attained matters less than the quality of the experience itself.

We now advance the proposition that, just as a nation's production indexes, whether industrial or biological, are often misleading, so the degree of a nation's talent for play is often the most dependable criteria of its health. Tense states develop occupational ulcers, just as tense Madison Avenue types do; and rather more dangerously.

By this criterion England seems to me a pretty healthy country. I do not mean that the English are a frivolous people. "The bias of the nation is a passion for utility," said my mentor Emerson in 1847; and the English are not apt to change passions in a mere 115 years. But a bias is not an obsession. A passion is not necessarily a ruling passion. To prevent it from ruling (says my theory), the English temper it with play, sometimes on a gigantic scale: Elizabethan drama has become such a solemn cloistered study that we forget it was once essentially a vast raree show for the people. The plays were play.

Take English eccentrics. I have written on this subject more than once. But it was not until I visited the Eccentrics' National Home that their complete function dawned on me. They are a kind of national resource, like coal or Shakespeare's birthplace, and England makes use of them to correct her utilitarian bias. Her eccentrics tend to keep her sane; her occasional wayward excursions make it possible for her to follow the middle path. Eccentrics are play corporealized; and when England feels the need to preserve them she throws up a Laurence Sterne or a Charles Dickens, who act like a kind of National Trust, expert in the eternizing of oddballs.

Or take journalism. I had long vaguely known that *The Times* is a great newspaper. But I did not realize just how remarkable it is until I became a regular reader and learned to use it as a shield to protect me from my fellow breakfaster. The greatness of *The Times* does not lie only in its organization, its accuracy, or the excellence of its prose style. It lies also in the largeness of its view of the human animal—which it recognizes to be an odd animal. Its first page is not devoted to the "important" news of the day (that is, to those events which for the most part show men to be monsters) but to Personals and Classified Ads, which show them to be winningly human.

I am now looking at page one, top right-hand column—rather valuable space. Here Messrs. R. & G. Cuthbert ("The nation's nurserymen since 1797") are requesting you to part with your pounds in exchange for Super Roses, Rockery Bulbs, and Wonder Strawberries. But the first three inches of this eleven-inch ad are devoted to Mr. R.'s (or perhaps Mr. G.'s) completely irrelevant observations on the life of a small Italian fishing village in which Mr. R. (or Mr. G.) was at the time staying—its fountains, its football-playing youths, the strange fish landed on its quays. Mr. R., or Mr. G., is a wise fellow. Though a nurseryman, he knows that life is more than a bed of roses.

The editorial page of our own *New York Times* features a daily light essay, often quite good. But the London *Times'* famous fourth leader (the one I'm looking at deals with Sunday country walks of fifty years ago—in other words, with play) is not included merely for "balance." It is almost always a small masterpiece in its own right, and I discovered to my amazement that Englishmen will turn to it first before bothering to read The Thunderer's leading editorial on mankind's latest disaster or stupidity or viciousness.

But not all Englishmen. Most of them will, exactly as we do, turn first to the sports pages. Now the English are just as much interested in sport as we are; I heard as much crashingly tedious conversation there about racing as one does here about baseball. Nevertheless there is a difference between the two nations.

In theory sport *is* play. We learn from Edward T. Hall's recent book *The Silent Language* that among the Pueblo Indians races are run in which young men, small boys, and old men all participate at the same time. "The function [I think Mr. Hall means "aim," but he's a social scientist] of the race is not to beat someone else but only 'to do one's very best.'" Here the noncompetitive play element is not merely paramount but exclusive.

The English are not Pueblos. They emphasize winning (don't let anybody persuade you to the contrary) but there's less emphasis on the emphasis. I, like most Americans, find it hard to understand cricket. We can grasp the rules and even the techniques (I've been told that an American is one of Oxford's ablest cricketers). What baffles us is the lack of ferocity, of hyperthyroid intensity—all the emotions we think proper to such primitive-religious rituals as baseball or football. What we cannot quite take in is that the English actually seem to be playing a *game*.

During my trip I spent a great deal of my time in pubs. (It is quite untrue that you can learn anything from New York taxi drivers, but it *is* true that you can learn a great deal from pub locals.) I didn't enjoy the beer but I did enjoy watching the game of darts, and I learned something from it. An arrangement whereby it is difficult both to make the first score and to "get out" gives the inferior player a chance to creep up on the superior player. In the long run (and to tell the truth often in the short) the better player will win—but only after he has been penalized for being better.

I got the bewildering impression that there is something morally wrong in being a champion; and, to generalize, that there is something a little infra dig about being Number One in any field whatsoever. Englishmen appear to believe that it is less important to do things well than to do them well in a fit of absence of mind. I suppose this is a by-product of the gentleman theory: Byron was ashamed of being such a good poet and wanted people to believe he wrote verses as a sport.

By the same token the Englishman, I felt, never quite wholeheartedly admires the leader in any important field unless he knows that that leader is good at something else, preferably useless, such as growing gladioli or turning out bad oil paintings. The vulgarity of being a singleminded professional can be moderated by the infusion of the element of amateurism, or play.

I'm not sure whether it was observation or merely my theory leading me by the nose, but I seemed to find this play impulse cropping up in English life in every direction. It suffuses the national character, keeping it more or less sweet and wholesome, just as Bigger-and-Betterism suffuses ours, keeping it vigorous and volatile. Playfulness breaks out in the correspondence columns of newspapers and magazines. It expresses itself in donnish humor (by contrast, for really first-rate dull conversation, characterized by extreme caution, try the faculty club at any good American college). It will even pop up in an occasional speech in the House of Commons. I find it in the porter in *Macbeth*, cracking jokes about the human bladder as the corpses multiply. (Where is his similar in Racine or Corneille?) I find it in the hundreds of droll old signs and inscriptions that meet the tourist everywhere and are preserved not only for antiquarian reasons but because the Englishman's funny bone is tickled by them, the more so as they grow more familiar and traditional.

The range of English playfulness extends even—and indeed most notably—to such seemingly refractory materials as brick and stone. The chimneys of the manor house of Compton Wynyates are twisted and turned for fun, to show how bricks may be made to tell a joke.

Architectural "follies" are to be found everywhere, of course, in our own country as well as in England. But in England they are virtually a standard feature of the landscape. Of them all, the most renowned is surely the Royal Pavilion at Brighton, built by Henry Holland and John Nash as a pleasure palace for the Prince Regent. Despite what the more solemn architectural historians may say, this pseudo-Mogul, pseudo-Chinese monstrosity can be defended only as an elaborate joke. But that is a sound defense. The Pavilion is kept in beautiful repair, at considerable expense to the taxpayer, not only as a museum of Regency taste, but as a magnificent nonutility. It is one of those freaks, in its way a work of genius, that somehow satisfies the Englishman's appetite for the splendidly playful.

Take a minor Folly, one of hundreds, such as Hadlow Castle in Kent. It was erected about 175 years ago merely to enable its overwealthy owner to glimpse the sea. This tower was of course a sheer extravagance, in both senses of the word. It cannot be defended on any grounds of social utility. But even today, though little more than a comic ruin, it gives the Englishman heartening evidence that man can be an irrational being. Such evidence helps to keep him mentally stable. Lunatic asylums are full of people who never learned to play.

The great popular attraction of Wells Cathedral is the clock invented by a Glastonbury monk named Peter Lightfoot. Every hour hundreds of visitors forsake the breathtaking interlacing vaulting, the fourteenth-century glass, "the heavenly stair" of the Chapter House to cluster around this mechanical fancy. With grave satisfaction they watch Jack Blandiver, a little wooden man, kick his heel against a bell to mark the hour; they watch four jousting knights canter out of a hollow above the dial. Peter Lightfoot's clock, all fun, is in a way as much a national monument as Westminster Abbey, a building completely devoid of a sense of humor.

For there can be quirky buildings as well as solemn ones. St. Paul's Cathedral, Sir Christopher Wren's masterpiece, built in an age of piety rather than of faith, is less notable as a house of worship than as an example of mathematical acrobatics in stone. The Whispering Gallery, the famous double dome, the corkscrew Geometrical Staircase without immediately visible means of support—these belong less to the history of religious architecture than to the history of mathematical recreations.

The English slope in the direction of play is often hard to measure because it is not necessarily connected with any outward show of hilarity. It is said that they take their pleasures sadly. This is not true; but it is true that one cannot always tell when they are enjoying themselves. Often, when they seem to be devoting themselves with brow-furrowed earnestness to some seeming triviality, they are actually having fun.

Take their grave, almost systematic delight in miniatures. It was shrewd of Swift to lead his readers into his terrible black world by way of Lilliput; he knew his Englishmen. So did Dickens, with his description of the shipshape toy house in which the Wemmicks of *Great Expectations* lived. Indeed the very words "snug" and "snuggery," to denote the smallish, semi-private room set apart for the regular customers of a pub, evidence the Englishman's grave-playful enjoyment of the reduced, the limited, the enclosed.

Windsor Castle is crowded with magnificences and monstrosities, appealing to both good and bad taste. But its most popular exhibit is not the Van Dyck Room or the Savill Gardens or St. George's Chapel. It is the Queen's Dolls' House, given by the nation to Queen Mary in 1923. The English take this complicated little fancy with the utmost seriousness, beneath which plays a quiet humor. The famous old wine firm of Berry Brothers and Rudd, at 3 St. James's Street, London, is no prouder of its honorable antiquity than it is of the fact that it supplied the Dolls' House with a miniature cellar, made accurately to scale (1,728 dolls' bottles make one ordinary wine bottle), and consisting of full elf-size cellar paraphernalia plus sixty-six dozens of wines, spirits, and liqueurs, including the finest vintages, all of them genuine.

If you travel from Hythe to Dungeness in Kent you may if you choose use "the smallest public railway in the world." It has fourteen miles of fifteen-inch-gauge track and its engineer stands about three feet above his locomotive, which is a beautiful thing indeed. I doubt that the railway pays its way, except in the intangible coin of the Englishman's affection.

Annually about 50,000 people visit the pleasant market town of Wimborne in Dorset so that they may wander through and peer down on a miniature model of part of the town—one acre of tiny streets, houses, gardens, shops, lawns, even Lilliputian shrubs and flowers, set alongside the banks of a tiny river, crossed by tiny bridges, with real fish swimming in its waters, and highlighted by the twin towers of Wimborne Minster, all of twelve feet high.

Showmanship? Publicity? Box-office income? Yes, the commercial motive is involved; the English are no nearer to the angels than we are. But much more deeply involved is the English play instinct, the urge to marry, when possible, the free-floating imagination to the utilitarian fact.

I felt this most keenly on my first evening in London. My friend and teacher W. D. H. McCullough (it is quite English that he should be not only a well-known broadcaster and an able businessman but also the coauthor of a very funny book on motoring, *You Have Been Warned*) took me to a pub in Northumberland Street. It is run by Whitbread & Co., brewers, and run for profit. The pub is small and snug. No neon lights guide you to it. It is called *The Sherlock Holmes.* As you enter the street-level bar your eye is caught by the head of a giant bloodhound, greenly lit in a glass showcase. All around you on the walls are Holmes memorabilia, photographs, manuscripts, including a specimen of the soil taken from the spot near Reichenbach Falls where Holmes and Moriarty struggled in deadly combat. You mount to the second-floor grill room, seat yourself at one of the half dozen or so tables, and look through a sheet of glass at a reconstruction of the living room at 221B Baker Street, as it appeared on an evening in 1897. It is complete with unanswered correspondence, chemical apparatus, a portrait of

Irene Adler, the violin, the pipes, the Inverness cape and deer-stalker hat on their pegs, and a wax decoy bust of the famous detective, with the bullet mark Moran had meant for the real Holmes. One feels the fog outside the window.

The spirit of the whole thing is one of playful, almost mock reverence, lit by genuine imagination. There is no touch whatso-ever of the hand of the public-relations man, though undoubtedly that hand has been and still is in operation.

There are New York restaurants, quite good ones too, that aim to incorporate in their décor this same play impulse. But in most cases there are telltale evidences of overbudgeting, or overorganization or overcuteness. As with the efficient humor of our TV comedians, the play shows work.

I have been trying to think of some one experience that crystallized for me the basic English attitude toward play. The best I can come up with is a recollection of a half-hour I spent under The Arches at Charing Cross Station.

From my New York childhood I can recall many heart-gladdening street entertainers, from the organ grinder with his monkey to the magnificent seven-piece German band. These seem to have disappeared. On the whole, American street enter-tainment, the theater without walls, decays and dies, a victim of our lust for organization. For organization, though it produces valuable tangible goods, sorts ill with the play spirit. Somehow it is difficult to hold in the mind simultaneously two ideas: that television is entertainment; and that RCA and CBS are bought and sold daily on the New York Stock Exchange.

Every visitor to London is fascinated, as I was, with the buskers, amateur entertainers (or perhaps jobless professionals) who beguile you as you queue up before a box office. Just for a moment, they seem to turn a drab twentieth-century street into a medieval market square.

Late one evening I wandered down to Charing Cross Station. Connected with it is the street-level tunnel known as The Arches. Inside this rather romantic cavern were three young musicians, a guitarist and two singers, looking like members of our Beat Generation, their handsome aggressive beards giving them that

Elizabethan aspect that is part of the tonality of modern London. They started with some blues. When a small audience had gathered, one of the buskers came over to us and said, with what seemed to my American ear extraordinary gentleness, "Please come closer so pedestrians can pass—it's regulation." We all obeyed, very quietly. Soon we were pretty numerous, yet we remained an audience, not a crowd. Under the echoing Arches the buskers strummed and sang, song after song, their voices clear, loud, and untrained.

To my naive ear these unpretentious jongleurs were fifty times as pleasing as Mr. Sinatra or Mr. Presley or Mr. Laine or Mr. Fisher, or any other of our well-organized business syndicates masquerading as entertainers. They did not moan, they did not whine, they did not wheedle the audience, they did not break into trick falsetto. They just sang as if they liked singing. Without a sound, indeed with little visible show of pleasure the English audience listened, gravely attentive. Their attitude seemed to show a recognition of the fact that the buskers were performing a useful function, the provision, in an almost playless world and century, of a grateful interlude of casual, unsystematic diversion.

When the hat was passed not one of the audience tried furtively to move away, though many were poorly dressed. As far as I could make out not one refused his mite of copper or silver.

To an American the atmosphere was a curious one. It had none of our go-ahead-and-show-me quality, inevitable in a people who receive so much organized entertainment that they end by feeling knowing, semiprofessional, almost competitive. I may not have it quite right, but I should say that the emotion dominating that English audience of stray passers-by was one of mingled respect and tranquil pleasure.

England's Inner Man

"It is too far north for the culture of the vine," wrote Emerson more than a century ago, "but the wines of all countries are in its docks." The sentence floated into my memory as we (my companion was the publisher and wine expert George Rainbird) rounded the abutments of London's Tower Bridge and emerged on Butler's Wharf. Tea and other cargoes are discharged here, but it is mainly a wine wharf. We noted a vessel from Cadiz unloading sherries, and at some other moment we might have seen carriers from Bordeaux, or freighters from Rotterdam and Amsterdam laden with German vintages.

Our goal was the vast Eagle Bonded Bottlers wine warehouse fronting Butler's Wharf and the timeless Thames. It is also the goal of a great deal of the wine of the world. We were shown about its Daedalian cellars by the managing director, Stanley Dennis, whose family has been in the wine trade for four generations. Here, bedded deep beside the river, lay two and a half million bottles, about 400,000 gallons of wine, resting before their release to the trade. They had been racked with marvelous ingenuity; the geometrical minds of bees could not have done better. In these dank passageways clarets and red burgundies will mature for perhaps five years, vintage ports for as much as fifteen. Here the wine is checked by the excise officials, tested, sterilized, examined four times annually for weevils and other pests, bottled, corked, put gently to sleep. The fine ethers and alcohols suspended in the cool air seem to have been there for centuries. But beyond a glass door lay the modern age, in the form of a chemical laboratory, presided over by a quiet, keen-faced East Indian. Seventy samples a day are analyzed, to guard against bacterial infections, excess sulfur, and all the thousand natural shocks that wine is heir to. Mr. Dennis tasted one sample in which too much iron had just been found. Thumbs down.

We lunched in the warehouse's small private dining room. It was pleasant to realize that on all sides we were surrounded by miles of bins, rich with their happy burdens. We were happy too: Mr. Rainbird; André Simon, the *doyen* of wine in England, as alert before a fine bottle as he has ever been; and our host, typical of the best men of his noble profession, holding in harmonious solution a vigorous commercial acumen and that capacity for general discourse found so frequently among English men of business, and so infrequently among our own. The lunch was superb, but I shall not catalogue it, except to mention, merely as a gesture of respect, a Corton '47, quite beautiful.

As you see, I am interested in wine. In the course of my English journey I was fortunate enough to enjoy the generous hospitality of several other wine men. In their cellared dining room Mr. Edward Tatham and his associates of the famous firm of Justerini and Brooks (Dickens, among others, bought from them)' fed me a perfect cold lobster, a pluperfect cold grouse. With a casualness that did not quite conceal legitimate pride they unveiled a series of vintages that included a Romanée Conti '52, a La Tâche '43, and two fantastic ports—the Warre '08 staggered even my experienced fellow lunchers.

Then there was Harvey's, famous for their Bristol Cream, but actually a great general wholesale house. Despite the mur-derous bombing which destroyed much of this ancient harbor town, Bristol is still rumorous with the ghost voices of the Cabots and other Elizabethan sea dogs.

But for me Bristol meant two things: the suicide of Thomas Chatterton, who, high up in the muniment room of the Church of St. Mary Redcliffe, claimed to have discovered the Rowley manuscripts; and the wine firm of Harvey and Sons. I visited both places on a rainy Bristol afternoon, and it is hard to say which moved me more.

I think it was Harvey's. The cellars distill not only the aroma of wine but the essence of courage. Part of the cellar is quite old, but much more than half is new. Bristol took a bad beating during the blitz, and Harvey's got the worst of it. Their stocks were largely destroyed, their cellars partly transformed into rubble.

Not many men, not even many Englishmen, would have had the courage to go on, particularly in the case of a luxury trade. It never occurred to Harvey's to quit. They replenished their stocks, they reconstructed the bombed-out cellars. Every fresh new bin is a monument to gallantry.

Mr. F. G. Cox, the vice-director, told me the story as though it were merely another chapter in the commercial history of the firm. Then he showed me Harvey's pride and joy, "The Unicorn," a delightful underground reconstruction of an old tavern. Its floor is original, perhaps about three hundred years old. Some of the paneling dates from James II. Even the old brick which forms the inglenook fireplace has been so laid as to represent the uneven settling that comes with the passage of the centuries. Most traditional wine merchants are proud of their collections of ancient flagons and bottles. For example, I admired an especially fine grouping in the world-famous Berry's, in St. James's Street in London. The Unicorn Room houses the unique Pemberton collection of bottles, the oldest dating from the reign of Charles II, and a few containing a little of the wine that originally filled them.

Mr. Cox invited me to a lunch which lasted three hours. Wine men always seem to have lots of time, and even more generosity of heart. The fare I do not recall, but I have no trouble in recollecting the Meursault Perrières '53, the Grands Echézeaux '49, and a crowning port, Sandeman '11, whose balanced splendors memorialized the pre-World War I period during which our twentieth century reached its brief and transient apogee.

Visits such as those I have mentioned are of course Grand Tour. My daily wine drinking was on a less exalted level. But in a different way it was no less enjoyable, for it convinced me that England is currently passing through the tentative opening stages of a genuine change in her wine-drinking habits. The change is all to the good. It will make Englishmen happier and incidentally it will make American and European visitors happier.

I do not mean that England is becoming a wine-drinking country, as France and Italy are. The national drink is beer, and beer it will remain, and to such fine old obstinacy I willingly raise my tankard. Nevertheless it seemed to me, who had thought of English wine drinking as traditionally confined mainly to the privileged and intellectual classes, that wine is making astonishing progress.

I ordered wine in half a hundred pubs, inns, and restaurants. Some of it of course was mediocre, much of it more expensive than it should have been. But the point is that it was widely available; it was generally ordered; and much of it was well chosen, properly described, and well served. Wine is becoming democratized.

Wine merchants can no longer depend on the old families that have known and collected wine for generations. There are too few of them left, and they are growing poorer. But as the old cellars go out, the new buyers come in. These are mainly young people who have spent their vacation money in France or Italy and come home filled with new ideas about food and drink. To this group we must add the tourists, for England is now a great tourist center. I noted with pleasure that among the many Americans I fell in with, mostly middle-class folk like myself, by far the greater number ordered wine with their meals. A third pressure-group working toward the democratization of wine is the enclave, by no means inconsiderable, of Europeans who have settled in England since the beginning of the Hitler era, and who have brought continental habits with them. Many indeed have gone into the hotel and restaurant business. I ate a superb meal and enjoyed a fine second-growth claret (I've forgotten the name) at the Mascotte in Brighton. The manager and part owner, with whom I had a most instructive conversation, turned out to be an ex-colonel of the Polish Army. He is now a first-rate restaurateur and his civilizing influence will be felt in Brighton, which can use it.

In our own country, too, interest in wine is growing. On the domestic plane, however, it is too often linked with Gracious Living and similar nonsense. And, more important, it is not backed by a corps of alert and knowledgeable provincial innkeepers. In England, particularly among the young who want a cheap drinkable wine and to the devil with labels, there is much less fuss; and, at least in the South where my travels led me, one finds any number of restaurants with wine lists ranging from the modest to the magnificent, and service that is generally, though not always, more intelligent than one encounters in our own relatively arid hinterland.*

In former days a certain *noli me tangere* atmosphere surrounded the more distinguished wine merchants; people of modest means hesitated before invading these aristocratic preserves. That is all breaking down now. The dealers know that their future lies with the young and, as the attrition of class barriers continues, with the many Englishmen who can hope to taste some of the pleasures formerly reserved for the few.

Other prejudices, too, are on the way out. Guy Prince, of the famous wine firm of Lebegue, three years ago organized the first Ladies' Wine Tasting Day. It was successful and has helped to explode the stuffy notion that wine is a man's game.

However, when all is said and done, wine drinking in England is still in the domain of art rather than of nature. What do Englishmen drink when they are giving no thought to what is trickling down their gullets?

---

* I recommend to any American tourist above the bicycle-and-rucksack level Raymond Postgate's excellent *Good Food Guide,* which lists about seven hundred places in Great Britain where sound food and wine may be enjoyed. This guide is not part of an advertising racket; it is honest, reliable, precise in its prices, and critical when criticism is called for.

Water, as with us? Hardly. My fallible observation led me to think that the natives have not changed much since the days of Henry VI, whose Lord Chief Justice Fortescue remarked, "The inhabitants of England drink no water, unless at certain times, on a religious score, and by way of penance." This penitential aura still surrounds the drinking of water, which now seems to be regarded as a kind of medicine. During the hundred years from about 1720 to about 1820, when you felt the need of a therapeutic toot you rode to Bath and, with all the formality of a Mozart minuet, "drank the waters." I, too, went to Bath and drank my glass of hot water from the amazing springs whose health-giving properties have been exploited since A.D. 54. It was Mr. Weller, you recall, who detected in the waters of Bath "a wery strong flavor o' warm flat irons." To my less cultivated palate they tasted just like hot water, with a faint suggestion of Jane Austen.

Though you have but to ask for it, water is not generally supplied with meals. The average Englishman takes his water in the form of beer. In some cases, I am constrained to say, he takes his beer in the form of water. Professor Armstrong, a technical expert, complains bitterly, "Beer is so immature and so weak that it has even lost its diuretic value." It's a pretty how d'ye do, I agree, when beer loses its diuretic value, but the evidence is not all on Professor Armstrong's side. One of the pleasantest features of travel in England is the popularity and ubiquity of the Conveniences. They are distinctively signed, easy of access, often prettily screened and trellised. Indeed, Facility Decorated is as English an art as Perpendicular Gothic. To English reserve (let us not call it prudery) we owe the superiority of their Convenience architecture to the High Visibility style of the more candid French.

To get back to beer: the subject is so complex that no American who has not lived in England and steadily sampled its beers and ales has much right to express an opinion. The excellent *Book of Beer,* by Andrew Campbell, indexes 134 distinct native beers, ales, and stouts, and there are hundreds more. I tried as many as I could and emerged from my tankards with three impressions. First, ordinary English draft beer is like ordinary American draft beer; if you're used to it, you like it. Second, for a truly distinguished beer you generally, as is the case in the United States, ask for a German or Danish high-grade import. Third, no one can deny that Guinness Extra Stout, popular throughout southern England, has a character all its own. It should make a special appeal to those who, like Joyce's Leopold Bloom, relish kidneys and kindred innards. In general, beer drinking in England is pleasant, less because of the excellence of the brew than because it is associated with an agreeable social ritual.

Myself something of a cider man, I looked forward to the ciders of the West Country, particularly Somerset. Perhaps I was unlucky, but I tasted nothing to compare with the good Yankee cider we bought at Fairty's Orchard a quarter of a mile up the Connecticut road I then lived on. The best available bottled cider (I was given some by my host at Harvey's) seemed to me vapid. Certain "green" ciders *will*, after two or three glasses, cause your knees to buckle. Those interested in knee buckling should by all means try these. I gave up after a few sips, my knees unbuckled and unbowed.

Except for beer, the most popular current English drink is Baby Cham. It is a gassed-up perry slyly packaged to resemble champagne. Unfortunately the champagne people have no legal redress, for the label of this decoction bears a picture of a small chamois—get it? The evasion is clever, the advertising campaign full of hidden persuasion.

Speaking of advertising, this innocent traveler was struck, as are most Americans, by the relative absence of billboards along the highway. The neon blight of course has hit London and other large cities, but the corruption has not gone as far as with us. One sign is omnipresent: DRINKA PINTA MILKA DAY. The sickly phrase (I mention it because it stands out as one of the few advertisement irritations you encounter) does not seem effective. I can't remember seeing any grownup ordering milk for himself; and on the one occasion when it was ordered for children, the little consumers turned out to be Canadian. I think we're ahead on the milk deal.

Socially, for class reasons too subtle for me to grasp, coffee ranks tea. But gastronomically tea ranks coffee. We Americans fuss over coffee as we do over Martinis, partly out of a kind of mandatory convention, but also because we genuinely love both. I could not feel that the English genuinely love either. The coffee is better than my fellow American coffee fuss-budgets had led me to expect, but if you want it hot, go to places patronized by Americans. The tea, however, is always hot, frequently delicious, and within seventy-two hours it had persuaded me of its superiority to coffee, whether as stimulant or tranquilizer. One American convenience not generally available in the provinces is caffeinless coffee. I should think a profitable market could be exploited in this area. All we need do is convince the English that they are as tense and jumpy as we are. This should not take long: three centuries should do it.

As for the presumably thorny subject of English food, the only safe judgment is that England is at the moment subject to the law of uneven development.

Part of its cuisine is still stuck fast in yesterday. There are many Englishmen of Cromwellian disposition who seem irritated, or at least baffled, by the fact that the feeding problem recurs three times a day, every day, with no letup in sight. The predilection for beef, bread, and beer (I suppose it goes back at least as far as *Beowulf*) is still strong. But the same forces operating to create a more civilized attitude toward wine are working to upgrade cooking and serving: tourists, the influence of the Continent, the disappearance of Puritanism before the New Bohemianism, and the activities of many dedicated groups, André Simon's Wine and Food Society among them.

The consequence of this lack of uniformity is that, unless you are guided by a Postgate, you are just as apt to stumble into a cuisine suitable to the era of the War of the Roses as into one proper to our century. This makes traveling a succession of in-

teresting surprises; in our own provinces you know what you
are going to get, and alas, you get it.

I recall stopping for lunch at a tiny inn called The Withies, at
Compton near Guildford. No more than sixteen guests, I should
judge, could crowd in. You sat on stools at a bar—comfortable
stools, a clean roomy bar. The menu was rigorously restricted, as
it should be in any small-scale restaurant. (One of the anomalies
of our democratic outlook is that, just as the student is permitted
to study what he likes, so the restaurant guest is encouraged to
eat what he likes, instead of what can be perfectly prepared.
Hence the art of the kitchen shades into the commerce of the five-
and-dime.) At The Withies you had small choice, but all was
first-rate. Among other incredibilities, the wine list proposed a
Martinez '27 port, which I sensibly accepted. After lunch we sat
outside at a little table. My neighbors' conversation, not listed on
the menu, was as good as the fare; and our cognac glasses, before
being filled, were dipped in lukewarm water. The bill, while not
modest, was little enough to pay for ninety minutes of civilization.

But civilization is no more uniform in England than it is in
our country, where pockets of feudal and even Stone Age mentality are easy enough to find. I was worsted by inns still mired
in the era of cut-off-the-joint-and-two-veg, with the joint Ar-
gentinian, the veg water-logged.

At an inn in the New Forest, where I lunched, mine host was
John Bull himself, and the getup, down to the cricket photos
on the walls, aggressively Old English. But there wasn't a piece
of Stilton to be had, only some apologetic importations from
Holland and Denmark.

At the Mitre at Oxford, probably the most professionally traditional inn in the British Isles, the waiter, in response to my
habitual query, knitted his brows in perplexity: "Ah—Stilton. . . .
All the Americans seem to ask for Stilton, but we—ah—don't
seem to have it." I got the impression that Stilton was in a class
with johnnycake or clam chowder. I was later told that most
of it goes to London or overseas. Pity.

In London I ate up and down the gastronomic ladder, from
a Lyons, where my two shillings for tea and meat pie were well

spent, to the Mirabelle, where the *tournedos Rossini* was incomparable. In the provinces I ranged from a pub's ham sandwich (in England, unlike our own luxurious land, when you ask for a sandwich that's what you get and not a damnable salad coffined in bread) to such deservedly famous places as the Hind's Head at Bray-on-Thames or—not famous, but it should be—the Dormy at Ferndown.

At the suavely cosmopolitan Dormy I felt sure that I had flushed a covey of continental cooks. Quite properly I was taken down several pegs when the *maître d'hôtel* informed me dryly that the six chefs plus the staff were pure English.

As I could eat only three meals a day my knowledge of the English public cuisine is admittedly scant. General impression: the English cook well what they love best and understand by instinct.

Their thick soups by and large are better than ours. The breakfast toast has had tenderness lavished on it and is served hot in lovely silver racks. For fish in general they have a subtle sentiment: Dover sole is poetry, our sole is not even bad journalism; the potted shrimps are first-class; and they can even create something out of plaice, a fish that tastes as if it had never had an interesting experience. They know how to braise celery, their smoked salmon is almost always delicious (about fifty times as good as our best Nova Scotia), and the humblest of shops will often supply the most delicious of afternoon teas, with neat sandwiches and excellent cakes.

Contrariwise, take eggs. An egg is not difficult to understand, even if one balks at loving it. We all know that the French both understand and love eggs, whereas I am not certain that the English do either. I often had scrambled eggs served to me molded like a perfect mammary gland and moving about uneasily on a shallow pond of aqueous matter. And a really *well*-poached egg apparently runs counter to the British Constitution.

Rough generalization: in London you can eat as well on all levels as you do in New York. In the provinces (at least in the southern counties—I am told things are different in the North and undiscussible in Scotland) you eat more interestingly than you do in our own nonmetropolitan areas, and frequently make exciting discoveries, which is not apt to happen in Arkansas, Tennessee, or Illinois.

Outstanding impression: English gastronomy is now engaged in a great civil war.

On one side are ranged the dark hordes of barbarism, on the other the bright armies of civilization.

The forces of barbarism include:

First, a basic English Puritanism, doubtless going back to Cromwell, and which we Americans have inherited. To the Puritan the other seat of sin is the stomach.

Second, a kind of sexual delusion by which a near-exclusive addiction to simplicities like bread, beef, and beer is identified with maleness.

Third, English conservatism: what was indigestible enough for father is indigestible enough for me.

Fourth, the cost of good cooks (£800 a year, Richards with bated breath informed me.)

Fifth, a traditional suspicion of continental "flummery."

Last, the fact that up to a short time ago the English were not interested in becoming tourist pleasers.

Against these are ranged the forces making for gastronomic civilization. They include:

First, the new desire to attract and please the tourist, which is evoking an entirely different attitude toward the pleasures of the public table.

Second, the activities of such determined groups as the Wine and Food Society, and of such determined men as the founder of the Good Food Club, Raymond Postgate, whose *Good Food Guide* is no Duncan Hines but the real thing.

Third, the leavening effect, as already noted, of the enclaves of Continentals who have settled in England since the beginning of the Hitler era.

Fourth, the new continentalism. More and more English, particularly young people, spend their vacations in France or Italy. They acquire a taste for wine and interesting food, return home, and sooner or later make their demands felt.

Fifth, the attrition of the old class barriers. Millions of Englishmen hope now to taste some of the pleasures that only thousands previously enjoyed.

My money is on the side of the forces of civilization. They have already, the American traveler will be happy to learn, won any number of tactical victories, both in London and in the provinces. The mop-up is not far distant.

Fish and chips in a paper bag, thou art doomed!

Perhaps I should add a word or two about English lodging. I divided my London stay between two hotels. To underscore their separation let us call them the Alpha and the Omega.

The Alpha, going back perhaps to the middle of the last century, had gone forward with reluctance. My large pleasant room, had it been possible to open its burglar-proof windows, would have been quite airy. It was furnished with eleven varied wooden structures. As none of these contained drawers suitable for the horizontal disposal of men's shirts, my room gradually assumed the look of a haberdashery. Also, though the room-service breakfast was excellent, I could never discover any article of furniture with a level surface at the proper height for the reception of the tray. The spacious bathroom had what the *Country Life* ads call "mild plumbing." (For mild plumbing three pulls are bogey. More difficult courses require six and occasionally you hit an unplayable one.) The toilet paper was standard Anglo-Saxon Glazed, with that sealed surface for which the English have so baffling an affinity.

There were seven lamps in my room, total wattage 150. For all his genius in theoretical physics it is conceivable that the Englishman has never quite mastered the idea of the incandescent lamp: though my request for a 60-watt bulb was at once acceded to, I was informed, in tones of gentle reproach, that it would have to be purchased from a shop that apparently specialized in such twenty-first-century supermechanisms.

As the English are rarely late for appointments, I was awakened each morning promptly at 6 A.M. by an authoritative roar from the Old World courtyard beneath my window. This came from the discharge into the cellar of what I took to be the previous day's yield of coal from the combined mines of England and Wales.

After a week of these amenities I removed, feeling mingled regret and shame, to the Omega. Regret because the Alpha was in many respects a delightful hotel. Shame because I was violating one of my rules of Travel: if you want to feel at home, stay home.

Run with American capital, the Omega caters to Americans. I fitted into it at once, like a penny in a slot. My room was as neat as a bandbox and slightly larger. All the furniture was built-in—in fact, it took only ten minutes before I felt built-in myself. Everything worked, including the toilet paper. I had what my secret American soul wanted—a food-and-shelter machine.

For our ideal hotel is an automatic vendor dispensing a hundred conveniences, from Gideon Bibles to stock-market tickers. It does not have an organic character of its own, like a tree or a human being, but aims rather to be a microcosm of our distribution society. It will even distribute good will. I had occasion to stay over recently at a hotel in the mid-South. I had just finished my dinner when the hostess approached on rails, registered a smile, and ejected a brisk "Are you happy?" Before I could sign a receipt for this neat package of cheer, she was off to make her next delivery.

To the Englishman a hotel is not a machine. He does not expect it to dispense the latest conveniences, though he may expect it to retain certain time-tested luxuries we do not enjoy, such as towels kept constantly warm by the steam pipes. The American would like his hotel to be more up-to-date than his home; he respects it when it is, and may feel for his favorite caravanserai something of the same near-religious fidelity he feels for his car. Not so the Englishman. In fact, up to perhaps fifty years ago a hotel was a bit infra dig anyway, like the continent of Europe. A gentleman *had* to use one on occasion, but it was hardly the sort of thing one boasted of. One's proper place was home. And so the traditional English hotel does its

best to supply a kind of ersatz home, complete with family re-
tainers. It will even, perhaps unconsciously, duplicate a few
inconveniences its patrons are attached to in their own houses.

It offers its special version of comfort, as opposed to our version of convenience, which is technology applied to the hotel
business. This notion of comfort is hard to pin down. It involves
a certain rather pleasing shabbiness, a conservative view of "improvements," and a marked disinclination to bother the guest.
The desk clerk will not flash a hotel-school smile. But he will
give you his whole attention—if you ask for it.

The English notion of comfort may even be associated with
conscious inefficiency. Inefficiency, if not carried too far, has a
certain value. Too much convenience, like the letter, killeth. A
little inconvenience, while it may waste time, somehow enhances
life, just as a small amount of friction makes ice skating possible.
It was because I did not understand this, I suppose, that I transferred from the Alpha to the Omega.

The move was a miniature recapitulation of one aspect of the
current evolution of English hotel keeping. For if well-estab-
lished Alphas are numerous, so are Alphas that hope to become
Omegas. I stayed at provincial inns quite suitable for the entertainment of Chaucer's pilgrims. But I stayed also at the Imperial
in Torquay, finding it to be the last word in elegance and convenience and yet preserving a certain cozy atmosphere of English comfort. Many hotels are in between the Alpha and the
Omega, with one foot in the twentieth, the other in the eighteenth
century, often giving the American tourist the sensation of loco-
motor ataxia.

There are genuine Tudor inns with hallways so laid out that
you might as well be in the Maze at Hampton Court; or which
have existed blissfully for hundreds of years without providing
a bathroom hook for your dressing gown. These inns are often
very beautiful. They seduce you into tolerance. And there are
brewery-run bogus Tudor taverns equipped with interior lava-
tories, neon lights, American bars, and I believe even juke
boxes. These taverns are often very hideous. They tempt you to
arson.

The crux of the matter is that England has only recently become a large-scale tourist center. In a way it has just been "discovered." Consequently its hotel-and-inn system is unbalanced. Part of it is stuck fast in the pretourist era, when it catered mainly to locals or to the unfortunate Englishman whose main desire was to get back home as soon as possible. Part of it is trying to ape America—I saw several motels quite as neat and depressing as anything we have to offer. Part of it (the best part) is taking its cue from the two greatest hotel civilizations in the world, the French and the Swiss, and is offering shelter and fare suitable for the most discriminating traveler. Mine English host is not advancing smoothly into our dubious century, but by leaps and stumbles. And this curious unevenness of development, which we have already noted in the matter of cuisine, is one of the many attractions of travel in England, each stopover being a small experience.

A Holiday in Time

I HAVE JUST RETURNED from the Dark Ages.

Now and then I take such brief excursions into history in order to rub off a little of what may be called the Pastless Look. This look is quite commonly found in our age and country—a wholesome, vacant expression that comes of living exclusively in the present, of perching unintermittently on today, like a sparrow on a telephone wire.

But before telling you about my trip to the Dark Ages perhaps I had better offer a general defense of these odd vacations. They involve no more than a few round trips between a shelf and a reading desk. During them I meet only dead people. From them I return without even a sun tan.

I believe that holidays not only may but should be taken in time as well as space. The imaginary lines generated by Greenwich Observatory and the Equator mark merely a bounded sphere spinning parochially in the present moment. To traverse only these latitudes and longitudes is to pace a narrow plot of real estate. Ten thousand other meridians and parallels lead back into an estate no less real, into the domain of the rich, recoverable past; and never to follow the gleam of their curves is to limit oneself to a life of semi-immobility.

I think it a sign of national health that we have as many ama-

257

teur time travelers as we do. A detailed, not to say fussy knowledge of the Civil War, for example, may be found, not only among students of history but among us plain citizens who may have no other claim to scholarship. There is hardly a whistle stop that cannot produce its corner druggist or hotel clerk ready to reanimate for you Shiloh's bloody ground or vehemently argue the *ifs* of Gettysburg. These history hobbyists are not in flight from the present. They have merely discovered the curious pleasure of being at ease in at least one inglenook of time other than our common hearth of today.

I do not urge that we bury ourselves in the past. I know that we prefer to be contemporaries, though on occasion I am puzzled by the intensity of this preference, for after all we share contemporaneity with the lowest idiot, and it is in any case a state hard to avoid. You may recall the obscure German savant whose mountainous researches gained him neither fame nor fortune and whose dying words were "Vell, at least I voss a gondemborary!"

No, I do not wish to wean any of us from the delights of being alive in this year of Our Lord. I merely suggest the pleasures that lie in living, if only sporadically and superficially, out of one's time.

Sign a lease on a time room of your own, enclosing some decade or era of the past, some crucial adventure of your forefathers, some salient dead hero, saint or knave. Make that room yours. Furnish it with reading and thought, the interior decoration that is always in good taste and resistant to the whims of fashion. Whenever the world is too much with you, unlock its door with your one-of-a-kind key. It really matters little how the nameplate on that door reads: Amenhotep IV or Eighteenth-Century Polynesia or Jeb Stuart or Mycenae or Aurignacian Man or Marie Antoinette or the Constitutional Convention. You are not setting out to become the curator of the House of History, but only to grow intimate with one of its many mansions, as a man may get to know and love each homely detail of his favorite bar.

Dilettantism? Granted. But this frivolity is not fatuity. The word *dilettante* is rooted in the Latin *delectare*, to delight; and I maintain that living out of one's time offers its own peculiar delights, to despise which is to cheat ourselves of part of our human inheritance.

As, in the course of many informal visits, you get to feel more and more at home in Pericles' Athens or Akbar's India or Jefferson's Virginia, these delights emerge so clearly that you can list them.

The first is the pleasure frowned on by those with a talent for frowning: that of escape. Few bore more successfully than the bores who are always facing facts. Soon their faces begin to look like the facts they face—and very dull facts to boot. Why not admit that much of living is escape, that some of our most ingenious inventions, from sport to distillation, are but engines of evasion? Perhaps escape from "the facts" is part of the make-up of man, a reflex as uncontrollable as that which closes his eyes when a blow threatens them. And so I feel no shame in an occasional retreat from a fascinating but noisy, disordered present to the arranged simplicities of a selected segment of the past.

Arranged? Of course they are arranged. And from this circumstance flows the second pleasure of our holidays in time. The past was at one time a work of nature, like our present. But for us (I am quoting from the late Max Beerbohm's seductive essay in *Mainly on the Air* on Lytton Strachey) "the past is a work of art, free from irrelevancies and loose ends. There are, for our vision, comparatively few people in it, and all of them are interesting people. The dullards have all disappeared—all but those whose dullness was so pronounced as to be in itself for us an amusing virtue. And in the past there is so blessedly nothing for us to worry about. Everything is settled."

The third pleasure is simply the satisfaction of curiosity. In a way all recorded history is but one vast murmurous back-fence gossip. We persist in writing and reading it because we long to understand but also because we love to eavesdrop. Behind Edward Gibbon's most classical periods hides a Nosy Parker. Circumstances and good manners will forever shut me off from knowing how my next-door neighbor lives; but nothing hinders me from getting a pretty clear idea of how Louis XIV lived. And as my neighbors appear to live lives, like my own, of appalling rectitude, Louis, even if those lives were open books, would get the nod anyway.

The fourth and fifth pleasures are linked: the sharpening of the sense of one's time, the sharpening of the sense of one's self. Asked the year, all of us would reply "1962." But that bare numeral means one thing to a teen-age jazz fan, quite another to Arnold Toynbee. To know *when* you are you must know at least one other point in time, better still several points, as the astronomer requires two remote ones to triangulate his star.

Similarly, to know *who* you are it is helpful to conceive of someone else, and preferably someone remote from your own condition. The lunatic is lost because he cannot know any soul other than his own, and this is especially true when he thinks he is Napoleon. He is entirely enclosed within himself, as you may see by the unnoticing expression of his eyes. To the degree that we refuse any understanding of or partial identification with the great majority who have preceded us (all living people are merely a temporarily privileged minority) we approach a state of lunacy. Visits to the past help to keep us balanced by enabling us to feel more clearly and intelligently our own identity.

They also enlarge us. They endow us with a kind of retrospective immortality, that curious sensation of backward duration that comes of being able to touch hands at will with our rich and varied past. This retrospective immortality I find more nourishing than the concept of any future immortality, which I cannot help feeling is touched with a Fat Boy greediness for mere endurance. I cannot arouse much enthusiasm for living in Eternity. But I would feel diminished if I could not live in Time, encompassing all our yesterdays as well as our today.

These pretty theories smugly laid out, I felt that in all conscience I should test them systematically. I resolved therefore to pass the spare time of two months in some other time and place, then return with a holiday report for my readers.

The time I chose was the Dark Ages which, you will recall,

lasted from about A.D. 500 to 900. With the aid of a couple of dozen books, some of which are listed at the end of the article, I focused on the latter part of the eighth century, the century climaxed by Pope Leo III's Christmas Day crowning of Charlemagne as Roman Emperor. (The seventh century would have been *too* dark; I wouldn't have been able to see a thing.) For my habitat I selected Gaul, a part of it not far from a small encampment we now call Paris. As I am fond of reading and writing and not good for much else, I conceived myself to be a lowly but not unobservant monk—I would have made a lubberly soldier, an atrocious minstrel, a bad serf, and a worse lord.

Why the Dark Ages you may ask. I admit that they hardly rank among the Gold Coasts of time travel. They are skirted by most tourists, who dismiss them as dull and barbarous. But their dismal reputation supplied me with one reason for a visit. Should these obscure and dun-colored centuries yield matter of some interest, my defense of living out of one's time would seem all the sounder. Besides, I thought it best to select a historical period generally thought of as in violent contrast to our own.

I do not propose to tell you in detail how I lived or who my neighbors were, but only to give you a few general impressions, as gleaned by the eyes and mind of one fresh from the mid-twentieth century.

Now that I look back upon my holiday in the Dark Ages what I remember most vividly is not what I found, but what I didn't find. I missed three dominating features of my own time. I missed things, movement, and change.

If by fullness we mean the prevalence of objects, the Dark Ages were empty. The number of different manufactured articles the average man might see or handle in the course of a day could be quickly enumerated. His environment was like the interior of the atom—mainly space.

But it was quite unlike that interior in another respect. Practically nothing moved. The old Roman roads in Gaul had been neglected. The victories of Islam had closed off the Mediterranean, reducing commerce to a pitiful internal trickle. There was a little illegal traffic in slaves. Down the rudimentary arteries of trade traveled modest quantities of wine, salt, and a few other necessities. Each civil or ecclesiastical demesne lived off its own fat, producing little, consuming little, exchanging virtually nothing.

The peasants hardly owned even themselves; lords and bishops did not own much more. As there were no commodities to make a profit out of, the profit idea simply did not enter my neighbors' heads, just as it is rarely absent from our own.

The world was small-scale, atomized; it seemed to be held together only by its own inertia; and of course I knew that after Charlemagne's death it was fated to fall apart. In the Latin Church it possessed a certain center and bond of union; in its vague vision of the Roman Empire it possessed a unifying myth. But these fealties fell short of creating any sense of control. During my stay with the Dark Agers I got the feeling that they cast themselves into the hands of God largely because no other hands were available.

Theirs was an empty world and still, as ours is cluttered and noisy. It was closed in on itself, windowless, unhistorical. My neighbors knew that a past had existed, but were incurious; and in any case could have found out very little about it. As for the future, man could not shape or control it, and it was better not to think of it, except as the afterlife.

The tribe was dying; the nation did not yet exist. There were no patriotisms. Charlemagne was the emperor, one heard, but one's real day-by-day loyalty was to the local lord or bishop on the one hand and to Christendom on the other.

Just as the nation did not exist, neither did the city. What the Dark Ages called the town was merely a camp or administrative center. In peacetime you might set down spade and mattock and hie to the town fair—the one in Paris lasted a month, during which all regular work stopped. But at bottom the town was an attempt to neutralize the nonpoliced wilderness that surrounded it. It was an enclosure, a shelter to which you fled for safety.

The relative absence of things, movement, and change in the Dark Ages seemed to reflect a basic inability to *fiddle*. The fiddling urge, our almost instinctive desire to change whatever exists, to move the mountain because it is *there,* marks us as modern men.

This urge has now led us to the point where we can at will change ourselves shortly into godlings or radioactive dust. A cliché, of course; but to sharpen your sense of its truth try a weekend with Early Medieval Man.

It was not that early medieval minds were so sluggish (though I think they were, compared with ours). It was that these minds worked in a way favoring the *status quo.* For us the world is—just the world. Therefore you can change it. For them the world was an allegory. Therefore you could do nothing but interpret it. Of course all my Dark Age neighbors didn't think this way, or their epoch would never have ended. Charlemagne, for instance, didn't; that's why today we can so readily feel his genius. But for most early medieval men things were not themselves but were to be understood as veils covering something else. Alcuin, the English scholar Charlemagne impressed into his service, provided the men of the Dark Ages with a book of popular riddles: "What is the word? The betrayer of the mind. . . . What is the tongue? The whip of the air." For us this is mere wordplay. For Alcuin's contemporaries it was that, too, but also something more.

During my brief stay in the eighth century I received the impression that a genius for allegory is connected with a lack of genius for humor. Humor is a technique by which the veils, or some of them, are removed from reality. My Dark Agers simply didn't appear to have this sense. Occasionally I overhead the raucous laughter of boasting and vilification; and there was plenty of horseplay, which is a form of humor that proceeds from the structure of our bodies rather than that of our minds. But of humor in our sense, a mode of viewing the world, there seems to have been little. An odd lack.

Another lack was what amounted to a visual defect. Though their natural world, being unspoiled, was far more impressive than ours, they did not appear to *see* it. It was not a usable thing as it is for us. It did not stimulate their sense of beauty, it did not console them, it was not poetry. When the seventh-century monk

Aldhelm describes his experiences during a storm in Cornwall, it strikes the student of the Dark Ages as notable. To this nature-blindness there are exceptions: the Irish poets of the period have as keen an appreciation of the external world as does Keats. But then the early medieval Irish seem in many ways not to have belonged to the Dark Ages at all, but to have been almost a race apart, more alert, more imaginative, more *personal* than the mainlanders.

On the whole I found Early Medieval Man far more remote from me than, on previous time holidays, I had found men who had preceded him by many generations—men of the time of Pericles, for example, or Augustus.

On the other hand certain of his habits reminded me of my own contemporaries. His superstition, for example, in which, as all the history books will tell you, he was sunk. He was too—sunk in an unhappy mix of gullibility and fear. Today we have rid ourselves of the fear, which means a net gain in sanity. But have we rid ourselves of the gullibility? Was my Carolingian peasant, with his amulet worn to ward off evil spirits, much more naive than the man who is secretly convinced that driving a Jaguar endows him with superiority? In his interesting *Madison Avenue, U.S.A.*, Martin Mayer argues that the well-advertised tooth paste or cosmetic really does have that extra value: to wit, the self-confidence it confers on the user. I think he is right. But I think also that Mr. Mayer is describing behavior not too unlike that of our eighth-century clod. Both clod and consumer in effect buy a little unreality and feel all the better for it. The difference is that the clod, wallowing in unreason, knew of no alternative conduct; we, confronted by magic and reason, choose the magic.

In at least one other and far more fundamental respect the men of the Dark Ages were like ourselves. They lived precariously, and so do we. Their margin of safety was narrower than it had ever been since the last Ice Age or would ever be until the day the atom was split. The culture of the past was saved, but only just saved, by the devotion of the Church, with considerable help from the Arabs. Our infinitely richer culture will probably survive one atomic war, but doubtfully two or three.

I came back from the Dark Agemen wondering whether, just as they founded monastery after monastery, we oughtn't to think of sinking time capsules in wholesale lots.

But it would be wrong to conclude this travel report on a doleful note. My visit was enjoyable, because it was interesting —just as any trip to a strange land is interesting. We go abroad not for the purpose of making moral judgments favorable to our own country, but to shake off, if only transiently, the all-too-familiar self of use-and-wont. Travel is a way of breaking up habit patterns.

I would suggest that living exclusively in the present is itself a habit pattern, and a dangerous one. The time-bound man, his glazed eyes fixed implacably on the current, is suffering from lockjaw of the imagination. I prescribe for him, as I occasionally do for myself, a brief tourist holiday, in any period of history that he is both ignorant of and curious about. The choice is wide. Scholars often select 4241 B.C. as the earliest date matchable with a specific event, marking the introduction of a calendar into use in Egypt. If we figure three generations to a century, that supplies our tourist with 206 generations of visitable ancestors. Some of them are mighty interesting people. And they're always home.

Some Useful Books

The Shorter Cambridge Medieval History, by C. W. Previté-Orton, 2 vols.

Economic and Social History of Medieval Europe, by Henri Pirenne.

Medieval Cities, by Henri Pirenne.

The Holy Roman Empire, by James Bryce.

Medieval People, by Eileen Power.

Medieval Essays, by Christopher Dawson.

The Medieval Mind, by Henry Osborn Taylor.

Thought and Letters in Western Europe A.D. 500 to 900, by M. L. W. Laistner.

A Note on a Brooklyn
Drugstore Boyhood

SOMEDAY someone will write a social history of the American drugstore. I should like to read it; and perhaps these frail reminiscences will supply it with material for a minor footnote. The saloon and the drugstore are both sensitive barometers of the social climate of the last half century, and perhaps the drugstore even more than the saloon. The depersonalization of our life is mirrored in the gradual transformation of the warm, dingy neighborhood drugstore into the highly efficient, glittering machine for selling that the large chain drugstore is today. Much has been gained; perhaps a few human values have been lost.

My childhood and early youth were in large part spent behind the counters of a series of drugstores in Brooklyn. My father was an old-line ethical pharmacist, rigidly conscientious, who worked from early morning till closing time—often nearly midnight—without any sense that this was not the normal way of mankind. The neighborhood druggist was not like other small shopkeepers. Not only was his working capacity presumed to be unlimited, but his social and communal obligations were equally vast. He had a special standing in the neighborhood, and often that was his major reward. I think this was particularly true in the various Brooklyns I was familiar with forty and more years ago.

Every ex-Brooklynite is another Mary Tudor; when he dies you shall find lying in his heart his own curious Calais. For him it is not only untrue that you can't go home again; the fact is he has never really left the place. This has little to do with local pride. You cannot be proud of a cosmos—and in my time Brooklyn was a cosmos, not a borough. Nor is it related to the common notion that *all* childhoods are vividly remembered. That notion is delusive. I have swapped recollections of earliest childhood with many a man whose memories turned out to be a non-Wordsworthian blur, and for the sound reason that his formative years had been dull ones. The novelist of the last century or so, a highly specialized animal whose main stock in trade consists of early impressions, has almost persuaded us that we are all equipped with a similar organ of total recall. It is not true. But it is often infuriatingly true of many former residents of Brooklyn.

I come of an old county family—Kings County. I do not mean that my family is rooted in Brooklyn's past. Our blood-lines are nonpatrician. I am a Brooklyn aristocrat only in the sense that I am a connoisseur of Brooklyn. I own it not by tradition but by knowledge. I have dwelt in so many of its realms and traveled so widely in the others that I may justly claim a kind of proprietary privilege. I have, as Chesterton said of Dickens, the key of the street.

I have stated that my father was titularly a druggist. But like so many Brooklynites he was, more profoundly, a practicing nomad. At the drop of a lease he would strike his window bottles of colored water and move in quest of the Brooklynite's Holy Grail, a "better neighborhood." Never out of Brooklyn, of course. Why confine oneself to the narrow limits of continental America when the world of Brooklyn was all before one, where one could choose one's place of rest, and Providence one's guide?

A Brooklyn characteristic distinguishing it from population centers of comparable density is the richness of its make-up. Most towns, even large ones, boast only a few neighborhoods:

the business district, the right side of the tracks, the wrong side of the tracks, the new development, and so forth. Social traffic is trammeled. Human life moves on rails. But Brooklyn is, or was, not a town, not a city, not a country. It was a world. It had a score of Main Streets. It had a hundred neighborhoods, each a nation in itself, each with its subtle class-and-income stratigraphy; and even today new localities open up, though they are marked increasingly by the monochrome of apartment house "projects."

In my era a Brooklyn family of Bedouin disposition was bound to live dangerously. It looked ahead beyond the horizon to an infinite vista of choices. Each choice entailed not merely a change of place, but of civilization. To move from the time-mellowed dignity of Brooklyn Heights to the Ultima Thule of Canarsie was equivalent to a shift from Beacon Street to the Andaman Islands.

In the course of my father's apothecarian flights we touched transiently on many wild coasts. Around the turn of the century we found ourselves in Bath Beach, then a watery waste just north of Coney Island. I have always considered us one of the First Families of Bath Beach and still think of my elder brother, who was born there, as the colony's Virginia Dare. The Bath Beach drugstore was often visited by the heavyweight chamuion Bob Fitzsimmons. Our family annals do not indicate that Mr. Fitzsimmons ever actually *bought* anything. As my father puts it, he just "dropped in," a phrase well suited to the drugstore of half a century ago.

In those days it combined some of the features of a recreation center, a New England town meeting, and the psychoanalytic couch. Among Brooklyn tribes the druggist ("Doc") enjoyed shamanistic standing. Felt to possess a Rosicrucian connection with life's mysteries, he was also felt to be more approachable than either physician or clergyman, to be more worldly, more man-to-man. Indeed, in order to appear as morally wholesome as my contemporaries whom Fate allotted sheltered, nonpharmaceutical childhoods, I have had to spend forty of my fifty-odd years systematically forgetting what at the age of twelve I had already learned by eavesdropping from behind the prescription counter. The drugstore was, of course, a retail establishment. But it was also a locus of neighborhood life. When I was eleven years old I might in the course of a single afternoon and evening overhear the marital confessions of a number of sorely perplexed customers; hold a mortar to catch the blood as my father, in anticipation of the doctor's arrival, bound up a badly cut arm; stealthily unlock a forbidden closet and read, with a wriggle of fearsome joy, the labels of dozens of preparations all marked with skull and crossbones and guaranteed lethal; enjoy the vivid shoptalk of the neighborhood physicians, all friends of my father, and—it is different now—blessed with plenty of time for leisurely gossip; learn the interesting techniques of rolling pills, preparing salves, making up powders—all now, with the advent of the new pharmacopoeic revolution, lost arts; learn intimately what is meant by remorse of conscience, as I watched my father sell, always unwillingly, patent medicines that he and I knew were at best harmless; as delivery boy, enter a dozen humble homes beset by illness and the fear of death.

All this sounds as if we were very busy. We were not always so, particularly in the early days. My father, as I have said, was a nomad. His commercial drives struggled continually with his Daniel Boone instinct for space and solitude. He liked quiet neighborhoods. What posed a more pressing problem to a druggist's family who could not be expected to subsist on Lydia Pinkham's Compounds, he liked *healthy* neighborhoods. As a matter of fact we often set up our therapeutic caravan near cemeteries, whose environs tended to the unspoiled and salubrious. To this day I retain a certain necropolitan *expertise* and can tick off the fine points of such varied mortuaries as Holy Cross, Greenwood, Cypress Hills, National, and Mt. Carmel—though some of these, I must admit, flourish in Queens, to whose then wildernesses we were at various times not strangers.

As a matter of fact I was born on Brooklyn's Seventh Avenue, a thoroughfare leading to Greenwood Cemetery, which lay conveniently not half a mile away from my cradle. Greenwood was to the south. To the east, two blocks by fast perambulator, stretched Prospect Park, with its tropical boscage, its sunny sheep-meadows, its Maggiorean lake, the lively fetors of its zoo, and its seductive grottoes, invitations to Cytherea from that day to this. Cemetery and park: the serenities of death, the amenities of life; to have both within easy reach is the happy lot of many a Brooklyn boy. Such a circumstance conduces to reflection. It is difficult to live in Brooklyn without becoming a deep thinker. New York's Socratic taxicab drivers almost invariably hail from Brooklyn, returning gratefully to its Athenian shades after a day in the philosophical shallows of Manhattan.

To the west, after one had traversed the Acheron of the Gowanus Canal, loomed South Brooklyn. Later on I came to know South Brooklyn as a place of fascinating dismalness, chiaroscuroed by elevated lines, pitted with the caverns of ice-coal-and-wood robber barons, rumorous with the conspiracies of street gangs. Somehow South Brooklyn always brings to my mind the haunting Carceri etchings of Piranesi, dark and dank with the effluence of what Aldous Huxley calls "metaphysical prisons." South Brooklyn was not merely a place to move from (any place in Brooklyn is a place to move from); it was a place to escape from. Kafka should have been born there.

I have noted that Brooklynites are philosophers. They are also ethnologists. Unless of a rooted disposition, in which case they are a rare species and belong in Staten Island, they sooner or later come in contact with many races. I must make one qualification: it was not until my college years that I met any considerable number of old-stock natives. I was baffled to discover that America was full of Americans and felt uneasily that somehow they stood in need of justifying their existence.

Following standard Brooklyn procedure, I lived a kind of roving ambassadorial life. During my first two decades of shifting drugstore locations I came to know Germans, Italians, Jews, Irishmen, Negroes, and Scandinavians, among others. At one time we lived not far from a colony of Turks, along Pacific Street.

I dare say I am one of the few living men whose knowledge of Italians is so intimate as to include an acquaintance with the fact that some of them like to drink citrate of magnesia as a social beverage. This racial trait, heretofore unrecorded, may have been confined, at about the time of World War I, to the denizens of Ozone Park, a mysteriously named *quartier* lying just beyond Brooklyn's eastern marches, to which we had penetrated during our Last Frontier or Lewis and Clark period. The Ozone Park descendants of Romulus drank citrate of magnesia, not so much for the taste as for the effect. During one of our cyclical commercial lulls the drugstore maintained its Dun and Bradstreet rating largely through the Saturday evening demand for this convivial tipple. At ten I was already Chief Cellarer, and even now I can re-evoke the thrill of prosperity I enjoyed Saturdays as I prepared and bottled vast lots of our profitable *vin du pays*. Particularly gratifying was the reflection that, Nature herself having built in a recurrent need, the addicts were bound to come back next week for more citrate of magnesia.

If I were asked for a single adjective that might suggest the atmosphere of a small neighborhood drugstore in those peaceful vanished days, I would choose one that may seem peculiar. The word is "medieval," or perhaps "gothic." The alchemical giant flasks in the window; the odd, squat, lovely jars in which so many pharmaceuticals, now less frequently to be seen, were kept; the remedies harking back to an earlier, darker age (I dimly remember selling leeches); the very smell of the drugstore, not neutral as it is today, but somehow reminiscent of dim laboratories of the Middle Ages; the respect, tinged with a little fear, in which that wonder-working sorcerer, the druggist, was held; even the curious, old-fashioned candies, such as horehound drops and rock candy, with their suggestion of a bygone era; the very way in which my father made up sodas at the new-fangled fountain, precisely as if he were carefully filling a prescription; the fact that, like most other small retail businessmen at that time, we lived "over the store," just as the medieval craftsman combined in one place his work and his home; the commercial ethics of the period, much more akin to the medieval notion of the just price than to today's cheerful gouge-the-customer philosophy; the dim lighting, so unlike the raw, efficient, hideous hospital glare of the modern up-to-date drugstore; the emphasis on *drugs*, which are magical and wondrous, rather than on mechanical toys, cheap cameras, fake cosmetics, and other imagination-paralyzing staples of our great latter-day chains: all this harked back somehow to some tradition hidden in the mists of a premodern age, to Paracelsus and Faustus and the bearded alchemists busy with their retorts and alembics.

The modern pharmacopoeia is of course a miracle as compared with that of fifty years ago, and I have no nostalgia for the therapeutic techniques of that vanished era. But something has been lost, some warmth of life, some precious oddity, with the disappearance of the old-fashioned drugstore of my childhood.

To Teach the Young Idea
How To Shoot

The Case for Basic Education

THE PRESENT educational controversy, like all crucial contro-
versies, has its roots in philosophy. One's attitude toward it depends on one's conception of man. It depends on one's view of
his nature, his powers, and his reason for existence.

If, consciously or unconscoiusly, one takes the position that
his nature is essentially animal, that his powers lie largely in
the area of social and biological adaptation, and that his reason for existence is either unknowable or (should he advance
one) a form of self-delusion—then the case for basic education,
and consequently for education itself, falls to the ground. By
the same token the case for physical, social, and vocational
training becomes irrefutable.

On the other hand, if one takes the position that man's nature
is both animal *and* rational, that his powers lie not only in the
area of adaptation but also in that of creation, and that his
reason for existence is somehow bound up with the fullest possible evolution of his mental and spiritual capacities—then the
case for basic education, and consequently for education itself,
is established, and further discussion becomes a matter, however interesting and important, of detail.

A crisis period is not necessarily marked by disaster or vio-
lence or even revolutionary change. Ours is; but it is also marked

275

by the absence of any general, tacit adherence to an agreed-upon system of values. Thus, of the two positions briefly outlined above, a minority adheres to the first. Another minority adheres to the second. But most of us waver between the two or have never reflected on either. Our present educational system quite properly mirrors this uncertainty of the majority. It mirrors our own mental chaos.

Now neither of the positions is logically demonstrable, though some have tried to bend them to logic, as well as to propaganda. They are faiths. Because all faiths are attackable, everything they say can be attacked. Indeed everything they say may be wrong. But the attack can only be sustained by the proclamation of an opposing faith. And if they are wrong, they are wrong only in the sense that no faith can be "proved" right.

Thus the *Metaphysics* of Aristotle opens with the well-known statement: "All men by nature desire to know." This is not a statement of fact in the sense that "All men are born with lungs" is a statement of fact. It is not statistically checkable. It is not a self-evident truth. Cursory observation of many men seems to give it the lie. Depending on whether we prefer the language of logic or the language of emotion we may call it either an assumption or a declaration of faith. If the assumption is denied, or the declaration countered by an opposing declaration, education itself becomes an irrelevancy. But in that case the cultural fruits of civilization also become an irrelevancy, because they would appear to flow, not from some blind process of unending adaptation, but from Aristotle's proposition. Any doubt cast on that proposition also casts doubt on the permanent value of culture.

It may be that the proposition *is* untenable. Perhaps all men do not by nature desire to know. We can then fall back on a second line of defense. We can say that at least men have acted *as if* they did so desire. Aristotle's dictum may be an illusion. But it looks like a creative illusion.

He has another dictum. He tells us that man is a social animal. Put the two statements together. Were man not a social animal but an anarchic animal, his desire to know would have both its origin and its terminus located in himself. But, as he is a social and not an anarchic animal, he socializes and finally systematizes his desire to know. This socialization and systematization are what we mean by education. The main, though not the only, instrument of education is an odd invention, only three thousand years old, called the school. The primary job of the school is the efficient transmission and continual reappraisal of what we call tradition. Tradition is the mechanism by which all past men teach all future men.

Now arises the question: If all men by nature desire to know, and if that desire is best gratified by education and the transmission of tradition, what should be the character of that education and the content of that tradition? At once a vast, teeming chaos faces us: apparently men desire to know and transmit all kinds of matters, from how to tie a four-in-hand to the attributes of the Godhead.

Obviously this chaos cannot be taught. Hence in the past men have imposed upon it form, order, and hierarchy. They have selected certain areas of knowledge as the ones that, to the exclusion of others, both *can* and *should* be taught.

The structure of this hierarchy is not a matter of accident. Nor is it a matter of preference. The teacher may not teach only what happens to interest him. Nor may the student choose to be taught only what happens to interest *him*. The criteria of choice are many and far from immutable. But there is an essential one. Basic education concerns itself with those matters which, once learned, enable the student to learn all the other matters, whether trivial or complex, that cannot properly be the subjects of elementary and secondary schooling. In other words, both logic and experience suggest that certain subjects have generative power and others do not have generative power. When we have learned to tie a four-in-hand, the subject is exhausted. It is self-terminating. Our knowledge is of no value for the acquisition of further knowledge. But once we have learned to read we can decipher instructions for the tying of a four-in-hand. Once we have learned to listen and observe, we can learn from someone else how to tie a four-in-hand.

It has, up to our time, been the general experience of men that certain subjects and not others possess this generative power. Among these subjects are those that deal with language, whether or not one's own; forms, figures and numbers; the laws of nature; the past; and the shape and behavior of our common home, the earth. Apparently these master or generative subjects endow one with the ability to learn the minor or self-terminating subjects. They also endow one, of course, with the ability to learn the higher, more complex developments of the master subjects themselves.

To the question, "Just what are these master subjects?" there is a traditional answer. That is, there exist, with modifications in each epoch, certain subjects that Western civilization has up to very recent times considered basic. That they are traditional is not an argument in their favor. One must be persuaded that they are sanctioned not only by use and wont but by their intrinsic value.

The word *intrinsic* is troublesome. Is it possible that, as the environment changes, the number and names of the basic subjects must also change? At a certain time, our own for example, is it possible that driver education is more basic than history? Many of us think so, or act as if we thought so. Again I would suggest that if we do think so, or act as if we thought so, it is not because we wish to lower the accident rate (though that is what we say) but because we unconsciously conceive of man primarily as an adaptive animal and not as a rational soul. For if he is primarily the first, then at the present moment in our human career driver education *is* basic; but if he is primarily the second it is, though desirable, not basic.

I think many persons would concede that with environmental changes the relative importance of the basic subjects will also change. It is obvious that a post-Newtonian world must accord more attention to the mathematical and physical sciences than did the pre-Newtonian world. But *some* science has at all times been taught. Similarly in a hundred years the American high school student may be universally offered Russian rather than French or German. But this does not affect the principle that *some* systematic instruction in *some* leading foreign language will remain a basic necessity.

In other words, however their forms may be modified, a core of basic or generative subjects exists. This core is not lightly to be abandoned, for once it is abandoned we have lost the primary tools which enable us to make any kind of machine we wish. Other subjects may seem transiently attractive or of obvious utility. It is pleasant to square dance, for instance, and it is useful to know how to cook. Yet we cannot afford to be seduced by such "subjects." Hard though it may be, we must jettison them in favor of the basic subject matters. And there is no time for an eclectic mixture: only a few years are available in which to educe, to educate the rational soul. We cannot afford bypaths. We cannot afford pleasure. All education, Aristotle tells us, is accompanied by pain. Basic education is inescapably so accompanied, as well as by that magnificent pleasure that comes of stretching, rather than tickling, the mind.

I have briefly outlined the standard case for basic education insofar as it rests on an unchanging philosophic faith or view of human nature. But there is a more urgent, though less fundamental, argument still to be advanced. In sum it is this: while basic education is *always* a necessity, it is peculiarly so in our own time.

Perhaps I can best make this clear by a personal reference which I hope the reader will forgive.

I am a very lucky man, for I believe that my generation was just about the last one to receive an undiluted basic education. I am fifty-seven years old. Thus I received my secondary school education from 1916 to 1920. Though I was not well educated by European standards, I was very well educated by present-day American ones. For this I am grateful to my country, my city, and my teachers. Of personal credit I can claim little.

My high school was part of the New York City system. It had no amenities. Its playground was asphalt and about the size of two large drawing rooms. It looked like a barracks. It made no provision for dramatics or square dancing. It didn't even have a psychiatrist—perhaps because we didn't need one. The students were all from what is known as the "underprivileged"—or what we used to call poor—class. Today this class is depended on to provide the largest quota of juvenile delinquents. During my four years in high school there was one scandalous case in which a student stole a pair of rubbers.

Academically my school was neither very good nor very bad. The same was true of me. As the area of elective subjects was strictly limited, I received approximately the same education my fellows did. Here is what—in addition to the standard minors of drawing, music, art, and gym—I was taught some forty years ago:

Four years of English, including rigorous drill in composition, formal grammar, and public speaking.

Four years of German.

Three years of French.

Three or four years (I am not sure which) of history, including classical, European, and American, plus a no-nonsense factual course in civics, which was dull but at least didn't pretend to be a "social science."

One year of physics.

One year of biology.

Three years of mathematics, through trigonometry.

That, or its near equivalent, was the standard high school curriculum in New York forty years ago. That was all I learned, all any of us learned, all all of us learned. All these subjects can be, and often are, better taught today—when they are taught at all on this scale. However, I was taught French and German well enough so that in later years I made part of my living as a translator. I was taught rhetoric and composition well enough to make it possible for me to become a practicing journalist. I was taught public speaking well enough to enable me to replace my lower-class accent with at least a passable one; and I learned also the rudiments of enunciation, placing, pitch, and proper breathing so that in after years I found it not too difficult to get odd jobs as a public lecturer and radio-and-television handyman.

I adduce these practical arguments only to explode them. They may seem important to the life adjuster. They are not important to me. One can make a living without French. One can even make a living without a knowledge of spelling. And it is perfectly possible to rise to high estate without any control whatsoever over the English language.

What *is* important about this old-fashioned basic education (itself merely a continuation and refinement of the basic education then taught in the primary schools) is not that it prepared me for life or showed me how to get along with my fellow men. Its importance to me and, I believe, to most of my fellow students, irrespective of their later careers, is twofold:

1. It furnished me with a foundation on which later on, within the limits of my abilities, I could erect any intellectual structure I fancied. It gave me the wherewithal for the self-education that should be every man's concern to the hour of his death.

2. It precluded my ever becoming lost.

In drawing the distinction between generative and self-terminating subjects we have already discussed the first point.

I want now to explain the second point because the explanation should help to make clear why in our time basic education is needed not only in principle but as a kind of emergency measure.

Again I hope the reader will forgive the intrusion of the autobiographical note.

Considered as a well-rounded American I am an extremely inferior product. I am a poor mechanic. I play no games beyond a little poorish tennis and I haven't played that for years. I swim, type, dance, and drive raggedly, though, with respect to the last, I hope nondangerously. I have had to learn about sex and marriage without benefit of classroom instruction. I would like to be well-rounded and I admire those who are. But it is too late. I take no pleasure in my inferiorities but I accept the fact that I must live with them.

I feel inferior. Well and good. It seems to hurt nobody. But, though I feel inferior, I do not feel lost. I have not felt lost since being graduated from high school. I do not expect ever to feel lost. This is not because I am wise, for I am not. It is not because I am learned, for I am not. It is not because I have mastered the art of getting along with my peers, for I do not know the first thing about it. I am often terrified by the world I live in, often horrified, usually unequal to its challenges. But I am not lost in it.

I know how I came to be an American citizen as of today; what large general movements of history produced me; what my capacities and limitations are; what truly interests me; and how valuable or valueless these interests are. My tastes are fallible but not so fallible that I am easily seduced by the vulgar and transitory—though often enough I am unequal to a proper appreciation of the noble and the permanent. In a word, like tens of millions of others in this regard, I feel at home in the world. I am at times scared but I can truthfully say that I am not bewildered.

I do not owe this to any superiority of nature. I owe it, I sincerely believe, to the conventional basic education I received beginning about a half century ago. It taught me how to read, write, speak, calculate, and listen. It taught me the elements of reasoning and it put me on to the necessary business of drawing abstract conclusions from particular instances. It taught me how to locate myself in time and space and to survey the present in the light of an imperfect but ever-functioning knowledge of the past. It provided me with great models by which to judge my own lesser performances. And it gave me the ability to investigate for myself anything that interested me, provided my mind was equal to it.

I admit this is not much. But it is something, and that a vital something. And that something—here we touch the heart of our discussion—is becoming ever rarer among the products of our present educational system.

The average high school graduate today is just as intelligent as my fellow students were. He is just as educable. But he is often lost, in greater or lesser degree.

By that I mean he feels little relation to the whole world in time and space, and only the most formal relation to his own country. He may "succeed," he may become a good, law-abiding citizen, he may produce other good, law-abiding citizens, and on the whole he may live a pleasant—that is, not painful—life. Yet during most of that life, and particularly after his fortieth year or so, he will feel vaguely disconnected, rootless, purposeless. Like the very plague he will shun any searching questions as to his own worth, his own identity. He will die after having lived a fractional life.

Is this what he really wants? Perhaps it is. It all comes round again to what was said at the opening of these remarks. Again it depends on one's particular vision of man. If we see our youngster as an animal whose main function is biological and social adaptation on virtually a day-to-day basis, then his fractional life is not fractional at all. It is total. But in that case our school curriculum should reflect our viewpoint. It should include the rudiments of reading so that our high school graduate may decipher highway markers, lavatory signs, and perhaps the headlines of some undemanding newspaper. It should include a large number of electives, changing every year, that may be of use to him in job hunting. And primarily it should include as much play and sport as possible, for these are the proper activities of animals, and our boy is an animal.

Yet the doubt persists. *Is* this really what he wants? And once again the answer depends on our faith. For example, the Rockefeller Report on Education (published in 1958 and called *The Pursuit of Excellence*) did not issue, except indirectly, from surveys, analyses, polls, or statistical abstracts. It issued from faith. The following sentences do not comprise a scientific conclusion. They are an expression of faith, like the Lord's Prayer:

> What most people, young or old, want is not merely security or comfort or luxury—although they are glad enough to have these. They want meaning in their lives. If their era and their culture and their leaders do not or cannot offer them great mean-

ings, great objectives, great convictions, then they will settle for shallow and trivial meanings.

There is no compulsion to believe this. If we do not believe it, and unqualifiedly, there is no case for basic education. Which means that, except for the superior intellect, there is no case for traditional education at all. In that event we should at once start to overhaul our school system in the light of a conception of man that sees him as a continually adjusting, pleasure-seeking, pain-avoiding animal.

The root of our trouble does not lie in an unbalanced curriculum, or in an inadequate emphasis on any one subject, or in poor teaching methods, or in insufficient facilities, or in underpaid instructors. It lies in the circumstance that somehow the average high school graduate does not know who he is, where he is, or how he got there. It lies in the fact that naturally enough he "will settle for shallow and trivial meanings." If nothing in his early education has convinced him that Newton, Shakespeare, and Lincoln are both more interesting and more admirable than Frank Sinatra, Jerry Lewis, and Pat Boone, he will find answers to his questions in Sinatra, Lewis, and Boone, and not in Newton, Shakespeare, and Lincoln. If he has learned little or no history, geography, science, mathematics, foreign languages, or English he will, naturally enough, learn (for even if all men do not desire to know, in Aristotle's sense, surely they desire to know *something*), golf, quail shooting, barbecuing, and some specialized technique of buying and selling.

In accordance with his luck and his temperament, he may become happily lost, or unhappily lost. But lost he will become. Lost he will remain. Lost he will die.

And if we allow these lost ones to multiply indefinitely, they will see to it that our country is lost also.

My Day in School

IT IS ON REALISTIC GROUNDS that I favor visits to my only inalienable possession: the past. I know that among the inalienables Mr. Jefferson lists Life, Liberty, and the Pursuit of Happiness. But as for Life, whose any moment may be terminal, what is it but the past? And as for Liberty and the Pursuit of Happiness, I care not what Mr. Jefferson says: they are no more than what we may call loans. The past alone counts as solid capital, its interest (excellent word) compounded with every passing year.

To use this capital well is not easy. That is why so few of us draw on it. We Western men prefer the future. To shape it seems to us the task best fitted for high-energy types. But is it any more so, I wonder, than understanding and organizing the past, even one's own small slice of it? Is Toynbee's effort to plan the past less formidable than, say, General Motors' effort to plan what is to come? And does not a man like Proust prize the past so highly as to devote to it his entire future?

Some time ago, with the aid of two 15-cent subway tokens, I subsidized and carried through a one-man expedition into the past. In an endeavor to find out who I was, I excavated a thin layer or two of my childhood. This childhood happened to be spent in Brooklyn, a spiritually independent state attached by statute to the City of New York. My aim was scientific, not nostalgic. I do not care to relive my youth, having learned to admire the wisdom of the tree, which takes no account of its rings. My least favorite character in fiction is Peter Pan.

The research into my own antiquity involved visiting every house and street I had lived in, from the age of one day (far and away the most interesting day of my life—I hate myself for not remembering it) to my early teens. As I come of a tribe of Brooklyn Bedouins, these places were too numerous to mention. In any case my experiences can interest only a specialized audience of one and so I shall not bore you with them. But, as it is linked to the subject of this discourse, which is schooling, I should like merely to mention my investigation of the schools I had attended (four of them) from the age of six to the age of twelve. What I hoped was to use the smell of chalk dust (it hadn't changed—in fact I think it was the same dust) somewhat as Proust used his recollective device, the madeleine dipped in tea. I succeeded fairly well. My more commonplace Combrais returned in recollection, entire architectures of school time experience rebuilt themselves in my mind. It is these exhumed memories that formed the background of a second expedition I made shortly thereafter. I should like to tell you about it.

This one was to the world of today, to a clean-lined, sun-filled school serving a small New England town. The expedition was as simple as the Brooklyn one: I merely spent a whole day in class. I wanted to see what youngsters were being taught, and how, and in what ways, if any, the process differed from my own schooling of forty years ago. I recommend such a day behind a desk to all parents, especially those with short legs and flat stomachs.

From 8:30 to 2:30 I attended six classes at—let us call it Sunville. I was also a communicant at the central sacrament of any proper P.T.A., namely, Hot Lunch. I still prefer (if this be treason, etc.) the lunch of my own Silurian period—a cold sandwich and a warm Hershey bar, disengaged from a back pocket. It was less messy, involved less noise, required neither kitchen nor dining room, and co-operated beautifully with the family exchequer. One can pay too high a price for a balanced meal.

The classes I attended included the sixth, seventh, and eighth grades, the pupils' ages ranging roughly from eleven through thirteen. The sixth grade was undepartmentalized. The others involved social studies (I think we used to call this civics, and it rated as the spinach of the curriculum), mathematics, science, and English. Of the six teachers, two were male—an improvement over my era in which the only man teacher was a forlorn shop instructor who spent a frustrated year of his life trying to show me how to countersink a hole. My feeling is that the faculty in general represented a real improvement over that of my time.

The classes averaged twenty-four pupils, a teachable number. The reader must, however, keep in mind that the school, situated in a favored community, is superior in this respect, as in some others, to most American schools. As the town grows, the ratio will become less happy. And the town will grow: my locality, a model study in Togetherness, is currently making a hobby of proliferation.

Today's school—at any rate the one I visited—is a beautiful example of first-rate packaging. Light and air abound, fire perils do not exist, the plumbing is almost seductive, all equipment is functional. Even the textbooks are no longer dog-eared. In some rooms, I noticed, desks and seats were movable, so that a small group could be detached from the main body of the class and, for seminar purposes, isolated in any desired corner. In my time the class Hercules would make a five-minute production out of opening and closing windows. Today's windows are all out of *House Beautiful.*

Whenever I saw a boy or girl rise and walk over to the pencil sharpener or the supplies cabinet, my blood froze. When I was twelve we were riveted to our seats as the Count of Monte Cristo was to his dungeon wall, and had no excuse to leave them except for that most compelling reason.

The casual to-and-fro, though conducted with decorum, nevertheless made for a Times Square atmosphere, quite different from the cryptlike climate of my own classroom. In 1916 cars and trucks were still less important than people; at our inky labors we heard them rarely. But now, even in this country town, vehicular noise was constant. During quiet intervals I could hear the lively *churr* of the pencil sharpener in the next room. I remembered my own school. It was ugly. It looked like an undefendable armory. It had candid plumbing. But on the other hand the architects of those days actually believed that interior walls should be built to keep out noise. In the interests of Togetherness (and overexpanded budgets) this absurd notion has now been discarded. A fine modern school has the grace, beauty, lightness, and substantiality of a soap bubble.

This is not intended as criticism. The fact is that these noises bothered no one but me, a time-traveler from another epoch. Indeed in one or two cases the hall door was apparently left open on purpose, so that student and teacher might enjoy the pleasures of high-decibel education. In forty years the American auditory canal has changed; no one can persuade me to the contrary. These youngsters, who cannot study at home without the help of the radio, would be frightened by stillness. It is consoling to reflect that as our century progresses they will encounter less and less of it. Soon the disturbing experience of silence will be confined to a few short months in the womb— until that too is wired for sound so as to precondition the little potential citizen to the jet-plane, juke-box paradise awaiting him.

Not only were the pupils untroubled by noise; they were untroubled by school itself. There lies the revolution: school is no longer disliked—which begs the question as to whether education is. In my day the normal relation between school and schoolboy was that between a knife and a throat. Unconsciously we thought of ourselves as versus classroom, book, assignment, teacher. This does not mean we refused to be educated. It means that our education was conducted in a climate of tension, the tension itself being part of the training process.

During my visit I detected no tension on the part of either teacher or pupil. Problems of discipline did not seem to exist. The pupils were formidably well-adjusted, far happier, more amiable, more casual than I remember myself and my contemporaries as being. But whether this chemically pure atmosphere, free of the toxins of conflict, is the best one for learning, I am not sure. Just as the novelist, we are told, should take care to equip himself with an unhappy childhood, so it may be that a certain amount of friction is good for the beginning student. Remembering my own school days, saturated with uncertainty and fear, I kept eying each class for the neurotic, the exhibitionist, the bad boy, the daydreamer, even the seeming dullard. (Such children are very valuable; they should be watched far more carefully than the three-letter man.) In each class there were of course several children brighter than what seemed to me a high average. What made me a bit uneasy was that the general atmosphere—so sensible, wholesome, democratic—was somehow not adapted to challenge the exceptional, the odd, the wayward in them. In brief I am arguing that our schools' job, among others, should be the regular production of a certain number of misfits.

I used to run a television show called *Quiz Kids*. The two questions most frequently put to me by viewers were "Is it on the level?" (Answer: Yes.) "Are the kids *normal?*" (Answer: Yes.) They always asked the second question with real anxiety and I always answered it as I knew I had to, even adducing the final overwhelming proof of normality: the Quiz Kids liked baseball. I am not ashamed of my answer to the first question, for it was an honest answer; but I am ashamed of my answer to the second. I should have said something like this: "Yes, most of them, I'm sorry to say, are quite normal. No better than any of us. One of them, though a delightful child, is, I hope, not normal; he may even have a streak of the most valuable commodity in the world —genius." That is what I should have said. But I didn't want to hurt the program. I hope I am wrong in feeling that some schoolteachers are similarly cautious. They too don't want to "hurt the program."

I do not wish, however, to suggest that Sunville is dominated by the make-the-children-happy dogma. The classroom atmosphere, though easygoing, was not slack, and the general level of attention far higher than I remembered it from my own school days. In my time each class had a fairly large proportion of Unreachables—those who simply did not want to learn. My guess is that the proportion of Unreachables in Sunville is very low indeed.

This excellent circumstance may flow from something almost unknown in my time: the involving of the students themselves in running the class, almost as if they were part-time teachers. Forty years ago the classroom relationship was still that of the Middle Ages: master and disciple, often master vs. disciple. This relationship has now been broken up. For example, one Sunville class began its day with a Bible reading—but by a pupil, not by the teacher. This same youngster administered the Pledge of Allegiance, with its (to me) novel addition "under God." (The assumption is that among children there exist no atheists, agnostics, or fire worshipers.) Another pupil led the class in the singing of the "Battle Hymn of the Republic" and then asked, "Any news?" Several children reported on something they had read in the newspaper. All this seemed to me a good thing. While its educational value was doubtful, it did create a sense of participation, so that the formal instruction that followed (a first-rate "old-fashioned" drill in fractions and decimals) met no emotional resistance.

It was interesting to compare this arithmetic period with another I attended, led by an equally competent teacher. The material was similar: percentages and averages. But the technique was more "progressive"—that is, instruction was conveyed through an analysis of the standing of the teams in the National League. The textbook fitted into this theory. It was called *Mathematics To Use*, and was packed with little stories and amusing pictures.

The danger here is that by featuring the concrete you run the risk of degrading the abstract. Arithmetic itself is far larger and more interesting than any of its applications, but this fact may never be suspected by the child who is convinced that some academic merit attaches to knowing who leads the league in batting. It is not that the child was not taught how to figure percentages. He was taught; in this particular class he was well taught. But he may receive the impression that somehow the value of his subject rests on its ability to submit to picturesque application.

Our national weakness in abstract thought may stem partly from our early schooling. My own teaching experience suggests to me that by nature the child is more interested in abstract questions than is the grownup. It is he, not you and I, who wonders why the world was made, who made it, how large the universe is, how long it will last, how it may be measured, what makes people different from animals, what it means to be brave or good or truthful.

I used to teach English to junior high school students. I found that I could interest them in poetry (this is supposed to be one of the pedagogical impossibles) through a preliminary study which had nothing to do with "appreciation" or "feeling the beauty" of specific poems. We considered the underlying esthetic and semantic justification of poetry in general (though of course none of this jargon was used). The general idea of rhythm, for example, was discussed. The child was asked to listen to his own pulse and heartbeat, and he himself came to the conclusion that rhythm has some connection with the way all living bodies are put together. Or I remember asking the class to prove or disprove this proposition: poetry is the most economical way of making certain difficult statements. Once you've caught the child on this *abstract* level, you can lead him to Keats or Robert Frost. In my case whatever success I had was not due to the quality of the teacher. It was due to the quality of the subject matter. All children naturally, if primitively, philosophize. It is ourselves and their teachers who have forgotten how.

I fear I am too reactionary to believe that a class can learn anything essential about medieval history by spending a month

(working as a Team, of course) constructing a lovely scale model
of Chartres Cathedral; or about the French Revolution by building a miniature guillotine. These examples are not, I add hastily,
drawn from my Sunville day. But one Sunville class, apparently
engaged in a study of World War I, did bewilder me by spending three pleasant, chatty minutes discussing the Kaiser's mustache; in another (social studies) a thirteen-year-old girl delivered
an instructive lecture on the interior of a submarine, a topic
which seems to me of no educational interest whatever; and in
an otherwise excellently conducted class in science, it was
thought necessary to open a perfectly intelligent discussion of
the nature of the earth's atmosphere by recounting the circumstances of Lindbergh's flight.

It is only we stupid grownups who have to be seduced into
attention by such tricks. To my mind the child is a child precisely because his experience is so thin that it is not worth "tying
into." The education *itself* must be the experience. The enlargement of the child's horizon from 8:30 A.M. to 2:30 P.M. should
ideally be of such a nature as to make everything else that happens to him appear relatively dull and trivial. If the nonschool
day (dating, television, sports, and so on) seems "realer" to the
child than the school day, then we cannot hope to turn out
scholars but only at best well-adjusted youngsters all possessed
of sufficient elementary skills to enable them to "get along in
practical life."

I think modern primary and secondary education in general
is now in a state of confusion (but it is a potentially fruitful
confusion) precisely because we are not sure whether we should
put our emphasis on forcing the child's mind to develop to the
absolute limit of its capacity—or on using education as a casual
adjunct to "real life." At the moment those who believe that life
reveals its reality only to the constantly inquiring mind are,
though vociferous, still in the minority.

Considerations such as these troubled me, for example, as I
listened to the youngsters delivering book reports, or talks on
the nature and function of oxygen, or recapitulations of something they had read in the papers. Far more time was devoted to

these formal oral recitations than in my own day; and an excellent thing too.

The youngsters also had an ease and a self-assurance that I am positive I and my contemporaries did not possess at twelve or thirteen. They were not awed by their subject matter; they were not awed by the teacher; they certainly weren't awed by me.

Why then did I feel a certain uneasiness, a sense of something missing? Finally I traced the source of my trouble. The pupils were all well-prepared, they were not nervous, and they were interested in what they were talking about. But, with some exceptions, they spoke so poorly, with such defective control of the language, with such slurred enunciation, and such general rhetorical looseness that their material "came across" only with difficulty.

In my day any error a child made in oral recitation was at once corrected, often overseverely, by the teacher. The result was twofold: (a) nervousness, (b) clear English, painfully arrived at. Here such corrections were infrequent. The result was again twofold: (a) self-assurance, (b) unclear English, which meant unclear ideas.

The teachers themselves without exception spoke well. I am positive they were better educated than were my own instructors. These men and women really seemed to be *teachers*, whereas most of my instructors were either gentle, rather withered, remote elderly ladies, or marriage-hungry chits who would have looked at home behind a counter at the dime store. It was apparent that these intelligent Sunville teachers refrained from correction on principle. The principle is that it is more important for the child to express himself than to express himself well. If carried too far, this notion, stemming from the most generous and sympathetic impulses, can be risky. It may produce a nation of sloppy talkers and in consequence sloppy thinkers, for we cannot think except in words.

I have long been convinced that while "literature" is a proper field of separate study, "English" is not. "English" should not be taught as a subject. Rather, it should be taught continuously all day long in every classroom. English is not a separate discipline. It is the medium the child has to use whether he is writing a formal composition or solving an equation. Hence, from kindergarten to college, *all* teachers should be teachers of English. The child should no more be permitted to express himself lazily or inaudibly than he should be permitted to loll in his seat. Composition and rhetoric should be woven into the entire curriculum from a child's first day in school. It cannot be left to the overworked "English" teacher, and should not be, for it is less a subject than an integral part of the way we live, like breathing or observing. It is, in a word, thinking. And that is what education is about, and why it cannot be painless or "entertaining."

I left Sunville feeling that my day had been well spent, that it was in many ways a better school than any I had attended forty years ago, that the taxpayers were being well served by a conscientious faculty. But I also ended my day in school with a sense that these youngsters could be worked even harder and more vigorously; that the teacher can on occasion have *too* much "respect for the child's personality"; and that an infusion of the intellectual rigor of the comparable French or English classroom might not be a bad thing.

What Makes a Teacher Great?

IN THE SECOND CENTURY of our era, while resting in the course of his arduous campaigns against the German barbarians, the Roman emperor Marcus Aurelius set down his famous *Meditations*. My favorite passages are contained in the opening Book in which he offers up thanks to those teachers who in his youth arranged for him to grow not into a mere emperor but into Marcus Aurelius.

If a cat may look at a king, an essayist may ape an emperor. In this one respect I match myself with Marcus Aurelius: though the results are not comparable, I too have had good teachers, and perhaps three or four great ones. That this realization should strike me forcibly thirty-odd years after my graduation from college is not strange, any more than it was strange for Marcus Aurelius to record his gratitude in his fifties. It takes at least a couple of decades for a man to discover that he was well taught. All true education is a delayed-action bomb, assembled in the classroom for explosion at a later date. I had a friend who, dying well and nobly, told me he drew his courage from something his philosophy teacher had said three decades before. And so an education fuse over thirty years long is by no means unusual.

A book I've been reading, *The Autobiography of Mark Van Doren*, is partly responsible for these reflections. Mr. Van Doren taught me English at Columbia long ago; and, as he is still talking and writing, though retired, he is still educating me, free of charge.

The *Autobiography* is a quietly, beautifully written account of as much as we are entitled to know concerning the life of a superbly civilized American. I might also point out that this book is something of an oddity. The converse of *The Education of Henry Adams,* it records the career of an unabashedly happy man.

When I try to think of what he taught me I cannot remember a thing. That is as it should be. The catalogue stated that he taught English. A catalogue however is not composed by teachers but by administrators who are fit for such chores. Mr. Van Doren of course taught English in the sense that he did not teach mathematics; but his real subject was one on which no examination could test you: human life. Mr. Van Doren is a poet, that rare being in whom passion and repose carry on a peaceful co-existence. In the classroom he never denied his vocation; he remained the poet, the poet as teacher. He taught us something simple, profound, sensible, and useful: that human life is enhanced if one can manage to see it with the imagination. There lay his subject, which the catalogue would label "Shakespeare" or "The Epic" or some other advertisable trade name.

In a way the great teacher—even the great mathematics teacher—does not teach anything quantitatively measurable. He performs certain actions, says certain things that create *another* teacher. This other teacher is the one hidden inside the student. When the master teacher (a one-man normal school alongside which most teachers' colleges seem rather a drain on the taxpayer) is finished, the newborn professor inside the student takes over, and with any luck the process of education continues till death. "The object of teaching a child is to enable him to get along without his teacher," said Elbert Hubbard.

This capacity, rather than acquired information, marks the legacy of the great teacher. The process is described more soberly in a private communication to me from Dr. Alvin C. Eurich, vice-president of the Fund for the Advancement of Education. Doctor

Eurich once taught psychology at the University of Minnesota. He prepared a comprehensive examination which he gave at the beginning and end of the course, and then again three, six, and nine months after the students had completed it. "I found in general that specific facts which the students learned rapidly disappeared on successive examinations, whereas general principles seemed to be retained by them." It is these "general principles" that, continuing their life, enable the student to meet new situations. The great teacher is the one who can pass on "general principles" that are quick with incessant generative power.

The great teacher is rarely "popular." He is interested in something more important than winning the affections of an unending anonymous procession of young people. The "beloved" teacher image is part of our American sentimental mythology: it expresses our willingness to pay homage to education provided it be painless—that is, noneducational. I have long maintained that any college can raise its standards simply by firing annually whichever professor is voted "Best Liked" by the graduating class.

Mr. Van Doren did not waste his valuable time by interesting himself in us as individuals. Unlike the teaching staffs of most of our "modern" schools he was willing to leave this job to Mamma and Papa. The great teacher does not bother to "love" or "understand" his students; he bothers to love their minds and understand their understandings. Mr. Van Doren did this by indirection. He reached us by paying attention, not to our trivial personalities, but to his subject and to the play of his own mind over his subject. He has put it thus: "The teacher whose love of truth is personal, is his own, is the teacher all students dream of encountering someday." *

You will remember Socrates' demonstration, in Plato's *Meno*, that an illiterate slave boy can prove the Pythagorean Theorem. It's just a question of education—that is, of *educing* the proof from the boy by asking the proper questions. All great teachers

---

* Address at the inauguration of Pres. Richard Glenn Gettell, of Mt. Holyoke College, November 9, 1957.

are smaller Socrateses. You may recognize them as much by what you say to them as by what they say to you. In her introduction to a collection of essays, *Snoring as a Fine Art and Twelve Other Essays*, by the late Albert Jay Nock, Suzanne La Follette recalls a friend's remark: "I don't know how he does it; but when you're with Albert Nock you find yourself coming out with things you didn't know you had it in you to say."

So with Mr. Van Doren. In his classes it was quite possible to be a poor student—that is, vulnerable to an examination—but it was harder to be a poor human being. He had then and has retained this curious faculty of making you say things you would swear were far beyond your mental capacity. Possibly he does not know to this day why he has always found human beings more interesting than they really are.

The secret of course lies in the fact that no great teacher is democratic, in the sense that a successful politician must be. (You recollect that Alfred E. Smith pronounced it *raddio* not because he didn't know any better, but because he felt his constituency demanded it of him. Since his day our political leaders have improved in moral integrity: their bad English is honest.) Mr. Van Doren calmly assumed a class composed entirely of heavy thinkers. At first this was embarrassing, for even in those days intellectuality and venereal disease enjoyed about equal prestige. After a while, however, you got used to it, and pretty soon you found yourself saying something practically publishable. I can remember philosophy classes, presided over by another fine teacher, the late Irwin Edman, in which football heroes suddenly, if impermanently, became adults simply because Edman refused to treat them as anything else. Memorable is that quick look of panic mingled with amazed delight that would spread over their pleasant open faces at the realization that they had given birth to an idea. By this look you may know that education is in process.

I have implied that the great teacher in a sense has no "department." I will go further. He may be unaware of what he is teaching. I once spent a year learning something from one of the finest teachers of my acquaintance, Harrison Ross Steeves, now retired. The something I learned was not what he taught—in fact, I cannot remember even the name of the course. Mr. Steeves was and, I believe, is an extraordinarily handsome person (he looked a little like a less aquiline Sherlock Holmes) with a carriage of such elegant rectitude that he would have improved our minds if he had done nothing but stand up straight for fifty minutes. From the mouth of this naturally aristocratic being there flowed, in lecture after lecture, a clear stream of the purest and most beautifully organized informal oral English prose that I have ever heard. Week after week he taught us, whatever his titular subject may have been, respect for our English tongue. He did this just by speaking perfectly; by assuming that beautiful speaking manners were preferable to ordinary ones; by treating each sentence, minute after minute, year after year, not as a passing jumble of vocables but as a small work of art. Since that classroom experience I happen to have made speaking part of my trade. Whatever trivial proficiency I have laboriously acquired is in part due to Mr. Steeves; in fact, I have been making a living out of him for years. He taught me and others to be ashamed of maltreating our magnificent English tongue. To implant that shame in perhaps fifteen thousand young men is a vast educational achievement.

I can think of at least one more mark of the great teacher. He often gains his best effects, not by iteration, not even by conscientious, steady pedagogy, but by strokes of lightning. The catalogue may say that he offers a year's course. But it may be as true to say that he offers a few magic moments. He may make an impression on the student's mind by a lengthy succession of small impacts. But the teachers we remember are those who suddenly set our minds on fire, and perhaps did so no more than a single time.

The late Oscar Hammerstein II, speaking of John Erskine, once recalled, "I attended his classes in 1916, and one day John read a poem. It came to me with a shock that poetry was intended to mean something. Whatever I've done in the theater I really owe to the way he read that poem."

James Newman, the brilliant editor of the now classic anthol-

ogy *The World of Mathematics,* once told Prof. Scott Buchanan
that a few words Buchanan had dropped in an evening class at
City College many years ago had started Newman's life-long pre-
occupation with mathematics. It is notable not only that Buchanan imparted to Newman this shock of recognition, but did so
in the course of teaching not mathematics but philosophy—
another evidence of the subordinate position occupied in the
mind of the great teacher by his "specialty."

At the moment there are three orders of men at work in the
American classroom: custodians, instructors, teachers.

The custodian is hired by the state to guard our children for
five or six hours a day until they are ready to be thrown on the
labor or marriage market. Because we are not happy with
the sound of the preceding sentence, we give the custodian the
name of teacher, often after he has completed courses guaranteed
to prevent him from becoming one in reality. Then we are
shocked to discover that the custodian's connection with education is minimal. Quite unfairly we attack him for doing precisely
the job we taxpayers have hired him to do: involve our children
in busy work so that they will not add to the burden of either
the traffic patrolman or the juvenile-delinquency officer. The
custodian is the necessary, inevitable, and perfectly guiltless
consequence of a society that prefers multiplication to the multiplication table.

The instructor, on the other hand, remains indispensable as
long as a fairly large number of Americans believe that the tools
of learning must be put into the hands of our young people. He
is master of a specific subject, or sometimes several subjects. His
job is to siphon learning out of his superior mind into the student's inferior one. Provided he obeys the rules of decent morality and good citizenship, it is not essential that he possess
qualities beyond this special ability.

Should he possess them he may turn out to be that invaluable
rarity, the teacher, perhaps even the great teacher.

The custodian teaches nothing, though he may put a class
through a series of exercises that have a shadowy resemblance
to the educational process. The instructor teaches a subject. The

teacher seems to teach a subject but is really engaged in doing a number of other things at the same time. We may define him as a human animal, specialized to think in public, to think in public before anyone, but particularly before young people who have not as yet learned even to think in private. He is an exhibitionist, willing, even eager to do an important part of his living, at stated intervals, for atrocious pay, before rows of plastic intellects.

The custodian keeps the student's body from getting into trouble. The instructor furnishes the student's mind. The teacher moves that mind. That movement, multiplied over time and space, adds up to a sum. The sum is civilization.

Eng. Lit. as She Is Taught

THERE APPEARED, some time ago, a delightful and irreverent essay, "The Myth of Eng. Lit.," by the brilliant novelist Aubrey Menen. Mr. Menen told us how he sat down in the library of the British Museum and, spurred on by his friends' praise of its magnificence, tried to bulldoze his way through the whole of English Literature—only to find the greater part of it "unreadable." He might, it is true, have chosen for his noble experiment a more favorable setting. He was somewhat in the position of a man seeking erotic excitement by contemplating the female figures at Madame Tussaud's. It can be done, but it helps to be inordinately susceptible to wax.

Be that as it may, Mr. Menen contended that the literati, the schoolmasters, and the critics have combined to put over a gigantic hoax on the public. Most of the celebrants of Eng. Lit., he felt, hadn't really read it. He went on to support his stand with telling references to Spenser, Shakespeare, Swift, Shelley, and Scott. He concluded by declaring that the bonzes have gone astray, not only because they haven't read what they claim to have read, but because they misinterpret the nature of the scribbling animal. Writers are not wingless angels, as the professors believe, but shameless rapscallions like Mr. Menen and me, faithful only to the great idol, Copy. If, Mr. Menen thinks, you look for mountains of moral elevation in pits of attractive perdition, you are bound to draw a misleading map of the literary terrain.

I once taught Eng. Lit. So Mr. Menen's remarks struck home, set me ruminating, and led to the reflections that follow.

There are at least five Eng. Lits.

There is the whole thing the entire corpus, a word cognate with corpse. From a variety of motives this corpus is studied by dedicated men who, because they partially identify it with their own lives, are bound to speak well of it. Similarly bankers look with favor on banking, though their vocation is to me the more mysterious, for they busy themselves with a mercurial insubstantiality known as money, whereas the literary scholar deals with real matters, such as people, emotions, and ideas.

Then there is the playground of the fake literatus, mainly an affair of names, references, and quotations.

Then we have the Eng. Lit. forcibly inserted into us by the average high school and college instructor.

There is still another Eng. Lit., hard to delimit, varying as tastes and styles and generations vary. This is the Eng. Lit. of the nonscholarly but curious reader. For him even a play by Dryden may be interesting if only because it shows how a first-rate mind can also contrive to be third-rate. The reader of this kind of Eng. Lit. is not primarily seeking "greatness," much less moral elevation. He is on the alert only for the flash, the quick flutter of human nature.

Finally we have Eng. Lit.'s glowing core, its actual living heart whose beat is audible to any open ear. In bulk this is perhaps one hundredth of the entire corpus. Yet, I swear by the bones of the Bard, Mr. Menen, it is just what your friends said it was—"a vast thing, filled with unending delights."

All credit to Mr. Menen for the courage to cry out that the emperor has no clothes on; but let us be sure we have the right emperor. Mr. Menen, who has a fastidious mind, should never have become involved in the often drear deserts of that Eng. Lit. which is the province of the dedicated, the votary. As readers of his subtle and accomplished fiction known, Mr. Menen is an ironist. An ironist lives and laughs by making comparisons; the votary lives, with less laughter, by worshiping an absolute, whether it be banking, baseball, or literature. The ironist and the votary are incompatible.

The eminent critic Lionel Trilling once observed that Shelley should not be read, but inhaled through a gas pipe. The votary of Eng. Lit., however, aiming at knowledge rather than delight, can inhale all of Shelley without fear of flatulence. So with Spenser's *Faerie Queene*. An ironist is bound to find it absurd; and indeed it is. But to the votary it is a monument not safely to be neglected; and indeed it is that too. And a third thing may be said: the *Faerie Queene*, amid its endless tropical tangle, contains a large but limited number of radiant sunlit clearings. Whether or not we seek them out depends on our time, energy, and temperament. No pundit dare tell us that we *must* seek them out.

Mr. Menen, in one of the most succinct literary summations ever recorded, says, "Scott stinks." I am not the man to question an olfactory judgment. Besides, I agree with Mr. Menen to this extent: Scott is largely a Name and so belongs largely to the votaries and the name droppers. Yet something may be said even for Mr. Menen's Old Stinky. In his day Scott, quietly and virtually single-handedly, supplied Americans and Western Europeans with what, with much *brouhaha,* the films, television, and the travel industry supply us today. He took his stay-at-homes to far times and places, described these times and places at what seems to us wearisome length, and also provided what is as necessary to the imagination as vitamins to the body: impossible heroes and heroines (also a few quite possible ones). For his time he was Hollywood, Radio City, and Pan Am all in one. If we can teleport our minds back 150 years and read him in this light, he takes on a curious, rather touching charm—and we will understand our forefathers and therefore ourselves a little better. Again, we don't have to do this. We may prefer to spend our lives racketing back and forth on the monorail of the contemporary. In that case we forego the charms of the kind of Eng. Lit. that, as I remarked a few paragraphs back, attracts the non-scholarly but curious reader who seeks no monuments but the gleam of human nature.

Mr. Menen has made out a case, both neat and diverting, against the Brahmins and the phonies. But they are not the villains under the educational bed. If the eyes of American youngsters glaze over when it's time to "take up" Shakespeare; if later on they go for *Gunsmoke* as against Chaucer—the fault lies neither with the Brahmins nor the phonies. At bottom the fault (if you consider it one) lies with a society that accords high prestige to *Gunsmoke* and its equivalents and low prestige to Chaucer. But, more concretely, the fault lies in the way the average teacher in the average high school and college teaches English.

The ideal classroom would be that in which the only Eng. Lit. taught is the living core of it, a classroom where a comatose content and tired teaching are changed to a series of absorbing experiences in reading, directed by a creative human being who has not been shanghaied from the Phys. Ed. department to "help out in English."

In many schools this transformation has long since taken place. Such schools are easily identified: the students talk about books and ideas (sometimes well, sometimes naively, it hardly matters) as unself-consciously as the "normal" boy or girl talks of basketball or the coming dance. But not all schools are of this order.

And not all reading lists. Who can tell how many of us today find essays (this very one, it may well be) unreadable because long ago we were compelled to study, in Mr. Menen's apt phrase, "two scrappy and often tired journalists called Addison and Steele"? Study what was perhaps, to meet a deadline, hastily scratched out over a splotched table at Button's or St. James's coffeehouse! There is no more reason for the young student to study Addison than to study the latest triviality by this morning's daily columnist.

Every generation or so a certain amount of Eng. Lit. dies. Why not cheerfully admit that *Ivanhoe* is dead, *The Lady of the Lake* dead, *Idylls of the King* dead, *Silas Marner* dead? In many high school classrooms these corpses are annually regalvanized. Is it any wonder that the young student goes on to assume that Eng. Lit. as a whole must be a cemetery?

The tendency today however is less to retain the deadwood than to feature the unseasoned. The bright young instructor is quite ready to chuck out *The Deserted Village* (and no great harm done either) but he is also quite ready to use as required or supplementary reading shoddy stuff from current magazines, digests, and transient books of popularization, as long as this stuff touches on matters "that affect the students' daily lives." Across my desk pass annually dozens of beautifully designed anthologies, full of pretty pictures and iridescent with colored inks, far more attractive than the drab textbooks of my own high school days. Many of these are excellent in content. But many are not. Often the editors, in making their selections, seem not to have asked, Is this first-rate writing by a superior mind? but rather, Is this writer, whoever he is, writing, however he writes, about matters that happen to be of moment to the teenager? Is he on mental all-fours with the young?

The whole purpose of education, one would suppose, is not to adjust its materials to the student, but to adjust the student to the materials. It is not to "meet his interests" but to *change* him, to *force* him out of childhood. To effect this I know no better way than to immerse him in literature that illuminates interests different from his own, larger and deeper than his own, literature couched in words and sentences that offer his mind, not the ease of the familiar, but the resistance of the difficult. And such literature is still to be found largely, though not entirely, in the works of men long dead.

"My child doesn't like to read" is the common complaint of parents. The reasons assigned are many; they have been discussed at wearisome length. One reason is rarely mentioned: the fact that literature is so often taught as if it were something that it is not. Eng. Lit. is not a "subject" as plane geometry or Latin are subjects. It can't be "covered"; in a very real sense you can't "learn" it. The teacher who does not cheerfully admit this at once is handicapping both himself and the student.

The class next to the Eng. Lit. classroom may be demonstrating the proof of the Pythagorean theorem. That is one kind of learning, and an essential kind. But the Eng. Lit. class is not, or should not be, engaged in this kind of learning at all. The reading and discussion of literature is less akin to what is going on in the adjacent classroom than it is to the experience of falling and being in love. Being in love is also a kind of learning, because it is concentrated, not desultory, living. As a by-product it gets you the girl or the boy, but its main value lies in the heightened awareness of life that goes along with it. Years later, recalling a love affair, we often fail to recollect the circumstances of its consummation; but quite frequently we remember how the whole experience made us feel more alive.

So is it with literature or any other fine art. It can be taught as a prelude to an examination, in which case most of the students will pass the examination, a few will fail, and only a tiny fraction will have habituated themselves to good reading as a necessary and permanent ingredient of a good life. Or it can be taught as if it were, like being in love, a concentrated mode of sensing what it means to be a human being.

We can put it in quite practical terms. Literature performs *work* on the teen-ager, and performs it more efficiently than does his so-called "practical experience." It makes him grow up. The Humanities are not a nosegay to put in one's buttonhole as a mark of "culture." They are, or should be, as much a part of a whole life as one's relation to one's family or one's chosen career.

The teacher who approaches his job from this angle must at once admit the truth: Eng. Lit. is not intended to be studied but to be read. Years ago, when I taught *Hamlet* to a class of sixteen-year-olds I began not by stating that it is considered the greatest play ever written (a declaration certain to antagonize any ordinary youngster) but by observing that its author thought so little of it that he never even bothered to preserve his plays for publication. I wanted to suggest that *Hamlet* was once an agitation in a man's mind, and to draw the student's attention *away* from the dismal fact that it is a "classic."

Then we proceeded to read *Hamlet* fast and superficially, just as the original theatergoers at the Globe listened to it fast and superficially. We tried to re-create in ourselves, by this slapdash

method, a little of the wonder, horror, and confusion that that
original audience must have felt. We even tried to feel something
of what Shakespeare himself may have felt when he wrote the
play. By that time the class, or a fair proportion of it, was caught.
Then we were in a position to read it all over again, trying to
discover what a dozen generations of men have since found in
it.

The habit of reading is got through reading. I therefore argue
for quantity, not thoroughness. The idea is to saturate the adolescent in the stuff, to open as many doors as possible, to dazzle
him, even to confuse him with scores of life perspectives that
he will never get from his daily experience. The high-school
graduate whose mind is a varicolored whirling chaos of ideas
and sentiments derived from five hundred (yes, five hundred)
hastily read good books is a more educable animal than the one
who can identify all the corpses strewn about the stage at the
close of *Hamlet*. To inform is a good thing. To inflame is a better.

At the very base of our reading trouble lies, as ever, a philosophical difficulty. In our time it is hard for any youngster not
to receive, quite unconsciously, the impression that men are not
spirits, but machine tenders, machine inventors, perhaps even
themselves machines. All the wonders that crowd in upon him,
everything he is commanded to admire, from television to space
satellites, are mechanical in essence. Even the most fate-fraught
actions of men appear to have something mechanical about
them: the heads of governments no longer produce free-swinging, bold, creative proposals, but act like chess players, even
mechanical chess players. The youngster is admonished to "fit
in." The phrase implies the existence of a nonmalleable structure,
larger than himself, superior to him, to which he must submit.

Now if we Americans truly believe that that is the way the ball
bounces, there is no need to read Eng. Lit. or any literature, and
whether Mr. Menen's complaint is justifiable is an irrelevant
matter.

I would argue, however, that this dull and frightful vision of
man at least be allowed to compete with a rival vision. In this
rival vision man, as Pascal reminded us, though a reed, is still a

thinking reed. He is central, splendid, and interesting precisely because he is so unlike a machine. And where is this rival vision most clearly represented? I would suggest, in all sound works of art, and particularly in those curious condensations of the human: books.

This is all better and more briefly put in a sentence you will find in Joseph Wood Krutch's *Human Nature and the Human Condition.* Here is the sentence:

> The great imaginative writers present a picture of human nature and of human life which carries conviction and this gives the lie to all attempts to reduce man to a mechanism.

Many teachers of Eng. Lit. have always known this to be true, and from that knowledge their students have benefited. The others might well engrave it on their hearts.

About the Author

CLIFTON FADIMAN was born in New York City in 1904, and got his A.B. from Columbia University in 1925. He has been a translator, a teacher, an adviser to Samuel Goldwyn, editor at Simon and Schuster, lecturer, platform reader, and book review editor of *The New Yorker*. During these years writing—and editing such books as *Reading I've Liked, The Short Stories of Henry James, The American Treasury, Fantasia Mathematica,* and other books and anthologies— played a concurrent part. His radio and TV chores have included: host of *Information Please,* M.C. of *This Is Show Business,* conductor of the NBC radio series *Conversation,* and book critic on *Meet the Press.* Mr. Fadiman is a member of the Board of Judges of the Book-of-the-Month Club, essayist for *Holiday* magazine, and one of the Board of Editors of the Encyclopaedia Britannica. He is the author of two books of essays, *Party of One* and *Any Number Can Play,* and most recently, *The Lifetime Reading Plan,* an original guide to one hundred books and authors.

This book was set in

Caledonia and Bulmer types by

Harry Sweetman Typesetting Corporation.

It was printed and bound at the press of

The World Publishing Company.

Design is by Larry Kamp.

Wilmington Public Library
Wilmington, N. C.

RULES

1. Books marked 7 days may be kept one week. Books marked 14 days, two weeks. The latter may be renewed, if more than 6 months old.

2. A fine of two cents a day will be charged on each book which is not returned according to above rule. No book will be issued to any person having a fine of 25 cents or over.

3. A charge of ten cents will be made for mutilated plastic jackets. All injuries to books beyond reasonable wear and all losses shall be made good to the satisfaction of the Librarian.

4. Each borrower is held responsible for all books drawn on his card and for all fines accruing on the same.